The Legacy of the Wimbledon Case

Queen Mary Studies in International Law

Edited by

Malgosia Fitzmaurice

VOLUME 57

The titles published in this series are listed at *brill.com/qmil*

The Legacy of the Wimbledon Case

Centenary of the First Judgment of the Permanent Court of International Justice

Edited by

Roman Kwiecień and Malgosia Fitzmaurice

BRILL | NIJHOFF

LEIDEN | BOSTON

The Library of Congress Cataloging-in-Publication Data is available online at https://catalog.loc.gov
LC record available at https://lccn.loc.gov/2024952145

Typeface for the Latin, Greek, and Cyrillic scripts: "Brill". See and download: brill.com/brill-typeface.

ISSN 1877-4822
ISBN 978-90-04-52899-4 (hardback)
ISBN 978-90-04-70797-9 (e-book)
DOI 10.1163/9789004707979

This book is printed on acid-free paper and produced in a sustainable manner.

Contents

Notes on Contributors

Michał Balcerzak
is Associate Professor at the Faculty of Political and Security Studies, Nicolaus Copernicus University in Toruń, Poland, and the Faculty of Law and Administration at the University of Szczecin. He served as a judge ad hoc at the European Court of Human Rights (2018–2022). Since 2022 he has been a member, vice-chair (2022-2024) and chair (2024-2026) of the UN Committee on the Elimination of Racial Discrimination.

Władysław Czapliński
is Professor of International and European law, Institute of Law Studies, Polish Academy of Sciences, and Professor at the University of Warsaw Center for Europe; Visiting Professor, Univertsities of Paris II and Paris XI, Nice-Cote d'Azur, Frankfurt/Oder (Viadrina), Rome (LUMSA) and Federal University of Minas Gerais, Belo Horizonte, Brazil. He was Rapporteur, ILA Committee on State Succession, and Chairperson, ILA Committee on Recognition/Non-Recognition. Currently he serves as a Co-Chair, ILA Committee on Abuses of International Law. Author of numerous publications on State responsibility, State succession, and theoretical problems of international law.

Malgosia Fitzmaurice
is Professor at the Department of Law, Queen Mary University of London and holds a chair of public international law. She is a full Member of the Institue de Droit International. In 2021 she was awarded the Doctorate Honoris Causa of the University of Neuchâtel. She specialises in international environmental law, the law of treaties, and indigenous peoples. She is Editor in Chief of International Community Law Review journal.

Michał Kowalski
is Professor of International Law at the Jagiellonian University in Kraków, Poland, Faculty of Law and Administration, Chair of Public International Law and Vice Dean for International Relations. Head of the doctoral program in law at the Jagiellonian University Doctoral School of Social Sciences. Conciliator at the OSCE Court of Conciliation and Arbitration in Geneva (2019–2025). Expert for the Human Dimension Mechanism appointed by the OSCE (2023-2029). Member of the Legal Advisory Committee to the Minister of Foreign Affairs of the Republic of Poland (2014-2021 and since 2024). Member of the International

Law Association's International Committee "Use of Force: Military Assistance on Request (Military Action with Consent)".

Roman Kwiecień
is Professor of Law at the Jagiellonian University in Kraków and holds a Chair of Public International Law at the Faculty of Law and Administration. He served as an arbitrator at the Permanent Court of Arbitration (2018–2024) and serves as an arbitrator at the OSCE Court of Conciliation and Arbitration (since 2019).

Agnes Rydberg
holds a Ph.D. in Public International Law from Queen Mary University of London, where she also completed an LLM. She also has a BSc in International Law from Orebro University in Sweden. She is a lecturer in international law at the University of Sheffield School of Law where she also serves as a Deputy Director of the Sheffield Centre for International and European Law and Deputy Director of Internationalisation.

Raphael Schäfer
holds his Dr. iur. from the Ruprecht-Karls-Universität Heidelberg. He is a Senior Research Fellow at the Max Planck Institute for Comparative Public Law and International Law, Heidelberg. He is also an Associate Fellow of the Royal Historical Society. His main fields of research include international humanitarian law, history and basics of international law, global history, national and international judiciary, comparative public law, legal theory, law and literature.

Barbara Stępień
holds a Ph.D. in Law from the Jagiellonian University in Kraków and is an Assistant Professor at the Chair of Public International Law, Faculty of Law and Administration, Jagiellonian University in Kraków. She is currently leading a research project titled 'Autonomous and unmanned vessels in international law: Yara Birkeland as a challenge to the law of the sea', funded by the European Union's Horizon 2020 program under the Marie Skłodowska-Curie grant No. 101038097.

Christian J. Tams
is Professor of International Law at the University of Glasgow and at Sorbonne Law School in Paris. He is a Vice-President of the European Society of International Law and sits on the Council of the German Society of

International Law. As an associate member of 11 King's Bench Walk, he regularly advises States in international legal proceedings, including before the International Court of Justice, the Iran-US Claims Tribunal and arbitral tribunals. Christian spent much of his early life in Northern Germany, often crossing the Kiel Canal, which the s.s. 'Wimbledon' was precluded from entering.

Introduction

Roman Kwiecień

2023 marked the 100th anniversary of the first contentious case decided by the Permanent Court of International Justice (PCIJ/Court). The PCIJ, as an international court of general jurisdiction, was the first judicial forum for authoritative stance on the relationships between various rules and principles of international law. Hence, the rise of the PCIJ was accompanied by great expectations regarding the development of international law. In general, the Court met these expectations, as evidenced by the relevance of its jurisprudence for both the International Court of Justice (ICJ) and the scholarly research to this day. The importance of the PCIJ jurisprudence for scholars is, for example, visible in the recently published comprehensive monographs concerning its impact on the development of international law.[1] It seems no exaggeration to say that the work of the Court has simply changed the way in which international law is approached, as Ole Spiermann phrased it.[2] In any case, the first advisory opinions and judgments issued by the Court may be regarded as the origins of the international judiciary, and the inspiration for other international courts and tribunals.

In the *Wimbledon* judgment, the Court referred to the legal issues that are important both for procedural and substantive international law, and which continue to attract the attention of States, courts and scholars. These include State sovereignty, sources of international law, interpretation of legal rights and obligations following from treaties and custom, 'objective regimes', 'self-contained regimes', or the status of international waterways. Moreover, the 2022 armed attack by Russia against Ukraine draws particular attention to the issues considered by the PCIJ in this case, that is, neutrality in armed conflicts and third-party participation in international adjudication. The latter is currently illustrated by the disputes pending before the ICJ between Ukraine and the Russia Federation, the Gambia and Myanmar or South Africa and Israel regarding alleged violations of the Genocide Convention.

1 See Spiermann O., *International Legal Argument in the Permanent Court of International Justice. The Rise of the International Judiciary* (CUP, Cambridge: 2005); Tams Ch.J. –Fitzmaurice M. (eds), *Legacies of the Permanent Court of International Justice* (Brill, Leiden: 2013).

2 Spiermann O., "The Legacy of the Permanent Court of International Justice – on Judges and Scholars, and Also on Bishops and Clowns" in Tams – Fitzmaurice (eds), *Legacies of the Permanent Court of International Justice* (n 1) 399, at 400.

 | DOI:10.1163/9789004707979_002

The traditional view of international law is that international courts and tribunals are not bound by their own precedents because there is no rule of *stare decisis* in this law. But the fact that decisions of international courts and tribunals are not binding precedents does not mean that they are not precedents at all.[3] In some cases, the judicial practice of various courts and tribunals, results in groundbreaking decisions that have permanently shaped the practice regarding the legal problems, which were the subject-matter of these decisions. Such decisions make impact not only upon scholars but also on various national and international officials, including judges. But the question arises whether the first judgment of a new court could be considered groundbreaking at all. It seems that this is possible, but only if such a decision permanently shapes the argumentative practice surrounding legal problems in judicial dispute resolution, i.e. it serves as a precedence in practice. This means such decisions pass the test of time, and is an important reason for the frequent referring to them by courts in the reasoning of their decisions. Therefore, the primary aim of the presented book is to respond to the question whether the first judgment of the PCIJ belongs to such decisions and, thus, to assess its relevance to the contemporary legal discourse and to the development of international law. The *Wimbledon* judgment is probably less known than the decisions in the *Lotus* and the *Chorzów Factory* cases. The *Wimbledon* case, however, has some peculiarities relating to both substantive international law and procedural law as well as the jurisdiction of the World Court. First, the reasoning of the Court given in its primary judgment *nolens volens* formed the path for the judicial application of international law. That is why, it can still be an important point of reference for shaping comprehensive argumentation for the impartial settlement of international disputes. Second, it was the initiatory case involving a national judge as a judge *ad hoc*. Third, it is the *Wimbledon* proceedings that was also the first case in which a State intervened under the procedure laid down in the Statute. And fourth, considering that these proceedings were initiated by the applicants not directly affected by the actions of the respondent, this case may be regarded as an evidence that interwar international law served not only to protect the individual interests of States, but also community interests, that is, the legal interests whose protection is not be based on reciprocity.

Both in the ICJ's activity and in the academia the problems decided by the PCIJ in the *Wimbledon* case have been constantly discussed. Therefore, the question arises whether the PCIJ's approach to these problems is still retained

3 Mahammed Shahabuddeen, *Precedent in the World Court* (CUP, Cambridge 1996) 2.

relevance under contemporary international law. Responding to this question, it is necessary to take into account a new, pioneering role played by judges who for the first time resolved a dispute in the forum of the first universal court of justice of general jurisdiction. There is no separate part of the book devoted to the working methods of the PCIJ's judges. This has already been thoroughly discussed.[4] However, it should be remembered that the role of an international judge was still being developed at that time and the judges adjudicating in the *Wimbledon* case had rather little in common. Another issue worth addressing is the stability of the normative structure of international law over last 100 years. In particular, it is interesting to discuss issues of continuity and changes in the ICJ's approach to the procedural and substantial legal problems decided by its predecessor in the *Wimbledon* judgment. Answers to these questions seem important for an assessment of the role of the judiciary of the World Court in shaping of the normative structure of the international legal order and legal certainty within it.

1 The Structure of the Book

The book is organized in ten sections, including this introduction and conclusion.

Chapter 1 is devoted to historical and legal background of the judgment, that is, the Versailles Treaty, and its reception in Germany as the respondent and Poland which intervened in the case due to its legal interest. In this chapter Raphael Schäfer seeks to examine the circumstances surrounding the dispute decided by the PCIJ and the legal claims of the parties submitted before the Court. The interpretation of rights and obligations following from the Versailles Treaty had been crucial both for the Court and for the applicants, the respondent and the intervener, which was clearly noticeable during the proceedings. The judgment is of particular importance not only because it was the first judgement of the PCIJ that inevitably led to a positioning of the role of the Court in international law. It was also the first international judgement based on the Treaty of Versailles, thus rendering the Treaty itself – even if only indirectly – the subject of proceedings. For this reason, the implementation of the Versailles Treaty in Germany and in Poland is recalled. Schäfer in his

4 See Spiermann, "The Legacy of the Permanent Court of International Justice – on Judges and Scholars, and Also on Bishops and Clowns" (n 2) 401–407; Spiermann, *International Legal Argument in the Permanent Court of International Justice. The Rise of the International Judiciary* (n 1) 15–23, 175–186.

chapter examines the historical background of the *Wimbledon* decision and sets out the historical singularity of the conclusion of the Treaty of Versailles. Building on this, he then shows the consequences of the peace settlement for Germany and Poland.

The findings of the PCIJ on parties to the proceedings, and more broadly, on the jurisdiction before the Court, as measures of protection of the legal interests of both States and the 'international community as a whole', seem to be an underestimated legacy of the judgment. Therefore, the special part of the book has been devoted to them. Christian Tams and Michał Balcerzak in Chapters 2 and 3 discuss issues of *locus standi* before the World Court. These procedural problems are still important in international law. The Statute of the PCIJ regulated contentious proceedings in its Chapters 2 and 3 but only four provisions (Articles 34–37) dealt with the 'contentious jurisdiction proper'. The PCIJ's contentious jurisdiction had features which characterise all contentious proceedings, that is, the Court settled disputes between parties, in proceedings submitted by one or both of them. The PCIJ's approach to contentious jurisdiction displays peculiar features. Framing this jurisdiction the PCIJ adopted a specific and, sometimes, broad reading of both the Statute's provisions and treaty jurisdictional clauses.[5] It was already visible in the *Wimbledon* case. In this judgment the Court implicitly accepted that where it had jurisdiction over substantive matters, this jurisdiction would cover disputes about reparation even though the jurisdictional title, Article 386 of the Versailles Treaty, had not mentioned reparation expressly. The Court's understanding of the 'legal interest' of the parties to the proceedings seems even more significant and is especially vital today. Discussing this problem aims at clarifying whether the applicant-states' legal interest to initiate the proceeding was just their individual interest or whether they might be rather seen as a common interest of the whole international society. Thus, it concerns the issue of the protection of individual and community interest in international law and the relationships between them. There is another significant problem: intervention before the Court. Its examination aims at answering the question about legitimacy of the institution itself and the status of an intervening State. This problem also concerns the protection of legal interests in international law as a request to the Court to intervene could, and still can be submitted before the ICJ when a State considers that "it has an interest of a legal nature which may be affected by the decision in the case" (Article 62 of the Statute).

5 See Tams Ch.J., "The Contentious Jurisdiction before the Permanent Court" in Tams – Fitzmaurice (eds), *Legacies of the Permanent Court of International Justice* (n 1) 11.

In Chapter 2, Christian Tams focuses on what he calls a 'prequel' to the ICJ's decisions regarding public or community interests and their protection in and through ICJ proceedings. Tams argues that this prequel is set in the 1920s, in the jurisprudence of the PCIJ, beginning with the *Wimbledon* case. He claims it is a prequel that lacks the drama of the *South West Africa* and the *Application of the Convention on the Prevention and Punishment of the Crime of Genocide* (The Gambia v. Myanmar) disputes before the ICJ. In the latter case the Court in its judgment on preliminary objections of 22 July 2022 concluded that "any State party to the … Convention may invoke the responsibility of another State party, including through the institution of proceedings before the Court, regardless of whether a special interest can be demonstrated".[6] But, as Tams argues, it is the *Wimbledon* decision that offers insights into an early approach to what might be called 'public interest litigation': an approach characterised by a degree of healthy pragmatism that would get lost afterwards, and that it is now perhaps possible to reclaim.

Chapter 3 is also connected with the problems of *locus standi* before the World Court. In this Chapter Michał Balcerzak addresses and focuses on the issue of intervention before the Court. An understanding of the 'legal interest' as a justification for interventions in the proceedings before the World Court is crucial. In particular, is this 'legal interest' an individual interest of a State or rather a common interest of all members of the international community? Needless to say it does matter in the pending disputes before the ICJ between Ukraine and Russia, the Gambia and Myanmar and South Africa and Israel regarding the Genocide Convention. Almost exactly a century after the PCIJ granted the Polish intervention in the *Wimbledon case*, on June 5th 2023, the ICJ allowed the intervention of no less than thirty-two State parties in the case concerning the *Allegations of Genocide under the Convention on the Prevention and Punishments Case* (Ukraine v. Russia).[7] It turned out that States request intervention in order to pursue the interests of the international community as a whole. At first glance it may seem that interventions in *Wimbledon* and the *Allegations of Genocide* cases have little in common. Nonetheless, Balcerzak discusses them in a broader context to arrive to more general remarks on the role of third-party intervention in the international litigation.

6 *Application of the Convention on the Prevention and Punishment of the Crime of Genocide* (The Gambia v. Myanmar), Preliminary Objections, Judgment, ICJ Reports 2022, 477, at 516, para. 108.

7 Order of the ICJ of 5 June 2023, *Allegations of Genocide under the Convention on the Prevention and Punishment of the Crime of Genocide* (Ukraine v. Russian Federation), available at: https://www.icj-cij.org/sites/default/files/case-related/182/182-20230605-ORD-01-00-EN.pdf.

2 The Substantive Problems of International Law in the *Wimbledon* case

Chapters 4-8 deal with the substantive legal problems. In Chapter 4 Malgosia Fitzmaurice and Agnes Rydberg address the problems of objective regimes, self-contained regimes, fragmentation of international law and the contemporary relevance of the Court's reasoning on these problems. According to Article 380 of the Versailles Treaty, 'the Kiel Canal and its approaches shall be maintained free and open to the vessels of commerce and of war of all nations at peace with Germany on terms of entire equality'. Article 380 established an objective legal regime of the Kiel Canal and changed its legal status. The Kiel Canal ceased to be an internal and national waterway and it became an international waterway for the 'benefit of all nations of the world'. The provisions of Article 380 which established this international and objective regime were self-contained for the Court. It was probably the first time this term had been introduced into the international legal vocabulary. Fitzmaurice and Rydberg in this chapter seek to answer the following questions: 1) has the *Wimbledon* judgment been a first clear sign of a phenomenon known as fragmentation of international law?; 2) what are the relationships between international objective regimes and self-contained regimes?; 3) and, finally, do the mentioned issues have a different legal expression and dimension today than they had 100 years ago? Their overall assessment of the *Wimbledon* case is that the judgment put the foundation of present international law in the above-discussed areas, even taking into consideration differences in approaches and structural considerations between legal circumstances then and now.

In Chapter 5 Władysław Czapliński deals with probably the best-known aspect of the *Wimbledon* case, that is, the statement on State sovereignty, and the relationship between international and national law. State sovereignty is still a crucial problem in theory and practice. For Hans Kelsen the issue of State sovereignty and the relationships between international law and national law are strongly interconnected and even interdependent on one another. The PCIJ referred to both problems in the *Wimbledon* case. The judgment is alluded as a famous example, of how to escape the difficulty or dilemma that results from the confrontation between the binding character of treaty obligations and the sovereign rights of States protected both in international law and national laws. The Court, on one hand, famously stated that 'the right of entering into international engagements is an attribute of State sovereignty' and 'sovereignty is not above law', and, on the other hand, it rejected the opinion that national legal acts could prevail over the treaty provisions. This chapter seeks to explore this understanding of State sovereignty and its influence on the relation of national law to international law. Thus, this chapter offers answers to the following questions, first, whether the *Wimbledon* judgment established an interpretative canon for understanding of State sovereignty in international law, second, whether this canon should be defended under the law, and, third, how the sovereignty issue affects the problem of mutual relations between international law and national law, which is especially visible in the time of populism.

Chapter 6 generally concerns the sources of international law. In this chapter Roman Kwiecień aims to discuss the following problems under the judgment: interpretation of legal obligations of States, including treaty obligations; the relationship between custom and treaties; a role of peremptory or categorical norms in the PCIJ's reasoning; and a normative hierarchy under the judgment, which concerns the 'relative normativity' issue under the judgment. According to the PCIJ, Article 380 of the Versailles Treaty contained the 'provision of a general and peremptory character'. The Court also considered the terms of Article 380 as 'categorical'. The Court had to respond to the relationships between Article 380 and other rules of international law, including customary rules, that is a situation when priority had to be given to a specific rule among several that might have been applicable to a legal matter or dispute. Thus, this chapter seeks to address the question whether the Court was in favour of the normative hierarchy in international law or of 'relative normativity' as labelled by Prosper Weil. Another question concerns the problem of formal source of the 'peremptory' or 'categorical' norms. In particular, could just treaty provisions be such a source? It is still a vital problem in international law. In the *Wimbledon* judgment legal reconstruction of rights and duties of parties to the proceeding was primarily grounded in the provisions of the Versailles Treaty. The Court's interpretation has been criticized for giving too much weight to the wording of Article 380. This was already indicated in the dissenting opinions by judges Anzilotti and Huber. Thus, an issue of interpretation of treaty rights and obligations arises, including the methods of interpretation, which is to be discussed in this chapter. There is one more crucial problem addressed in this chapter. It concerns the relationship between treaty obligations and unwritten sources of international law, that is, custom and general principles of law. Therefore, this chapter also seeks to answer the question of the formal source of general international law, in particular whether treaties could be seen as its source or merely source of legal obligations to their parties.

Neutrality in armed conflicts is a topic of Chapter 7. In this Chapter Michał Kowalski seeks to answer how neutrality affects the rights and obligations of States. The Court claimed that the use of international waterways could not be regarded as incompatible with the neutrality of the riparian States. According to it, the legal rules that governed the international canals showed that when an artificial waterway connecting two open seas had been "permanently dedicated to the use of the whole world", such waterway was assimilated to natural straits so that even the passage of a belligerent man-of-war did not compromise the neutrality of the sovereign State having jurisdiction over the respective waters. That is why the Court decided that the neutrality order of Germany would not apply to the case. For the Court a neutrality order issued by an individual State could not prevail over the treaty provisions aimed at a free and open passage through the Kiel Canal. As a consequence, Germany's neutrality orders could not be advanced against the obligation following from Article 380 Versailles Treaty. For these reasons the Court decided that it was not necessary to consider whether the state of war between Russia and Poland had or had not terminated at the date of the incident. But such an interpretation of neutrality and rights and obligations of States affected by armed conflicts is disputed and may be questionable. Doubts were already raised in the dissenting opinions of the judges. Michał Kowalski in his chapter argues that it is definitely advantageous to look at the *Wimbledon* judgement and its legacy in the context of neutrality as this issue strikingly shows the development and transformation of international law throughout the past one hundred years. He claims that the case of neutrality also illustrates how strongly the scholarship of international law still remains confined within traditional – or rather old-fashioned – legal concepts and is reluctant to admit their today's inadequacy and decline. As Kowalski argues, the function of neutrality was substantially different in international law before the UN Charter era – i.e. when international law was not based on the general prohibition of the use force. Neutrality has been thus evolving and – in consequence of this transformation –diminishing. According to him, whether and to what extent it has preserved its significance remains debatable and the *Wimbledon* case seems to be a good reference point for such a debate. The issue of neutrality seems especially topical nowadays when the international community is confronted with Russian aggression against Ukraine and some States again tend to advocate the neutrality concept as a desirable approach towards that armed conflict. Kowalski poses important questions in the light of this conflict: Is neutrality towards aggression legally possible in international law as it now stands? Or is it again – as in fact it used to be one hundred years ago – a useful legal excuse to protect individual States' interests preferred over community interests and masked with a pacifist legal narrative? In connection with these questions, he presents in his chapter contextual illustrations of neutrality approaches towards two armed conflicts separated by a hundred years but, at least to some extent, similar: the Polish– Soviet war of 1919–21 and the Russian aggression against Ukraine of 2022. At any case, different opinions presented in the judgment and the dissents seem to be a good reference point for discussing international legal status of neutrality in armed conflicts today, including the armed conflict in Ukraine.

In Chapter 8 Barbara Stępień discusses legal status of international and internal waterways. Article 380 of the Versailles Peace Treaty established an 'international and objective legal regime' within the Kiel Canal and changed its legal status. The Kiel Canal ceased to be an internal and national waterway and it became an international waterway for the 'benefit of all nations of the world'. The problem of the legal status of the Kiel Canal is connected with other legal issues addressed in the previous chapters of the book as 'self-contained regime', the relationship between treaties and custom, State sovereignty or neutrality in armed conflicts. This chapter seeks to discuss the very legal status of international waterways as 'objective legal regime', its normative source(s) and rights and duties of States within it. The Court considered the terms of Article 380 as 'categorical' and 'self-contained'. Discussing the legal status of the Kiel Canal, the Court referred to previous treaties on other international waterways, that is the Suez and Panama Canals. It did that mainly due to the rights and duties of riparian States, including their neutrality. The Court arrived at the conclusion that the legal regime of the Suez and Panama Canals invalidated the argument of Germany based on its neutrality. It recognized this regime as an illustration of "the general opinion according to which when an artificial waterway connecting two open seas has been permanently dedicated to the use of the whole world, such waterway is assimilated to natural straits in the sense that even the passage of a belligerent man-of-war does not compromise the neutrality of the sovereign State under whose jurisdiction the waters in question lie". A question thus arises on a normative source of such legal status of international waterways. Is it a treaty or a custom? The PCIJ speaking of 'the general opinion' seemed to incline to the latter. But this part of the judgment was strongly criticized for an unconvincing treatment of the issue, since the relevant State practice was based only on two treaties that had a limited number of parties. Besides, there was a weak similarity between the Suez and Panama treaties and Article 380 of the Versailles Treaty. That is why, Judges Anzilotti and Huber rejected in their dissenting opinion the comparison between them because the Suez and Panama Canal treaties entailed the precise regulation of situations of war which were omitted in the provisions on the Kiel Canal. Thus, this chapter discusses a legal basis for 'objective legal regimes' such as international waterways. Are these 'objective regimes' really objective? Does their status follow from general international law based on custom? Or is it possibly based on treaty regulations and, in consequence, fragmentated, and not objective and general? And how does it affect duties of riparian States and protect both their rights and rights of third States? Another problem addressed in this chapter concerns a legal qualification of 'free passage' through the international canals. The PCIJ failed to decide the question whether this right within the Kiel Canal amounted to a servitude by international law resting upon Germany. The Court just confined itself to indicate that it was not called upon to take a definite attitude to the question "whether in the domain of international law, there really exist servitudes analogous to the servitudes of private law". These are the research problems addressed in Chapter 8.

CHAPTER 1

Shadows of Peace: the Reception of the Treaty of Versailles in Germany and Poland

Raphael Schäfer

Abstract

The Chapter is devoted to the historical and legal context of the Wimbledon judgment, that is the Versailles Treaty and its reception in Germany and Poland. This chapter provides guidance for a clearer examination of the context surrounding the dispute decided by the PCIJ and of the legal statements of the parties submitted before the Court. The interpretation of rights and obligations following from the Versailles Treaty had been crucial both for the Court and for applicants and respondent, which was clearly noticeable during the proceedings. The judgment is of particular importance not only because it was the first judgement of the PCIJ that inevitably led to a positioning of the Court in international law. It was also the first international judgement based on the Treaty of Versailles, thus rendering the Treaty itself – even if only indirectly – the subject of proceedings.

1 Introduction

For 21 March 1921, the logbook of the S.S. Wimbledon – a French chartered British steamship on its way to the Polish Naval Base at Danzig with a cargo of 4,000 tons of military material – contains the following entry: '11.35 a.m. Kiel Canal Commission boarded, examined manifest, and stated that vessel could not go through the canal on account of cargo.'[1] The German authorities justified the denial of free passage through the Kiel Canal, to which the Wimbledon was entitled prima facie under Article 380 of the Treaty of Versailles, with the argument that 'German regulations regarding neutrality forbade the transit across German territory of war material'.[2]

1 Wolgast E., *Der Wimbledonprozeß* (Berlin: 1926) 16.

2 Application Instituting Proceeding 7. Article 1 of the Order of 25 July 1920, issued '[i]n consequence of Germany's neutrality in the war which has arisen between the Republic of Poland and the Federal Socialist Republic of the Russian Soviets' reads: 'The export and transit of

 | DOI:10.1163/9789004707979_003

The Wimbledon requested passage at a time when the Polish–Soviet war had formally ended with the Treaty of Riga on 18 March 1921, but peace was still not really trusted.[3] For Germany – the guardian of the Kiel Canal – the incident came at a period of extreme uncertainty and only fragile domestic stability. In 1921, the Reich was psychologically still under the immediate impact of the conclusion of the Treaty of Versailles and the overall political future seemed uncertain.[4] Due to the unstable domestic political situation, the government was dependent on maintaining strict neutrality towards the Russian–Polish war if it wanted to preserve the fragile constitutional body of the Weimar Republic. This was especially true for Kiel, where the 1918 uprising originated.[5]

Strong sections of public opinion were already calling for a German participation in the Polish–Soviet War – depending on the political persuasion on one side or the other.[6] Therefore, already on 2 August 1920, the German Foreign Minister, Werner Simons (1861–1937), had declared in an influential article in the *Deutsche Allgemeine Zeitung* that the German government would be very careful not to make either mistake: 'It will remain honestly neutral, and what prevents it from doing so I hope confidently that the German consequences will be a united defence,' Simons wrote.[7] This solemn declaration, however, could not hide the fact that German neutrality worked *de facto* in Russia's favour, as it blocked any arms deliveries to Poland.[8] Of course, Germany was aware of this,

... articles of war material is prohibited in so far as these articles are consigned to the territories of the Polish Republic or of the Federal Socialist Republic of the Russian Soviets.' Already on 20 July 1920 Reich president Friedrich Ebert issued the following declaration: 'In the warlike entanglements which have arisen between the Polish Republic and the Russian Soviet Republic, Germany, which is at peace with both States, has observed and will continue to observe full neutrality. Accordingly, I point out that it is the duty of everyone abroad to refrain from any action contrary to the neutrality of Germany.' Reproduced in Wagner G., *Deutschland und der Polnisch-Sowjetische Krieg 1920* (Wiesbaden: 1979) 76.

3 Wolgast, *Wimbledonprozeß* 102 et seq.

4 Ibid. 21.

5 Ibid. 22 and 41 et seq. However, this was met with distrust by the Allies. The Daily Telegraph of 23 July 1920, eg, wrote: 'The correct Dr. Simons may utter sonorous platitudes about strict neutrality, but we can have no confidence that the ruling influences in Germany will resist the temptation to use Bolshevism when they see a chance, in order to reverse the Treaty of Versailles and nullify the effects of the Allied victory.', reproduced in Wagner, *Polnisch-Sowjetische Krieg* 183.

6 Wolgast, *Wimbledonprozeß* 20. On the importance of the Peace of Riga of 18 March 1921, cf. ibid. 102 et seq.

7 Ibid. 20.

8 Erich Eyck, *Geschichte der Weimarer Republik*, vol. 1 (Zurich: 1954) 231. Cf. also Wagner, *Polnisch-Sowjetische Krieg* 60 and 79.

not least from a report in the Times.[9] To be fair, however, it also has to be stated that Germany found itself in a catch-22 situation: had it allowed the transit of weapons, it would have unilaterally disadvantaged Russia.[10] Nevertheless, it cannot go unnoticed that volunteers in East Prussia were ready to intervene on the Russian side in the war.[11]

Nevertheless, Germany seemed to be more favourably disposed towards Russia than towards Poland.[12] '[W]e ourselves have suffered too much from being treated as pariahs', Foreign Minister Simons recalled in the Reichstag, 'to want to inflict this treatment on [Russia].'[13] This seems all the more serious because in the same plenary session he continued with a threat, albeit indirectly, against Poland: 'I believe that Poland will have a very bleak, uncertain and unhappy future if it considers its task to be the barrier between Russia and Germany.'[14]

Irrespective of German neutrality, Great Britain, Italy and Japan perceived the denial of passage as a violation of the Treaty of Versailles. They were concerned – probably not without reason – that Germany wanted to indirectly ally itself with Russia at the expense of Poland.[15] Consequently, on 16 January 1923, they asked the PCIJ to adjudicate on the basis of Article 386 para. 1 of the Treaty of Versailles, inter alia, '[t]hat the German authorities wrongfully refused on March 21st, 1921, free access to the Kiel Canal of the steamship Wimbledon'.[16] The judgment is of particular importance not only because it was the first judgement of the Permanent Court of International Justice that inevitably led to a positioning of the Court in international law. It was also the first international judgement based on the Treaty of Versailles, thus rendering the Treaty itself – even if only indirectly – the subject of proceedings.

As we know, the verdict was unfavourable to Germany. The Court held in its judgment of 17 August 1923 that 'Germany was perfectly free to declare and regulate her neutrality in the Russo–Polish war, but subject to the condition that she respected and maintained intact the contractual obligations which

9 Available at: https://www.reichstagsprotokolle.de/Blatt2_w1_bsb00000028_00271.html. Cf. on this speech also Wagner, Polnisch-Sowjetische Krieg 90 et seq.

10 Ibid. 79.

11 Lehnstaedt S., *Der vergessene Sieg. Der Polnisch-Sowjetische Krieg 1919–1921 und die Entstehung des modernen Osteuropa* (Munich: 2019) 157.

12 So on this also Wagner, *Polnisch-Sowjetische Krieg* 224 et seq.

13 Available at: https://www.reichstagsprotokolle.de/Blatt2_w1_bsb00000028_00271.html.

14 Available at: https://www.reichstagsprotokolle.de/Blatt2_w1_bsb00000028_00272.html. Cf. also Wagner, *Polnisch-Sowjetische Krieg* 142 et seq.

15 Wagner, *Polnisch-Sowjetische Krieg* 172 et seq. and 183 et seq.

16 Application Instituting Proceedings 7.

she entered into at Versailles on June 28th, 1919.'[17] Not surprisingly, German scholars blamed the Court's insistence on the mere wording of Article 380 which allowed it to justify an unreasonable result on the overall 'spirit of the treaty': 'The impression of the Versailles Treaty as an instrument of gagging Germany weighs too heavily on the world and even on the highly distinguished members of the League of Nations Court,' Ernst Wolgast concluded in 1926.[18] Still in 1962, Ingo von Münch argued that it was precisely the 'nature of the peace treaty as a submission of the vanquished to the victor' that made it possible to 'reserve minor administrative interests for the vanquished state in a certain area, but deprive it of the freedom to decide on much more important matters – such as the observance of neutrality'.[19]

Against this background, it is necessary to examine the historical background of the Wimbledon decision. To do so, this chapter follows a three-step approach: First, it sets out the historical singularity of the conclusion of the Treaty of Versailles from a history of emotions perspective (1.). Building on this, it then shows the consequences of the peace settlement for Germany (2.) and Poland (3.). A final part concludes (4.).

2 The Hall of Mirrors at Versailles: Moments of Fear, Revenge and International Law

The Hall of Mirrors in Versailles is one of the places in which international law has manifested itself several times throughout history. It was there, on 18 January 1871, 170 years after Frederick III's self-coronation in Königsberg as King in Prussia, where the Prussian King William I was proclaimed German Emperor. This deliberate humiliation of France was intended as revenge for the German sufferings under Louis XIV and Napoleon I.[20] The 'hereditary Franco-German enmity' thus sealed henceforth determined the fate of the European continent and was decisive for the emergence of the First World War. It is therefore no great surprise that France insisted on Versailles with its

17 Judgment p. 30.

18 Wolgast, *Wimbledonprozeß* 175, cf. also p. 9 where he suspects, without further justification, 'that certain extraneous considerations may have played a role in the decision'.

19 Münch I., "Wimbledon-Fall!", in Strupp K. – Schlochauer H.-J. (eds.), *Wörterbuch des Völkerrechts*, vol. 3 (Berlin: 2nd ed. 1962) 850, 853.

20 Cf. also März P., *Nach der Urkatastrophe. Deutschland, Europa und der Erste Weltkrieg* (Cologne: 2014) 79 et seq.

Hall of Mirrors as the place for the signing of the treaty that would officially end the 'Great War'.

As a matter of fact, France took every opportunity to make the peace settlement a far more historic event than the mere signing of a treaty. The celebration of victory, that it was to supposed to become for France, as the newspaper *Le Petit Parisien* reported, could not meaningfully take place in any other venue, as French foreign minister Stephen Pichon (1857–1933) has declared already before the armistice.[21] However, the choice of Paris as the conference venue was not without controversy among the Allies. However, for fear of being labelled pro-German, and not least for the want of other suitable venues, no thoroughgoing opposition arose.[22]

Historians widely agree today that the treaty signing ceremony was 'a highly symbolic political staging'.[23] Already the peace terms were announced to the German government – with which there had been no personal contact since the signing of the armistice of 11 November 1918 – on 7 May 1919, the fourth anniversary of the sinking of the Lusitania on 7 May 1915.[24] This was a pivotal moment in the course of the First World War as it triggered the so-called 'Lusitania Effect', a catalyst moment 'for reconsiderations of American neutrality and innumerable exhortations of action against the German Empire'.[25] It also was no coincidence that the Paris Peace Conference began on 18 January 1919, the anniversary of the Proclamation of the German Empire in Versailles. The Treaty itself was to be signed on 28 June 1919, the fifth anniversary of the Sarajevo assassination. The official peace ceremony would take place on the French National Holiday, 14 July.

The symbolism, however, was not limited to calendrical dates. It was also present in the Hall of Mirrors itself, both conceptually and personified, paying

21 Allain J.-Cl., "Le château de Versailles", in Möller H. – Morizet J. (eds.), *Allemagne-France. Lieux et mémoire d'une histoire commune* (Paris: 1995) 75–84, 81. See also Le Petit Parisien (29 June 1919) 1. Cf. Conze E, *Die große Illusion. Versailles 1919 und die Neuordnung der Welt* (Munich: 2020) 349.

22 Nicolson H, *Peacemaking 1919* (London: 1933) 76 et seq. Cf. also Conze, *Versailles 1919* 201 et seq.

23 Conze, *Versailles 1919* 9. Cf. also Leonhard J., *Der überforderte Frieden. Versailles und die Welt 1918–1923* (Munich: 2018) 1020 et seq.

24 Schiff V., *So war es in Versailles …* (Berlin: 1929) 46; Protasio J., *The Day the World Was Shocked: The Lusitania Disaster and Its Influence on the Course of World War I* (Havertown: 2011); Larson E., *Dead Wake. The Last Crossing of the Lusitania* (New York: 2016); Jasper W., *Lusitania. Kulturgeschichte einer Katastrophe* (Berlin: 2015).

25 Trommler F., "The Lusitania Effect. America's Mobilization against Germany in World War I", *German Studies Review* (32) 2009, 241. Cf. also Graebner N. – Bennett E., *The Versailles Treaty and Its Legacy. The Failure of the Wilsonian Vision* (Cambridge: 2011) 16 et seq.

reference to Hegel's concept of 'world history as the Last Judgment'. With over 1,000 people the hall was completely full. Onlooking military personnel and politicians who had no longer found access to the Hall of Mirrors stood on stools, tables and chair backs in front of the glazed doors.[26] 'This robs the ceremony of all privilege and therefore of all dignity,' wrote Harold Nicolson (1886–1968), member of the British delegation, in his diary.[27] In the middle of the room was 'a horseshoe table for the plenipotentiaries' and in front 'like a guillotine, ... the table for the signatures.'[28] To underline that both of the government-bearing parties supported the signing of the treaty, the German delegation consisted of foreign minister Hermann Müller (SPD) and minister of transport Johannes Bell (Zentrum). Minister of finance, Matthias Erzberger, was not available for a signature, as he had already become a target of right-wing nationalist circles by signing the armistice agreement. His reluctance was not unfounded; on 26 August 1921 he was assassinated by members of the extreme right-wing 'Consul' organisation.[29]

The journalists present were prepared, as Jörn Leonhard points out, to make the signing a 'global media moment'.[30] A moment, described by Nicolson, as 'most painful', governed by 'general tension'.[31] However, the charge against Germany was not limited to the arrangement of the hall, the accusation was also represented in the room personally in form of the delegation of the so-called 'gueules cassées', five facially disfigured French soldiers of the First World War. They were standing behind the table where the Treaty was ready to be signed. The German delegation therefore had to walk past the deformed serviceman and turn their backs on them when signing the treaty.[32] These people, deliberately chosen for their distressing appearance, were 'witnesses of the war, plaintiffs and judges' and represented the suffering of the war, for which Germany was supposed to atone.[33] Jörn Leonhard sees in this a 'concretely

26 A photo is reproduced in *Der Vertrag von Versailles* (Munich: 1978) 112.

27 Nicolson, *Peacemaking 1919* 367.

28 Ibid. 366. Cf. also Schiff, *Versailles* 48.

29 Schiff, *Versailles* 136. Cf. on this, in more detail, Hüetlin T., *Berlin, 24. Juni 1922: Der Rathenaumord und der Beginn des rechten Terrors in Deutschland* (Cologne: 2022).

30 Leonhard, *Der überforderte Frieden* 1024.

31 Nicolson, *Peacemaking 1919* 368 et seq. Cf. also Payk M., *Frieden durch Recht? Der Aufstieg des modernen Völkerrechts und der Friedensschluss nach dem Ersten Weltkrieg* (Berlin: 2018) 426.

32 Audoin-Rouzeau S., «Die Delegation der ‚gueules cassées' in Versailles am 28. Juni 1919», in Krumeich G. (ed.), *Versailles 1919. Ziele – Wirkung – Wahrnehmung* (Essen: 2001) 281–287, 281.

33 Le Petit Parisien (29 June 1919) 1. Cf. also the statement by one of the soldiers, reproduced in Le Petit Parisien (30 June 1919) 1: 'En nous choisissant, dit-il, le gouvernement français a

visible symbol of German war guilt', a personification 'of war as a crime against humanity, of the search for peace as an indictment of Germany and of the conclusion of peace as an act of atonement before the eyes of the whole world'.[34] And, as Stéphane Audoin-Rouzeau argues, the wounded were to 'literally embody by their ruined faces the part of the treaty that had the greatest symbolic value: Article 231,'[35] which established Germany's 'responsibility [for] all the loss and damage to which the Allied and Associated Governments and their nationals have been subjected as a consequence of the war imposed upon them by the aggression of Germany'.

The whole ceremony had made German utter powerlessness obvious.[36] Maybe even more than necessary, as the signing of the Treaty was perceived as highly degrading by (and for) Germany at the time. 'I had a feeling of sympathy for the Germans who sat there quite stoically', Edward House, advisor to the President of the United States, noted on 28 June 1919:

> It was not unlike what was done in olden times, when the conqueror dragged the conquered at his chariot wheels. To my mind, it is out of keeping with the new era which we profess an ardent desire to promote. I wish it could have been more simple and that there might have been an element of chivalry, which was wholly lacking. The affair was elaborately staged and made as humiliating to the enemy as it well could be.[37]

The 'lacking of chivalry' determined the contact between the Allies and Germany since the conclusion of the armistice. German officials were entirely excluded from the negotiations of the conditions of the peace to prevent a repetition of the Congress of Vienna, where Charles-Maurice de Talleyrand-Périgord (1754–1838), as representative of defeated France, was able to set the victorious Allies against each other, thereby weakening their alliance.[38] Instead, the entire process was characterised by a lacking will of communication of the

tenu à montrer aux délégués allemands les consequences douloureuses de la guerre qu'ils ont provoquée et attester en même temps que la victoire que nous célébrions avait été chèrement achetée.'

34 Leonhard, *Der überforderte Frieden* 1033.

35 Audoin-Rouzeau, 'Delegation der „gueules cassées"' 287.

36 Cf. also Platthaus A., *Der Krieg nach dem Krieg. Deutschland zwischen Revolution und Versailles 1918/19* (Berlin: 2018) 355.

37 Seymour C., *The Intimate Papers of Colonel House*, vol. 4 (London: 1928) 502.

38 März, *Nach der Urkatastrophe* 105; Conze, *Versailles 1919* 276; Krüger P., Versailles. *Deutsche Außenpolitik zwischen Revisionismus und Friedenssicherung* (Munich: 1986) 19.

Allies with Germany.[39] Consequently, the official role of the German delegation was reduced to a mere reception carrier of the allied peace terms. It is therefore not surprising when Ulrich von Brockdorff-Rantzau (1869–1928), first foreign minister of the Weimar Republic and head of the German delegation, said upon receipt of the conditions of peace on 7 May 1919:

> We do not deceive ourselves about the extent of our defeat, the degree of our powerlessness. We know that the violence of German arms is broken. We know the force of the hatred that confronts us here, and we have heard the passionate demand that the victors should at the same time make us pay as the overcome and punish us as the guilty.[40]

The Allies did not miss any opportunity to lend weight to their accusation: On their way to Paris, the train of the German delegation was slowed down to walking speed when it reached the former battlefields in order to show the Germans the extent of the destruction the Allies held their country responsible for.[41] Having received the conditions of peace, Brockdorff-Rantzau delivered his speech of reception sitting down, which the Allies perceived as an affront and proof of incorrigible German arrogance.[42] If this behavior was supposed to symbolise German strength, his 'policy of open resistance' only succeeded in strengthening the already fragile solidarity between the Allies.[43] As Sally Marks stated, 'German leaders were unrealistic about their country's situation, more than ordinarily incapable of putting themselves in the shoes of other nations, and themselves oblivious to their effect on others.' At least after Brockdorff Rantzau's speech it became obvious that the German position was based on the conviction that 'Germany should not suffer and that reparation … could only occur when and to the degree convenient.'[44]

39 Leonhard, *Der überforderte Frieden* 1027. Cf. also Schiff, *Versailles* 63 et seq.

40 Speech of Foreign Minister Brockdorff-Rantzau on 7 May 1919 in the Hotel Trianon, Paris, reproduced in Brandt S., *Das letzte Echo des Krieges. Der Versailler Vertrag* (Ditzingen: 2018) 226.

41 Brandt, *Versailler Vertrag* 103. For a historical account of the journey, see Schiff, *Versailles* 25.

42 Leonhard, *Der überforderte Frieden* 1046; Conze, *Versailles 1919* 350; Kolb E., *Der Frieden von Versailles* (Munich: 2nd ed. 2011) 86; Zimmermann L., *Deutsche Aussenpolitik in der Ära der Weimarer Republik* (Göttingen: 1958) 57; Fink C., *Defending the Rights of Others. The Great Powers, the Jews, and International Minority Protection, 1878–1938* (Cambridge: 2004) 209.

43 Kolb E. –Schumann D., *Die Weimarer Republik* (Berlin: 2022) 33.

44 Marks S., "Smoke and Mirrors: In Some-Filled Rooms and the Galerie des Glaces", in Boemeke M. – Feldman G. – Glaser E. (eds.), *The Treaty of Versailles. A Reassessment after*

Only a short time later, Reich Minister President Philipp Scheidemann (1865–1939), used in the first meeting of the Weimar National Assembly on 12 May 1919 the famous words 'What hand should not wither that puts this fetter on itself and on us?' that would soon become a catchphrase in Germany.[45] Unwilling, to accept the terms of the 'Schandfrieden', the government resigned on 20 June 1919.[46] The scale of disappointment was perfectly captured by the theologian Ernst Troeltsch (1865–1923), who called the time between the armistice and the announcement of the peace terms 'the dreamland of the armistice period, where everyone could imagine the future fantastically, pessimistically or heroically without the conditions and real factual consequences of the impending peace'.[47]

In the end, however, there was no realistic way to avoid signing the Treaty of Versailles. For the ultimatum expired on 23 June 1919, after which there was the threat of a resumption of hostilities with an expected occupation of the territory of the Reich, the German military would be unable to counter.[48] In addition to this, the British naval blockade was continued beyond the armistice and could always be intensified if necessary. The hardliners among the Allies even hoped for a German rejection in order to be able to realise their stricter plans for partition of Germany after all.[49] It is reasonable to assume, therefore, that a refused signature would have ultimately led to the disintegration of German unity.[50] Eventually, any German government had no other option but to accept the new realities that ended the Troeltschian 'dream land'. Not much has changed since 6 February 1919, where Reich President Friedrich Ebert (1871–1925) had declared in his speech at the opening of the National Assembly that the government

75 Years (Cambridge: 1998) 337, 358 et seq. Cf. also Smith L., *Sovereignty at the Paris Peace Conference of 1919* (Oxford: 2018) 62.

45 Winkler H.-A., *Weimar 1918–1933. Die Geschichte der ersten deutschen Demokratie* (Munich: 4th ed. 2005) 91.

46 Krumeich G., *Die unbewältigte Niederlage. Das Trauma des Ersten Weltkriegs und die Weimarer Republik* (Freiburg: 2018) 176. Cf. also Graebner N. – Bennett E., *Versailles Treaty* 58.

47 Troeltsch E., „Nach der Entscheidung (Juli 1919)", in Hübinger G. (ed.), *Ernst Troeltsch. Spectator-Briefe und Berliner Briefe (1919–1922)* (Berlin: 2015) 125, 131.

48 Erzberger M., *Erlebnisse im Weltkrieg* (Stuttgart: 1920) 372 et seq.

49 Kolb, *Versailles* 85; Kolb –Schumann, *Weimarer Republik* 34.

50 Zimmermann, *Deutsche Aussenpolitik* 65; Erzberger, *Erlebnisse im Weltkrieg* 372 et seq. But cf. also with arguments against a continuation of war Payk, *Frieden durch Recht?* 418 et seq.

> was shocked to learn from the last communication of the Allied and Associated Governments that they are determined to use extreme force to force Germany to accept those peace conditions which, without having any material significance, are intended to deprive the German people of its honour. The honour of the German people is not affected by an act of violence. After the terrible sufferings of the last few years, the German people have no means of defending it against the outside world. Giving way to overwhelming force, and without thereby abandoning its view of the outrageous injustice of the peace terms, the Government of the German Republic therefore declares that it is prepared to accept and sign the peace terms imposed by the Allied and Associated Governments.[51]

German resistance was therefore limited to what little Germany was still capable of. Consequently, it was primarily of a symbolic nature: On 21 June, the battleships of the Imperial Fleet, interned in the natural harbour of Scapa Flow in Scotland, sank themselves in order to avoid being seized by the British and on 23 June, *Freikorps* soldiers publicly burned French flags captured in the war of 1870/71, which should have been returned to France in accordance with the Treaty of Versailles.[52] Shortly before the ultimatum expired, the Allies received a telegram from Reich Chancellor Hermann Müller announcing the Government's intention to sign, in extreme protest against the 'act of violence' that could not deprive the German people of its honour.

3 A Carthaginian Peace? Germany and the Treaty of Versailles

It is too easy to subscribe unreflectedly to the 'traditional' critique of the Treaty of Versailles. From the very beginning, Germany staged the 'Versailles' as a 'national drama and dictate threatening its existence'.[53] It was a diffuse, differently accentuated and utilised common national sentiment across all party lines that German imperial power would have to be restored by revising the Treaty of Versailles.[54] But it was especially anti-democratic forces that

51 Note der deutschen Friedensdelegation an Clemenceau vom 23. Juni 1919 über vorbehaltlose Annahme der Friedensbedingungen, in *Materialien, betreffend die Friedensverhandlungen*, Teil IX, Dok. Nr. 14. Cf. also the speech by Paul Löbe on 22 June 1919 in the German National Assembly, reproduced in Schiff, *Versailles* 123 et seq.

52 Kolb, *Versailles* 82; Leonhard, *Der überforderte Frieden* 1017 and 1019; Brandt, *Versailler Vertrag* 154 et seq.

53 Payk, *Frieden durch Recht?* 428.

54 Krüger, *Deutsche Außenpolitik* 80.

instrumentalized the Treaty of Versailles for their agitation against the Weimar Republic.[55]

This poisoned mood could only be created by down-playing the extent of Germany's military defeat. A first (or last) success of Germany's military leadership was to conceal that the armistice was not a mere cease fire but an actual surrender[56] The surprise of the German people, who was constantly promised that their armies were on the verge of victory, was reinforced by the German legend (or better: lie) of the stab in the back (the infamous 'Dolchstoßlegende').[57] It was established by none other than the famous Field Marshal General Paul von Hindenburg (1847–1934), who declared on 18 November 1919 before the Parliamentary Committee of Inquiry:

> An English general rightly said: 'The German army has been stabbed in the back'. The good core of the army is not to blame. ... Where the blame lies is clearly proven. If any further proof were needed, it is to be found in the English general's statement and in our enemies' utter astonishment at their victory.[58]

However, there were also several prominent voices from the side of the Allies, criticizing the Versailles Treaty. By far the biggest impact – up to this day – had the book 'The Economic Consequences of the Peace', written by John Maynard Keynes (1883–1945) who was part of the British Delegation in Paris. 'The Treaty', he wrote,

> includes no provisions for the economic rehabilitation of Europe, nothing to make the defeated Central Empires into good neighbours, nothing to stabilise, the new States of Europe, nothing to reclaim Russia; nor does it promote in any way a compact of economic solidarity amongst the Allies themselves; no arrangement was reached at Paris for restoring

55 Conze E., „Verhasster Vertrag. ‚Versailles' als Propagandawaffe gegen die Weimarer Republik", *Aus Politik und Zeitgeschichte* 69 (2019) 45. Cf. also Barth B., *Dolchstoßlegenden und politische Desintegration. Das Trauma der deutschen Niederlage im Ersten Weltkrieg 1914–1933* (Düsseldorf: 2003) 451.

56 Marks S., "Mistakes and Myths: The Allies, Germany, and the Versailles Treaty, 1918–1921", *The Journal of Modern History* 85 (2013) 632, 634. For a historical account, see Delbrück H., *Der Friede von Versailles* (Berlin: 2nd ed. 1930) 15.

57 See on this in greater detail Barth, *Dolchstoßlegenden* passim.

58 14. Sitzung des 2. Unterausschusses, Dienstag den 18. November 1919, in *Stenographische Berichte über die öffentlichen Verhandlungen des 15. Untersuchungsausschusses der Verfassunggebenden Nationalversammlung nebst Beilagen*, vol. 2 (Berlin: 1920) 695, 701.

> the disordered finances of France and Italy, or to adjust the systems of the Old World and the New.[59]

Admittedly, tough peace terms were imposed on the German Empire and in particular of a quality that no other European nation had yet experienced. In sum, Germany was about to lose roughly 12.5 % of its territory with 10 % of its population, 15 % of its agricultural production, 50% of its iron ore supply and 25% of its hard coal deposits, and finally all its colonies. Furthermore, Austria was banned from joining the Reich to prevent compensation for Germany's lost territories. The Saar region was to come under the administration of the League of Nations for 15 years, Danzig became an independent state as a Free City under the protection of the League of Nations, the Rhineland was demilitarized and occupied for 15 years. Most of Posen and West Prussia, with the exception of a few peripheral areas, went to Poland. With the so-called 'Corridor', the restored Polish state gained access to the Baltic Sea.[60] As a result, however, East Prussia was detached from the Reich's core territory.[61]

In military terms, general conscription was abolished, the General Staff was dissolved, fortresses in the demilitarised Rhineland were demolished and modern weapons such as aircraft and tanks were banned. The military equipment Germany was allowed to possess was regulated in detail by the Treaty. The land army was limited to 100,000 soldiers, the navy to 15,000. Compliance with these provisions was to be monitored by an Inter-Allied Commission, the costs of which were to be borne by the German government. Furthermore, the German government had to extradite all persons accused of violating the laws of war for the purpose of prosecution by the Allies. The German Kaiser was publicly arraigned for a supreme offence against international morality and the sanctity of treaties and was supposed to be tried by a special tribunal. All German foreign assets were confiscated and all German submarine cables had

59 Keynes J., *The Economic Consequences of the Peace* (London: 1920) 211. Cf. also Conze, *Versailles 1919* 476 et seq.; Churchill W., *The Second World War. The Gathering Storm* (Boston: 1948) 6 et seq.: 'The economic clauses of the Treaty were malignant and silly to an extent that made them obviously futile. Germany was condemned to pay reparations on a fabulous scale. These dictates gave expression to the anger of the victors, and to the failure of their peoples to understand that no defeated nation or community can ever pay tribute on a scale which would meet the cost of modern war.'

60 See on this in greater detail Smogorzewski C., *Poland's Access to the Sea* (London: 1934) passim.

61 For the importance of East Prussia on German identity, cf. März, *Nach der Urkatastrophe* 107. For a critical account of the peace terms, cf. Smith, *Paris Peace Conference* 85 et seq. who uses the image of a 'frustrated parent disciplining a truculent teenager'.

to be ceded. The major German rivers were internationalised and all states with which Germany was not at war were granted the right to navigate the Kiel Canal. Until the final amount of damages was determined, Germany had to pay 20 billion gold marks.[62]

It was, by all means, a hard peace and it is easy to understand why it was perceived as disgraceful in Germany. However, the Treaty of Versailles must also be put in relation to German practice. It was not an Allied version of Brest-Litovsk that truly deserved the name 'dictate'. In this treaty, which lost its validity as a result of the Treaty of Versailles, Germany deprived Russia of 34 percent of its population, 54 percent of its industry, 89 percent of its coal reserves, and all its production of oil and cotton.[63] Furthermore, if one takes the power fantasies of a German 'Mitteleuropa' as formulated in the 'September Progamme' of 1914 by Reich Chancellor Theobald von Bethmann Hollweg (1856–1921) seriously, Germany was met with incomparably milder conditions in Versailles than Germany would have imposed on France in the event of its victory.[64]

Zentrum politician Adolf Gröber (1854–1919) was one of the few Germans who saw the chances the Versailles Treaty was offering: immediate return of the prisoners of war, end of famine caused by the naval blockade, rebuilding the German economy and preservation of the unity of the German Reich.[65] Of course, these opportunities had to be sought for actively, they did not impose themselves. Especially as the principle of 'charitable oblivion', the basis of previous peace treaties, was replaced by moralised categories of crime, guilt and punishment.[66] Therefore, active attention must be devoted to those provisions that the Treaty did not adopt in the end: Germany was not separated, its territories left of the Rhine where neither given to France nor transformed into a buffer state, East Prussia remained German and did not become an independent 'East State'.[67] Of course, these concessions were not the result of

62 Kolb, *Frieden von Versailles* 59 et seq. Cf. also Brandt, *Versailler Vertrag* 136 et seq.; Hildebrand K., *Das vergangene Reich. Deutsche Außenpolitik von Bismarck bis Hitler 1871–1945* (Munich: 2008) 399 et seq.

63 Wehler H-U., *Deutsche Gesellschaftsgeschichte*, vol. 4 (Munich: 2003) 152.

64 Fischer F., *Germany's Aims in the First World War* (New York: 1967). For a more modern interpretation of the Treaty of Versailles, cf. Sally Marks, "Smoke and Mirrors" 360 et seq. For the German plan of 'Mitteleuropa', see Naumann F., *Mitteleuropa* (Berlin: 1915) passim.

65 Quoted in Probst R., „Wir kennen die Wucht des Hasses" (Süddeutsche Zeitung of 28 June 2019). Cf. also Schiff, *Versailles* (Berlin: 1929) 135 et seq.

66 Leonhard, *Der überforderte Frieden* 901 et seq. and 1266 et seq.; Brandt, *Versailler Vertrag* 143; Conze, *Versailles 1919* 383 et seq.

67 Conze, *Versailles 1919* 280 et seq. Cf. also Birdsall P., *Versailles Twenty Years After* (Hamden: 1962 [1941]) 177 and 201.

Allied generosity towards Germany. While France wanted to see Germany as weakened as possible, Britain advocated the European balance of power.[68] In particular, as Lloyd George dramatically outlined in his famous 'Fontainebleau Memorandum' of 25 March 1919, the defense against Russian Bolshevism required Germany not to be weakened excessively.[69] Already from an economic perspective, it was common ground that Germany had to remain in a position to be able to fulfil the reparations, on which Great Britain in turn was dependent in order to pay its loans to the US.[70] As a consequence 'Germany's productive capacity and industrial potential were left intact' which allowed the Reich to remain Europe's 'industrial power-house'.[71]

Unlike the Habsburg and Ottoman empires, the German Empire continued to exist as such. Admittedly, the Treaty eliminated Germany's position as a great power for the moment, but did not make it impossible for Germany to regain it.[72] As Russia ceased to be a German competitor for the time being, Peter März even argued that this amounted to a 'serious improvement in its geostrategic position in Europe': between the Baltic Sea and the Black Sea, Germany had, according to März, gained new room for political action, provided the Reich was able to choose a peaceful foreign policy that accepted the new borders set by the Treaty of Versailles.[73] And indeed, with the conclusion of the peace, the already traditional German angst of an encirclement by hostile states was no longer justified – none of its neighbouring states could realistically pose a threat – and it even gave Germany and Russia a chance to

68 See on this, more generally, Jackson P., *Beyond the Balance of Power. France and the Politics of National Security in the Era of the First World War* (Cambridge: 2013) 290 et seq. Cf. also Fry M., "British Revisionism", Boemeke M. – Feldman G. – Glaser E. (eds.), *The Treaty of Versailles. A Reassessment after 75 Years* (Cambridge: 1998) 599 et seq.

69 Smith, *Paris Peace Conference* 137; März, *Nach der Urkatastrophe* 103; Conze, *Versailles 1919* 303. The memorandum is reproduced in Nowak K., *Versailles* (Berlin: 1927) 145 et seq. (in German).

70 März, *Nach der Urkatastrophe* 103; Kleine-Ahlbrandt W., *The Burden of Victory. France, Britain and the Enforcement of the Versailles Peace, 1919–1925* (Lanham: 1995) 105. Cf. also Allbert Dayer R., "The British War Debts to the United States and the Anglo-Japanese Alliance, 1920–1923", *Pacific Historical Review* 45 (1976) 569.

71 Steiner Z., *The Lights That Failed. European International History 1919–1933* (Oxford: 2005) 67. Cf. also Hildebrand, *Deutsche Außenpolitik* 407.

72 Hillgruber H., „Unter dem Schatten von Versailles – Die außenpolitische Belastung der Weimarer Republik: Realität und Perzeption bei den Deutschen", in Erdmann K. – Schulze H. (eds.), *Weimar. Selbstpreisgabe einer Demokratie. Eine Bilanz heute* (Düsseldorf: 1980) 51, 57; Steiner, *European International History* 67. Mai G., *Die Weimarer Republik* (Munich: 2009) 45 argues that Germany kept the position as a Great Power.

73 März, *Nach der Urkatastrophe* 103. Cf. also Steiner, *European International History* (Oxford: 2005) 67; Hildebrand, *Deutsche Außenpolitik* 408 et seq.

get closer to each other as it happened with the Treaty of Rapallo on 16 April 1922.[74] Even the Versailles Treaty itself, as the classic compromise between the Allies that it was,[75] left a certain margin for revisions.[76] This, in turn, led to a stronger juridification of European relations than ever before. As Marcus Payk has shown, Germany and its foreign policy invested more than ever in building up and expanding expertise in international law.[77]

A final word should be said on article 231, the infamous 'War Guilt Clause'. Throughout the war, the Reich leadership had presented Germany's situation on the battlefield much better and more legitimate in terms of international law than it actually was.[78] As the German public has been and still was constantly told that the Reich was waging a just war of pre-emptive self-defense, the outcry was all the greater when they learned that Germany (together with its allies) was to assume sole responsibility for the war. One of the immediate consequences was the creation of the Centre for the Study of the Causes of the War in Berlin, funded by the German Foreign Office.[79] The Kaiser Wilhelm Institute for Comparative Public Law and International Law (now the Max Planck Institute for Comparative Public Law and International Law) was founded in 1924/1925 to build up the expertise in international law necessary for a practical legal campaign against the Treaty of Versailles. The staff of the Institute, which was mainly financed by the Reich, answered specific legal questions posed by the Foreign Office, so that 'German representatives could draw on a high level of expertise before the arbitration tribunals of the Treaty of Versailles'.[80]

Article 231 never ceased to be a source of agitation and polemics. Still tied to the political thought of the 19th century, Germany, incapable of pursuing a dispassionate and rational policy, saw its honour and prestige affected in an unbearable way.[81] For Germany, Article 231 was one of the main reasons why

---

74 Winkler, *Weimar* 97; Steiner, *European International History* 67; Hildebrand, *Deutsche Außenpolitik* 424 et seq.

75 Steiner, *European International History* 68; Conze, *Versailles 1919* 276; Leonhard, *Der überforderte Frieden* 1042 and 1156; Birdsall, *Versailles* 295.

76 Wüest E., *Der Vertrag von Versailles in Licht und Schatten der Kritik. Die Kontroverse um seine wirtschaftlichen Auswirkungen* (Zurich: 1962) 45 et seq.

77 Payk, *Frieden durch Recht?* 428.

78 Boemeke M. – Feldman G. – Glaser E., "Introduction", in Boemeke M. – Feldman G. – Glaser E. (eds.), *The Treaty of Versailles. A Reassessment after 75 Years* (Cambridge: 1998) 538.

79 Herwig H., "Clio Deceived. Patriotic Self-Censorship in Germany after the Great War", *International Security* 12 (1987) 5, 21.

80 Lange F., „Wider das ‚völkerrechtliche Geschwafel' – Hermann Mosler und die praxisorientierte Herangehensweise an das Völkerrecht im Rahmen des Max-Planck-Instituts", *Zeitschrift für ausländisches öffentliches Recht und Völkerrecht* 75 (2015) 307, 316.

81 Leonhard, *Der überforderte Frieden* 1041.

the Treaty of Versailles was not a peace of law ('Rechtsfrieden') but a peace of force ('Gewaltfrieden').[82] Seen unemotionally, however, the provision was supposed to serve as a mere legalistic element in a treaty that was full of historically unique 'legal complexity and prescriptive detail'.[83] Article 231 was the first provision of Part VIII on Reparations and therefore, already from a systematic point of view, restricted itself to provide the legal foundation for Germany's general reparation obligations addressed in the following articles of the treaty. As Alan Sharp pointed out, the clause only affirmed Germany's 'theoretical responsibility for the entire cost of the war' while the following Article 232 limited the actual claim to an amount within Germany's capacity to pay.[84] While there cannot be any reasonable doubt the Allies were convinced of German 'guilt' for the outbreak of the war, the primary sources do not suggest that it was their intention to force a corresponding recognition from Germany.[85] Interestingly, even Friedrich Berber, one of the Nazis' crown lawyers, apologist for German violations of international law and foreign policy propagandist of Joachim von Ribbentrop could not question this.[86] Then as now, the term 'responsibility' stood for a classical legal concept that does, as such, not entail any moral judgement.[87] In the whole article 231, the word 'guilt' does not appear. The same wording was used in the treaties with the German allies, e.g. in article 177 of the Treaty of Stain-Germain, where it did not become a problem because the respective states decided not to make it one.[88]

82 Anlage zur deutschen Mantelnote vom 29. Mai 1919, reproduced in Graf Brockdorff-Rantzau U., *Dokumente und Gedanken um Versailles* (Berlin: 1925) 88, 93 et seq. Cf. also Krumeich, *Die unbewältigte Niederlage* 168 et seq.

83 Payk, *Frieden durch Recht?* 381.

84 Sharp A., *The Versailles Settlement. Peacemaking in Paris, 1919* (London: 1991) 86. Cf. also Macmillan M., *Paris 1919. Six Months That Changed World* (New York: 2003) 193; Birdsall P., *Versailles* 254; Platthaus A., *Der Krieg nach dem Krieg.* 310 et seq.; Kolb, *Frieden von Versailles* 94; Conze, *Versailles 1919* 321; Smith, *Paris Peace Conference* 71 et seq.

85 Berber F., *Das Diktat von Versailles. Entstehung – Inhalt – Zerfall. Eine Darstellung in Dokumenten*, vol. 2 (Essen: 1939) 1257.

86 Toppe A., *Militär und Kriegsvölkerrecht. Rechtsnorm, Fachdiskurs und Kriegspraxis in Deutschland 1899–1940* (Munich: 2008) 217 et seq.; Pauly W., „Das Öffentliche Recht an der Berliner Juristischen Fakultät 1933–1945", in Kloepfer M. – Paulus C. – Schröder R. – Werle G. (eds.), *Festschrift 200 Jahre Juristische Fakultät der Humboldt-Universität zu Berlin. Geschichte, Gegenwart und Zukunft* (Berlin: 2010) 773, 783; Weber H., „Die politische Verantwortung der Wissenschaft. Friedrich Berber in den Jahren 1937 bis 1945", in Krause E. –Huber L. –Fischer H. (eds.), *Hochschulalltag im „Dritten Reich". Die Hamburger Universität 1933–1945*, vol. 3 part II (Berlin: 1991) 939, 940.

87 Cf. also Mommsen W., "Max Weber and the Peace Treaty of Versailles", in Boemeke M. – Feldman G. – Glaser E. (eds.), *The Treaty of Versailles. A Reassessment after 75 Years* (Cambridge: 1998) 535, 538.

88 Macmillan, *Paris 1919* 466.

As a matter of fact, the actual debate on guilt only came into focus due to the German response to the allied peace terms – the Allies themselves did not expect the clause to be of any peculiar difficulty.[89] It was the emotional German protest that caused the Allies – also due to public pressure at home[90] – to accentuate the thesis of German war guilt much more sharply, which was now 'formulated as a moral verdict against Germany'.[91] After Germany's public challenge of the self-inferred war guilt interpretation, of Article 231, 'it was politically impossible for the Allies to say that they did not mean war guilt.'[92] Their response of 16 June 1919 states, in the most relevant parts:

> The Allied and Associated Powers therefore feel it necessary to begin their reply by a clear statement of the judgment passed upon the war by practically the whole of civilized mankind. … Germany's responsibility … is not confined to having planned and started the war. She is no less responsible for the savage and inhuman manner in which it was conducted. … The conduct of Germany is almost unexampled in human history. The terrible responsibility which lies at her doors can be seen in the fact that not less than seven million dead lie buried in Europe, while more than twenty million others carry upon them the evidence of wounds and sufferings, because Germany saw fit to gratify her lust for tyranny by resort to war. The Allied and Associated Powers … treat this war … as a crime against humanity and right.[93]

The German government itself had thus brought about the verdict of German guilt based on the accusation that the Reich had 'planned a criminal war and

89 Ibid. 193. Cf. also Conze, *Versailles 1919* 354 et seq.; Marks, "Smoke and Mirrors" 357.

90 Cf. on this Goldstein E., "Great Britain: The Home Front", in Boemeke M. – Feldman G. – Glaser E. (eds.), *The Treaty of Versailles. A Reassessment after 75 Years* (Cambridge: 1998) 147 and Soutou G-H., "The French Peacemakers and Their Home Front", in Boemeke M. – Feldman G. – Glaser E. (eds.), *The Treaty of Versailles. A Reassessment after 75 Years* (Cambridge: 1998) 167.

91 Kolb –Schumann, *Weimarer Republik* 34. Cf. also Leonhard, *Der überforderte Frieden* 1008 et seq.; Brandt, *Versailler Vertrag* 106.

92 Marks, "Smoke and Mirrors" 357.

93 Papers Relating to the Foreign Relations of the United States, The Paris Peace Conference, 1919, vol. VI, Paris Peace Conf. 185.1/260, available at: https://history.state.gov/historicaldocuments/frus1919Parisv06/d93 (last accessed on 16 August 2023). See on this, historically, Schiff, *Versailles* 69 et seq; Nowak, *Versailles* 288 et seq., explaining a German translation mistake in the Lansing note of 5 November 1918. There, Germany accepted its obligation of compensation for all damage caused by its 'aggression'. However, Germany has translated this erroneously only as 'Angriff' (attack).

waged it like criminals' and on top of that made these 'Ehrenpunkte' (points of honour) even the basis of the Versailles Treaty.[94] SPD politician Carlo Mierendorff (1897–1943) saw in the reactions regarding article 231 'a unique autosuggestion of an entire people, which interprets a treaty article to its disadvantage, feels humiliated and demands revision.'[95] While European history is full of examples of revision of peace treaties,[96] Germany bears considerable responsibility for the fact that 'the odium of the moral defamation of the German people by the Treaty of Versailles became one of the pillars of the political self-destruction mechanism of the Weimar Republic'.[97]

4 Polonia Restituta: a State in Between

The most obvious consequence of the Treaty of Versailles on Poland was the restoration of its statehood. Interestingly, this was based on the unique circumstance that the powers responsible for the three partitions of Poland in 1772, 1793 and 1795 – the German Empire, Austria-Hungary and the Russian Tsarist Empire – were now the losers of the Great War, creating a power vacuum in Eastern Europe that could now be filled by Polish self-determination.[98]

Due to the military pressure they were under, the German Empire and Austria-Hungary decided on 5 November 1917 to install the 'Kingdom of Poland' on the territory of Congress Poland, previously dominated by Russia.[99] Contrary to the solemn language of the proclamation, however, the Central Powers 'founded' the Polish state out of necessity. They clearly indicated that they expected military support in return for the liberation from Russia.[100] Beyond that Germany even issued an 'Ordinance on the Combating of work-shyness' as an instrument of forced recruitment to replace German

94 Krumeich, *Die unbewältigte Niederlage* 174; Schiff, *Versailles* 118 et seq.

95 Quoted by Kolb, *Frieden von Versailles* 94. Cf. also Heinemann U., *Die verdrängte Niederlage* (Göttingen: 1983) 99 et seq.

96 Hildebrand, *Deutsche Außenpolitik* (Munich: 2008) 419.

97 Quoted by Kolb, *Frieden von Versailles* 87.

98 Leonhard, *Der überforderte Frieden* 495; Orzell L., "A 'Hotly Disputed Issue': Eastern Galicia at the Paris Peace Conference, 1919", *The Polish Review* 25 (1980) 49; Birdsall, *Versailles* 173.

99 Wandycz P., "The Polish Question", in Boemeke M. – Feldman G. – Glaser E. (eds.), *The Treaty of Versailles. A Reassessment after 75 Years* (Cambridge: 1998) 316. Cf. also Verordnungsblatt für das GGW, 51/1916, reproduced in Polsakiewicz M., *Warschau im Ersten Weltkrieg. Deutsche Besatzungspolitik zwischen kultureller Autonomie und wirtschaftlicher Ausbeutung* (Marburg: 2015) 153.

100 Polsakiewicz, *Warschau im Ersten Weltkrieg* 153.

workers who were now fighting in the army.[101] Reich Chancellor Theobald von Bethmann-Hollweg (1856–1921) stated that it would be his duty 'to make use of everything that can be of any help to us in the event of a longer duration of the war. We must mobilise all the means at our disposal, and this includes the forces that a Poland … can provide.'[102] A useful Polish army, however, could realistically only be created against the promise of Polish statehood.[103]

This 'kingdom' was not allowed to conduct an independent foreign policy, remained subordinate to German military legislation, and forced into the German Customs Union and insofar into the German-Austrian alliance. It was little more than a vassal state of the Central Powers.[104] At that time, the 'Kingdom' even was without set borders and, most importantly, without a king. The German-installed Polish Executive Committee was without real competences. When the Petrograd Council of Workers' and Soldiers' Deputies acknowledged on 27 March 1917 Poland's right 'to complete independence in terms of state and international affairs',[105] a Provisional State Council was created in response. However, it was primarily of an advisory nature only being competent to examine draft laws and to submit non-binding motions. One of its main tasks was to prepare the installation of further state institutions in the 'Kingdom'.[106]

In the end, this Polish 'state' was not meant to last but its creation was of key importance for the actual Polish state that would replace it: The Central Powers brought the Polish question back to the international level[107] and caused nearly all governments of the warring parties to take position on Polish independence.[108] Moreover, with Polish independence from their former

---

101 Ibid. 157.

102 Reproduced in ibid. 156. Cf. also Smogorzewski, *Access to the Sea* 83 et seq.

103 Polsakiewicz, *Warschau im Ersten Weltkrieg* 150; Templin W., *Revolutionär und Staatsgründer. Józef Piłsudski – eine Biographie* (Berlin: 2022) 220.

104 Geheime Aufzeichnungen der Wiener Verhandlungen vom 11. und 12.08.1916, reproduced in Polsakiewicz, *Warschau im Ersten Weltkrieg* 151.

105 Leinwand A., "Soviet Propaganda and the Independent Polish State", *Studia z Dziejów Rosji i Europy Środkowo-Wschodniej*, (54) 2020, 81, 85.

106 Thakur-Smolarek K., *Der Erste Weltkrieg und die polnische Frage. Die Interpretation des Kriegsgeschehens durch die zeitgenössischen polnischen Wortführer* (Berlin: 2014) 371; Polsakiewicz, *Warschau im Ersten Weltkrieg* 163.

107 Fink, *Rights of Others* 81; Gmurczyk-Wrońska M., "'Not Russia, but France and England Shall Decide about Poland': The Diplomatic Action of Roman Dmowski in 1916–1917", *Studia z Dziejów Rosji i Europy Środkowo-Wschodniej* (2017) 27, 38; Alexander A., *Kleine Geschichte Polens* (Stuttgart: 2008) 265.

108 Leinwand, "Soviet Propaganda" 88; Gerson L., *Woodrow Wilson and the Rebirth of Poland 1914–1920* (New Haven: 1953) 22.

masters, the overarching principle of the right of peoples to self-determination became virulent for entire Europe. Woodrow Wilson, e.g., stated in his famous 'Peace without Victory Speech' to the Senate on 22 January 1917:

> No peace can last or ought to last, which does not recognize and accept the principle that governments derive all their just powers from the consent of the governed, and that no right anywhere exists to hand peoples about from sovereignty to sovereignty as if they were property. I take it for granted … that statesmen everywhere are agreed that there should be a united, independent and autonomous Poland, and that henceforth inviolable security of life, of worship and of industrial and social development should be guaranteed to all peoples who have lived heretofore under the powers' of government devoted to a faith and purpose hostile to their own.'[109]

These considerations were incorporated directly into Wilson's 14 Points. Consequently, Point 13 demanded that:

> [a]n independent Polish state should be erected which should include the territories inhabited by indisputably Polish populations, which should be assured a free and secure access to the sea, and whose political and economic independence and territorial integrity should be guaranteed by international covenant.[110]

On close examination of the wording, however, the Polish statesmen were disappointed about the rather weak formulation: the term 'should' was met with unease, especially when compared to Point 7, which stated that 'Belgium … must … be restored.'[111] An independent Poland seemed not to be of primary importance in the allied programme.

When the Great War ended, it was mainly the remaining German troops that shielded Poland from the Bolsheviks.[112] However, the Entente powers

109 Reproduced in Kusielewicz E., "Paderewski and Wilson's Speech to the Senate, January 22, 1917", *Polish American Studies*, 13 (1956) 65, 66. On Wilson's role in the recreation of a Polish state, see, in more depth, Wolff L., *Woodrow Wilson and the Reimagining of Eastern Europe* (Stanford: 2020).

110 See, on the historical background of this point, Gerson, *Rebirth of Poland* 82 et seq; Landau R., *Ignace Paderewski. Musician and Statesman* (New York: 1976 [1934]) 101 et seq.

111 Basu S., "The Question of Polish Freedom and Wilson's Fourteen Points", *Proceedings of the Indian History Congress* 39 (1978) 941, 943.

112 Leonhard, *Der überforderte Frieden* 1189.

recognised the need for a regional stabilizing force because of the power vacuum in 'East Central Europe' that was expected to arise when the German forces withdrew.[113] Pursuing its own national (security) interests, France, e.g., saw in a strong Poland a replacement for the lost alliance to Russia.[114] It wanted to create a 'Barrière de l'Est' against German eastern expansion[115] and in the same time a 'cordon sanitaire' against the Russian Revolution.[116] For Russia, in turn, Poland represented the 'red bridge' that had to be crossed to connect Russia with Germany and bring the Bolshevik revolution the West.[117]

Because of local unrest in Warsaw, the particularly popular statesman Józef Piłsudski (1867–1935), who was in political prison in Magdeburg for refusing to take the oath of allegiance to the future Polish king and refusing military allegiance to Germany and Austria-Hungary, was brought back on 10 November 1918 at the request of the German Governor General Hans von Beseler (1850–1921).[118] Already on 11 November the Central Powers transferred him the command of the Polish army. German forces withdrew from 12 November onwards and Piłsudski became Provisional Head of State on 14 November.[119] Although Poland now had a preliminary leadership the situation of the new state remained precarious.[120]

As the Allies lacked the means and also the political will to effectively intervene in the revolutionary dynamics of the east, the young Polish state was left to its own devices.[121] Not only did its government have to clarify its political position towards the Bolsheviks, but also its factual position towards the

113 Ibid. 724.

114 Marks S., "Mistakes and Myths" 649. Cf. also Kornat M., "The Victors and the Polish Cause at the End of the Great War. 104th Anniversary of the Polish Independence", available at https://polishhistory.pl/the-victors-and-the-polish-cause-at-the-end-of-the-great-war (last accessed on 17 August 2023).

115 Dessberg F. La France et l'Europe centrale à Versailles: Objectifs stratégiques et combinaisons diplomatiques. *Guerres mondiales et conflits contemporains* 282 (2021) 15; Alexander, *Geschichte Polens* 276.

116 Hildebrand, *Deutsche Außenpolitik* 385; Kornat, "The Victors and the Polish Cause"; März, *Nach der Urkatastrophe* 142; Conze, *Die große Illusion* 104 and 296.

117 Davies N., *Im Herzen Europas. Geschichte Polens* (Munich: 2000) 106.

118 Templin, *Józef Piłsudski* 220 et seq.; Davies, *Geschichte Polens* 104 et seq.; Landau, *Ignace Paderewski* 133 et seq.; Zamoyski A., *Warsaw 1920. Lenin's Failed Conquest of Europe* (London: 2008) 4 et seq.

119 Michael H., *Zwischen den Kriegen. Polens Außenpolitik 1919–1939* (Berlin: 2022) 37; Gnauck G., *Polen verstehen. Geschichte, Politik, Gesellschaft* (Stuttgart: 2018) 36.

120 Leonhard, *Der überforderte Frieden* 489. Cf. also Debo R., *Survival and Consolidation. The Foreign Policy of Soviet Russia, 1918–1921* (Montreal: 1992) 191.

121 Payk, *Frieden durch Recht?* 170; Borodziej W., *Geschichte Polens im 20. Jahrhundert* (Munich: 2010) 118.

disputed eastern border areas.[122] Ironically, it was this at first sight weak state, abandoned by equally unwilling and unable allies that defended the Versailles settlement.[123]

Piłsudski's geopolitical project Międzymorze ('Between-Seas') envisaged the wishful thinking of a restoration of the historical Jagiellonian Polish-Lithuanian Commonwealth in a Polish Confederation.[124] All areas lying between Poland and Russia, while not necessarily having belonged to Poland, must be denied to Russia.[125] Because of the erosion in the east the areas which where inhabited by a majority of Lithuanians, Belarusians and Ukrainians were to be incorporated in the Polish-dominated federation in order to shift the eastern border as far east as possible in order to establish a security cordon between Poland and Russia.[126] Piłsudski expected that the common fear of Russia would serve as a stable unifying bond between all the entities concerned.[127] In the long run, however, this would mean that Poland was to 'replace Russia as the great power of eastern Europe'.[128] However, this project failed because of the resistance in both Lithuania and Ukraine, who saw Poland as just another occupying power and aggressor.[129] But there was also a lack of support among the Polish population. With the assassination of Poland's first federalist oriented president, Gabriel Narutowicz, on 16 December 1922, not only antisemitism in Poland came to a peak but also the federal ideas came to an end.[130]

122 Leonhard, *Der überforderte Frieden* 1189.

123 Zamoyski, *Warsaw 1920* 2.

124 Wandycz P., "Poland's Place in Europe in the Concepts of Piłsudski and Dmowski", *East European Politics and Societies* 4 (1990) 451, 453. Cf. also Chinburg Z., "Halting the Revolution: Poland and the 'Miracle at the Vistula'", *Constructing the Past* 16 (2015) article 4.; Wandycz P., "The Polish Question" 329; Gerson, *Rebirth of Poland* 111. 453. See on this project in more detail Ištok R. – Koziak T., "Międzymorze as a Polish Geopolitical Concept", *Folia Geographica* 14 (2009) 89.

125 Zamoyski, *Warsaw 1920* 8.

126 Leonhard, *Der überforderte Frieden* 488; Michael, *Polens Außenpolitik* 139.

127 Davies, *Geschichte Polens* 106; Jaworski R. – Lübke C. – Müller M., *Eine kleine Geschichte Polens* (Frankfurt am Main: Suhrkamp 2000) 296.

128 Debo, *Foreign Policy of Soviet Russia* 59.

129 Leonhard, *Der überforderte Frieden* 1189; Snyder T., "Federalism and Nationalism in Polish Eastern Policy", *Georgetown Journal of International Affairs* 4 (2003) 111, 114; Wandycz, "Poland's Place in Europe" 458 et seq.; Nowak A., "Between Imperial Temptation and Anti-Imperial Function in Eastern Politics: Poland from the Eighteenth to Twenty-First Century", in Matsuzato K. (ed.), *Emerging Meso-Areas in the Former Socialist Countries: Histories Revived or Revisited* (Sapporo: Hokkaido University 2005) 247, 268; Michael, *Polens Außenpolitik* 92 et seq.; Wagner, *Polnisch-Sowjetische Krieg* 24.

130 Snyder, "Federalism and Nationalism" 114; Brykczynski P., "Anti-Semitism on Trial: The Case of Eligiusz Niewiadomski", *East European Politics and Societies* 28 (2014) 411–439. Cf.

Piłsudski's great rival, Roman Dmowski (1864–1939), Paris-based leader of the National Democrats and recognised by the Entente as the Polish representative,[131] articulated an opposing idea of Poland's future. Instead of remodeling the multi-ethnic Polish–Lithuanian Commonwealth, he believed to find the necessary continuity not in the Polish state but in the Polish nation[132] Unlike Piłsudski, he identified Germany as the most imminent threat for Poland, not Russia. Accordingly, the geographical centre of the territory of the Polish state should be in the west, following the historical precedent of the Piast dynasty.[133] Dmowski calculated with borders that 'were based on a combination of ethnic, historic, strategic, and … economic claims while seeking to preserve Polish majority of at least sixty percent' in order to make a 'gradual Polonisation' of the incorporated minorities work.[134] As geopolitical realities required a strong state between Germany and Russia, this state had not only to be 'geographically extensive' but also needs to 'possess the means to influence international relations'. According to Dmowski, only an internally strong state would be able to do so.[135] A proponent of a 'homogeneous ethno-cultural nation',[136] the aim of his policy was to absorb all the areas in the east with a Polish majority into as large a nation state as possible. The non-Polish population groups were to be assimilated as quickly as possible.[137] His state would ot allow any form of mixed, or multilayered, national identity.[138] In the end, the notorious antisemite and social Darwinist Dmowski[139] envisaged a form of ethnic cleansing.[140]

Even though only Piłsudski as commander-in-chief had the military means to fight for his vision, Dmowski's National Democrats held the majority in the national assembly. Moreover, as the representative of Poland in Paris, he had

---

also Kiel M., *The Jews of Częstochowa. The Life and Death of a Community, a Concise History* (Berlin: 2023) xxi, xxiii.

131 Payk, *Frieden durch Recht?* 631; Fink, *Rights of Others* 104.

132 Dabrowski P., "Uses and Abuses of the Polish Past by Józef Piłsudski and Roman Dmowski", *The Polish Review*, 56 (2011) 73, 94.

133 Gnauck G., *Polen verstehen* 37; Jaworski – Lübke – Müller, *Eine kleine Geschichte Polens* 295 et seq. Cf. also Smogorzewski, *Access to the Sea* 74.

134 Wandycz, "Poland's Place in Europe" 457.

135 Ibid. 456.

136 Walicki A., "The Troubling Legacy of Roman Dmowski", *East European Politics and Societies* 14 (2000) 12, 15.

137 Leonhard, *Der überforderte Frieden* 488.

138 Walicki, "Roman Dmowski" 20.

139 Macmillan, *Paris 1919* 209; Walicki, "Roman Dmowski" 18 and 27; Gerson, *Rebirth of Poland* 12 et seq.

140 Curp T., "'Roman Dmowski Understood': Ethnic Cleansing as Permanent Revolution", *European History Quarterly* 35 (2005) 395.

the opportunity to persuade the Allies of his political aims.[141] Both leaders, however, understood that the Allies would not serves as agents of their respective visions for the Polish state. The position of the Entente towards Poland was less a result of a genuine interest in the new state than a consequence of the Entente's position towards Germany and Russia.[142] It was clear to the Allies that Poland needed compulsory access to the Baltic and had to be put in possession of economically important territories, especially in Upper Silesia, the 'industrial heartland of East Central Europe', to be viable.[143] Beyond this, the Allies were critical of Polish territorial claims.[144] However, for the time being the Allies were only able to determine the course of the border in the west. The eastern border, in contrast, could be influenced by Polish military successes.[145] To improve its political position in the border question Poland had to create a fait accompli as early and decisive as possible.[146] This, of course, did not go unobserved by the Allies: 'The Poles', Arthur James Balfour (1848–1930) stated, 'were using the interval between the cessation of war and the decisions of the Peace Congress to make good their claims to districts outside Russian Poland.'[147]

On the brink of defeat after initial significant successes in the beginning, Poland managed to halt the Russian advance on Warsaw in August 1920 and with it the Russian Revolution in Eastern Europe (so-called 'Miracle on the Vistula').[148] Due to the overall military situation in the east, however, Piłsudski was in the end obliged to come to an agreement with revolutionary Russia 'to partition Ukraine and the old Duchy of Lithuania territories'.[149] The final borders established by the Treaty of Riga were a classical compromise.[150] On the one hand, they went beyond the Curzon line foreseen by the Entente,[151] which

141 Walicki, "Roman Dmowski" 12.

142 Kornat, "The Victors and the Polish Cause".

143 Leonhard, *Der überforderte Frieden* 724; Kusielewicz, "Paderewski and Wilson's Speech" 71; Birdsall, *Versailles* 177; Payk, *Frieden durch Recht?* 614 and 616.

144 Eberhardt P., "The Curzon Line as the Eastern Boundary of Poland: The Origins and the Political Background", *Geographia Polonica* 85 (2012) 5, 7.

145 Borodziej, *Geschichte Polens* 110; Leonhard, *Der überforderte Frieden* 494.

146 Leonhard, *Der überforderte Frieden* 493 and 1202; Michael, *Polens Außenpolitik* 151.

147 Quoted by Macmillan, *Paris 1919* 215.

148 Chinburg Z., "Halting the Revolution"; Eberhardt, "Curzon Line" 13; Davies N., *White Eagle, Red Star: The Polish–Soviet War, 1919–20 and 'the Miracle on the Vistula'* (London: 2003); Zamoyski, *Warsaw 1920* 64 et seq.; Stephan Lehnstaedt, *Der vergessene Sieg* 163 et seq.

149 Nowak, "Poland from the Eighteenth to Twenty-First Century" 269.

150 März, *Nach der Urkatastrophe* 144; Wandycz, "Poland's Place in Europe" 461 et seq.

151 Eberhardt, "Curzon Line" 5.

cut off a significant number of Poles living east of it.[152] On the other hand, it was the definitive end of Piłsudski's Międzymorze, a 'third Europe' between the West and Russia, since it fell short of the 1772 borders. He had failed to establish an 'intermarium' as Poland had to recognise the existence of the Belarusian and especially Ukrainian Soviet republics.[153] With the incorporation of Western Ukraine and Western Belarus into Poland, Piłsudski unintentionally realized at least partially the conception of Dmowski, what led to the triumph of nationalism in Poland.[154] With '4 million Ukrainians, 2 million Jews and a million Byelorussians', the Treaty of Riga added in the end 'even more minorities to [the Polish] population'.[155] Even though the new borders made Poland the dominating state in East-Central Europe,[156] the price was considerable: the Second Polish Republic was at enmity with almost all neighbouring states.[157] Also the internal political situation was hardly better as Poland's national law consisted of a confusing mixture of the old Tsarist regime, German occupation orders and new legislative measures from the young government.[158]

Additionally, the argument was raised that the new Polish state had been created in contrast to the principle of self-determination: its territory was populated also by Germans, 'Latvians, Lithuanians, Belarusians, local people without a national identity, Ukrainians who had been influenced differently by Russia and Austria, and Jews'.[159] In sum over 30 percent of the population was part of a minority.[160] The Allies retreated to a pragmatic realism and succinctly declared: 'The restoration of the Polish State is a great historical act which cannot be achieved without breaking many ties and causing temporary difficulty and distress to many individuals.'[161]

In this context, a final word should be said on how the principle of self-determination was understood by the Allies. As Marcus Payk stressed, self-determination was not 'an offer to ethnic groups of various kinds to freely decide on their own autonomy'. Rather, it was a euphemism 'for the stabilisation

152 Wołos M., "A New Order in Central and Eastern Europe: Polish–Soviet Negotiations and the Peace of Riga (1920–1921)", *Zapiski Historyczne* 86 (2021) 97, 108 et seq.

153 Borodziej, *Geschichte Polens* 117.

154 Michael, *Polens Außenpolitik*; Wagner, *Polnisch-Sowjetische Krieg* 25.

155 Macmillan, *Paris 1919* 228.

156 Lehnstaedt, *Der vergessene Sieg* 181.

157 Alexander, *Kleine Geschichte Polens* 281.

158 Lehnstaedt, *Der vergessene Sieg* 160.

159 Borodziej, *Geschichte Polens* 110.

160 Beyrau D., "Antisemitismus und Judentum in Polen, 1918–1939", *Geschichte und Gesellschaft* 8 (1982) 205, 217.

161 Quoted by Payk, *Frieden durch Recht?* 615. Cf. also p. 632.

of the international community through sovereign statehood'.[162] According to the allied reasoning, states that 'could rely on the participation and consent of the ruled were more reliable, balanced and peaceful ... than autocratic regimes whose internal repression would always turn into external aggression.'[163] Self-determination, therefore, was granted for the 'ability to predictable and orderly self-government'. Otherwise, the Entente saw itself entitled to intervene.[164]

Especially against this backdrop, the increasing pogrom-like anti-Jewish violence in Poland[165] was a cause of concern for the Allies.[166] With all reason, Jewish leaders reminded the Allies that the Jewish population was a particularly vulnerable group in the new states.[167] Given these circumstances, allied intervention was inevitable. Already 'unstable and conflict-ridden' not only the question of the Polish borders 'but also its internal configuration had to be declared an international affair.'[168] To prevent the Polish minority policy from destabilising the region and to forestall Dmowski's 'Polonization efforts of the minorities in the Polish state',[169] the Allies forced the young Republic to sign the Polish Minority Treaty (or 'Little Treaty of Versailles'). Already the 'big' Treaty of Versailles stated in Article 93:

> Poland accepts and agrees to embody in a Treaty with the Principal Allied and Associated Powers such provisions as may be deemed necessary by the said Powers to protect the interests of inhabitants of Poland who differ from the majority of the population in race, language, or religion.

The core provision of this Little Treaty of Versailles was Article 7. It established that '[a]ll Polish nationals shall be equal before the law and shall enjoy the

162 Ibid. 594 et seq. Cf. also Conze, *Versailles 1919* 411 et seq.
163 Payk, *Frieden durch Recht?* 596.
164 Ibid. 599 and 647.
165 Cf., e.g., Fink C., "The Minorities Question at the Paris Peace Conference: The Polish Minority Treaty, June 28, 1919", in Boemeke M. – Feldman G. – Glaser E. (eds.), *The Treaty of Versailles. A Reassessment after 75 Years* (Cambridge: 1998) 249, 264 and 267; Fink, *Defending the Rights of Others* 106 et seq, esp. 110 et seq. Cf. also Wolff, *Reimagining of Eastern Europe* 199 et seq.; Miller M., "The Forgotten Pogroms, 1918", *Slavic Review* 78 (2019) 648, 653.
166 Miller, "Forgotten Pogroms" 651. Cf. also Smith, *Paris Peace Conference* 159 et seq.; Payk, *Frieden durch Recht?* 635; Hagen W., "The Moral Economy of Ethnic Violence: The Pogrom in Lwów, November 1918", *Geschichte und Gesellschaft* 31 (2005) 203.
167 Smith, *Paris Peace Conference* 160. Cf. also Wolff, *Reimagining of Eastern Europe* 176 et seq.
168 Payk, *Frieden durch Recht?* 630.
169 Wynot E., "The Polish Germans, 1919–1939: National Minority in a Multinational State", *The Polish Review* 17 (1972) 23, 24.

same civil and political rights without distinction as to race, language or religion' and continued:

> Differences of religion, creed or confession shall not prejudice any Polish national in matters relating to the enjoyment of civil or political rights, as for instance admission to public employments, functions and honours, or the exercise of professions and industries
>
> No restriction shall be imposed on the free use by any Polish national of any language in private intercourse, in commerce, in religion, in the press or in publications of any kind, or at public meetings.
>
> Notwithstanding any establishment by the Polish Government of an official language, adequate facilities shall be given to Polish nationals of non-Polish speech for the use of their language, either orally or in writing, before the courts.

Article 12 qualified the question of the Polish minorities as 'obligations of international concern' and placed them 'under the guarantee of the League of Nations.' It was especially the combination of an imposed treaty obligation which was in a second step put under international supervision that made the Little Treaty of Versailles in the eyes of the Polish a 'painful encroachment on the sovereignty they had just won'. Poland was particularly disappointed about the mistrust associated with this legal construction.[170] Despite all the Polish military successes, the Allies left no doubt that Poland was a state of their grace. Already the preamble in its very beginning stated that 'the Allied and Associated Powers have by the success of their arms restored to the Polish nation the independence of which it had been unjustly deprived', making unequivocally clear that 'perquisites of statehood depended on recognition, and that would not be granted unless and until the wording of the minority protection clause was agreed upon.'[171] That Poland's survival as a state depended on the goodwill of the Allies was clearly communicated to Poland beyond the text of the treaty when Clemenceau demanded from the Polish Prime Minister, Ignacy Jan Paderewski (1860–1941), the signature of the treaty with the reminder that

> it is thanks to the efforts of the countries on behalf of which I am honored to address you that the Polish nation is regaining its independence. …

170 Leonhard, *Der überforderte Frieden* 1188.

171 Meyer H., "The World Court, Minority Treaties, and Human Rights", *International Journal on World Peace* 14 (1997) 71, 74.

> Whether Poland can safely possess the territories depends on the support of the assets these countries shall bring into the League of Nations.[172]

With the signing of the treaty, Clemenceau stressed, Poland would receive 'in its most explicit and binding form the confirmation of her restoration to the family of independent nations'.[173] For Paderewski, however, this was again just another unfortunate example 'of the policy of external interference and foreign domination', from which Poland has already suffered in the past.[174] He saw in the treaty proof that 'the Polish nation was regarded as a nation of a lower level of civilization'.[175] And indeed, as Leonard V. Smith has pointed out, the minority treaties 'produced a hierarchy of states, in which some states had their national sovereignty circumscribed by international protections, and others not.'[176] Above all, it remained incomprehensible to Poland, not without any reason, that Germany did not have to sign a corresponding treaty.[177]

In the end, Clemenceau's indirect threat proved that in European International Law admission to the 'family of nations' was only granted upon the completion of certain preset conditions by the Great Powers. In signing the Polish Minority Treaty, Poland proved its capacity for self-determination – at least in the interpretation of the Allies.[178] The near future, however, would show, that the minority treaty – even though under the guarantee of the League of Nations – was a welcome instrument for the home states to intervene in Polish affairs.[179] Especially Germany would base 'its crusade for minority rights' on said treaty to undermine Poland's legitimacy.[180]

---

172 Kornat, "The Victors and the Polish Cause". Cf. also the statement by Lloyd George, reproduced in Gerson, *Rebirth of Poland* 136: '[Poland] has won her freedom, not by her own exertions, but by the blood of others; and not only has she no gratitude, but she says she loses faith in the people who won her freedom.' See also Larry Wolff, *Reimagining of Eastern Europe* 190 et seq.

173 Quoted by Smith, *Paris Peace Conference* 162.

174 Payk, *Frieden durch Recht?* 642; Leonhard, *Der überforderte Frieden* 1202. Cf. also Michael, *Polens Außenpolitik* 78; Wolff, *Reimagining of Eastern Europe* 206.

175 Borodziej, *Geschichte Polens* 108.

176 Smith, *Paris Peace Conference* 143.

177 Michael, *Polens Außenpolitik* 75.

178 Payk, *Frieden durch Recht?* 598.

179 Conze, *Versailles 1919* 441. But cf. also Michael, *Polens Außenpolitik* 76.

180 Fink, "Polish Minority Treaty" 274. Cf. also Gnauck, *Polen verstehen* 57.

5 Conclusion

The Wimbledon case was the first proceeding for Germany before an international court. For contemporary observers, the proceedings unsparingly exposed German insecurity on the international legal stage. The plaintiffs' conduct of the case was described as a 'well-conceived whole carried by a fresh optimism and a secure attitude to life'.[181] The Japanese representative, e.g., stated: '[T]he line of demarcation between modern international law and ancient international law may be found in the degree of freedom which is given to his development of human activity' – such as the passage through the Kiel Channel.[182] Ernst Wolgast believed to recognise in their pleadings not only 'the spirit of the American Declaration of Independence and the Declaration of the Rights of Man and of the Citizen', but also 'the proud consciousness of freedom and truth and the feeling of standing on solid ground'.[183] The German pleadings were, however, 'inconsistent, wavering between legal standards and, as a result, much less on point'.[184] For him, Germany was teetering between two extremes: state-egoism on the one hand and moral-religious standards on the other.[185] By doing so, he believed that Germany unconsciously presented itself as the defeated of the war even though this fact was without any relevance for the legal question before the Court. Psychologically, the Reich wanted to see it confirmed that the spirit of the Treaty was not the mutual recognition as 'entités politiques indépendantes' but the embodiment of the subjugation of Germany.[186] This view was based in particular on the following passage of the judgement

> The intention of the authors of the Treaty of Versailles to facilitate access to the Baltic by establishing an international régime, and consequently to keep the canal open at all times to foreign vessels of every kind.[187]

This autosuggestion seemed to prove true what Admiral Ludwig von Reuter – responsible for the sinking of the German fleet interned in Scapa Flow – wrote in 1921 in the People's Commentary on the Versailles Treaty: 'With the articles

181 Wolgast, *Wimbledonprozeß* 179.
182 Discours prononcé par M. Ito a la séance du 6 Juillet 1923, 293, 294.
183 Wolgast, Wimbledonprozeß 179.
184 Ibid.
185 Ibid.
186 Ibid. 143 und 145.
187 Judgment p. 23.

of the Treaty, the Entente has achieved that the Kiel Canal has become a safe, always available access route to the Baltic Sea.' What was left to Germany was merely, in the dramatic words of Reuter, to pay the maintenance costs of the proof of its engineering skills.[188] In his pleading before the Court, the French representative, Jules Basdevant, put it in the following words:

> Surely Germany, sovereign over the Kiel Canal, is no more in the same position now as she was before the conclusion of the Treaty of Versailles. Before, by virtue of that sovereignty, she could close the Kiel Canal. Now she can no more do so, as the Treaty of Versailles imposes on her definite conventional obligations limiting her freedom. To say that Germany is sovereign over the Kiel Canal does not mean that she may do what she wants. She may still legislate, she may exercise jurisdiction and may take administrative measures with regard to that territory, but all this on the understanding that certain limitations exist for her by virtue of the provisions contained in the Treaty of Versailles.[189]

However, this historical swan song does not capture the judgment in its entirety. It cannot go unsaid that it created a new awareness in Germany of the importance of international law. As the main reason for the defeat in Court was found to be that 'the opponents had a far superior command of international law and its legal methods', the judgment sparked the development of expertise in international law.[190] The Institute for International Law of the University of Kiel – directed by the German judge ad-hoc in the Wimbledon case, Walther Schücking, from 1926 onwards – studied extensively international jurisdiction as well as the legal consequences of the Great war. By 1924, the Kaiser Wilhelm Institute for Comparative Public Law and International Law had taken up its work in Berlin-Dahlem, which entered into 'productive competition' with the Kiel institute.[191]

188 von Reuter L., "Abschnitt 6. Bestimmungen über den Kieler Kanal", in von Lersner K. (ed.), *Versailles! Volkskommentar des Friedensdiktats* (Berlin: 1921) S. 87.

189 Discours prononcé par M. Basdevant a la séance publique du 5 Jullet 1923, 190, 215.

190 Wolgast, *Wimbledonprozeß* 176.

191 https://www.wsi.uni-kiel.de/de/institut/institutsgeschichte/i.-von-der-gruendung-bis-zum-ende-der-weimarer-republik (last accessed on 26 September 2023).

Acknowledgements

I am indebted to Alexandra Kemmerer for her most helpful comments on previous versions of this chapter. I owe special thanks to the one of a kind support provided by MPIL's librarians, especially Sara von Skerst and Stefanie Meier.

Bibliography

Alexander A., *Kleine Geschichte Polens* (Stuttgart: 2008).

Allain J.-Cl., «Le château de Versailles», in Möller H. – Morizet J. (eds.), *Allemagne-France. Lieux et mémoire d'une histoire commune* (Paris: 1995) 75.

Allbert Dayer R., "The British War Debts to the United States and the Anglo-Japanese Alliance, 1920–1923", *Pacific Historical Review* 45 (1976) 569.

Audoin-Rouzeau S., «Die Delegation der „gueules cassées" in Versailles am 28. Juni 1919», in Krumeich G. (ed.), *Versailles 1919. Ziele – Wirkung – Wahrnehmung* (Essen: 2001) 281.

Barth B., *Dolchstoßlegenden und politische Desintegration. Das Trauma der deutschen Niederlage im Ersten Weltkrieg 1914–1933* (Düsseldorf: 2003).

Basu S., "The Question of Polish Freedom and Wilson's Fourteen Points", *Proceedings of the Indian History Congress* 39 (1978) 941.

Berber F., *Das Diktat von Versailles. Entstehung – Inhalt – Zerfall. Eine Darstellung in Dokumenten*, vol. 2 (Essen: 1939).

Beyrau D., „Antisemitismus und Judentum in Polen, 1918–1939", *Geschichte und Gesellschaft* 8 (1982) 205.

Birdsall P., *Versailles Twenty Years After* (Hamden: 1962 [1941]).

Boemeke M. – Feldman G. – Glaser E., "Introduction", in Boemeke M. – Feldman G. – Glaser E. (eds.), *The Treaty of Versailles. A Reassessment after 75 Years* (Cambridge: 1998) 538.

Borodziej W., *Geschichte Polens im 20. Jahrhundert* (Munich: 2010).

Brandt S., *Das letzte Echo des Krieges. Der Versailler Vertrag* (Ditzingen: 2018).

Brykczynski P., "Anti-Semitism on Trial: The Case of Eligiusz Niewiadomski", *East European Politics and Societies* 28 (2014) 411.

Chinburg Z., "Halting the Revolution: Poland and the 'Miracle at the Vistula'", *Constructing the Past* 16 (2015) article 4.

Churchill W., *The Second World War. The Gathering Storm* (Boston: 1948).

Conze E., „Verhasster Vertrag. 'Versailles' als Propagandawaffe gegen die Weimarer Republik", *Aus Politik und Zeitgeschichte* 69 (2019) 45.

Conze E., *Die große Illusion. Versailles 1919 und die Neuordnung der Welt* (Munich: 2020).

Curp T., "'Roman Dmowski Understood': Ethnic Cleansing as Permanent Revolution", *European History Quarterly* 35 (2005) 395.

Dabrowski P., "Uses and Abuses of the Polish Past by Józef Piłsudski and Roman Dmowski", *The Polish Review*, 56 (2011) 73.

Davies N., *Im Herzen Europas. Geschichte Polens* (Munich: 2000).

Davies N., *White Eagle, Red Star: The Polish–Soviet War, 1919–20 and 'the Miracle on the Vistula'* (London: 2003).

Debo R., *Survival and Consolidation. The Foreign Policy of Soviet Russia, 1918–1921* (Montreal: 1992).

Delbrück H., *Der Friede von Versailles* (Berlin: 2nd ed. 1930).

Dessberg F. La France et l'Europe centrale à Versailles: Objectifs stratégiques et combinaisons diplomatiques. *Guerres mondiales et conflits contemporains* 282 (2021).

Eberhardt P., "The Curzon Line as the Eastern Boundary of Poland: The Origins and the Political Background", *Geographia Polonica* 85 (2012) 5.

Erzberger M., *Erlebnisse im Weltkrieg* (Stuttgart: 1920).

Eyck, Erich., *Geschichte der Weimarer Republik*, vol. 1 (Zurich: 1954).

Fink C., "The Minorities Question at the Paris Peace Conference: The Polish Minority Treaty, June 28, 1919", in Boemeke M. – Feldman G. – Glaser E. (eds.), *The Treaty of Versailles. A Reassessment after 75 Years* (Cambridge: 1998) 249.

Fink C., *Defending the Rights of Others. The Great Powers, the Jews, and International Minority Protection, 1878–1938* (Cambridge: 2004).

Fischer F., *Germany's Aims in the First World War* (New York: 1967).

Fry M., "British Revisionism", in Boemeke M. – Feldman G. – Glaser E. (eds.), *The Treaty of Versailles. A Reassessment after 75 Years* (Cambridge: 1998) 599.

Gerson L., *Woodrow Wilson and the Rebirth of Poland 1914–1920* (New Haven: 1953).

Gmurczyk-Wrońska M., "'Not Russia, but France and England Shall Decide about Poland': The Diplomatic Action of Roman Dmowski in 1916–1917", *Studia z Dziejów Rosji i Europy Środkowo-Wschodniej* (2017) 27.

Gnauck G., *Polen verstehen. Geschichte, Politik, Gesellschaft* (Stuttgart: 2018).

Goldstein E., "Great Britain: The Home Front", in Boemeke M. – Feldman G. – Glaser E. (eds.), *The Treaty of Versailles. A Reassessment after 75 Years* (Cambridge: 1998) 147.

Graebner N. – Bennett E., *The Versailles Treaty and Its Legacy. The Failure of the Wilsonian Vision* (Cambridge: 2011).

Graf Brockdorff-Rantzau U., *Dokumente und Gedanken um Versailles* (Berlin: 1925).

Hagen W., "The Moral Economy of Ethnic Violence: The Pogrom in Lwów, November 1918", *Geschichte und Gesellschaft* 31 (2005) 203.

Heinemann U., *Die verdrängte Niederlage* (Göttingen: 1983).

Herwig H., "Clio Deceived. Patriotic Self-Censorship in Germany after the Great War", *International Security* 12 (1987) 5.

Hildebrand K., *Das vergangene Reich. Deutsche Außenpolitik von Bismarck bis Hitler 1871–1945* (Munich: 2008).

Hillgruber H., „Unter dem Schatten von Versailles – Die außenpolitische Belastung der Weimarer Republik: Realität und Perzeption bei den Deutschen", in Erdmann K. – Schulze H. (eds.), *Weimar. Selbstpreisgabe einer Demokratie. Eine Bilanz heute* (Düsseldorf: 1980) 51.

Hüetlin T., *Berlin, 24. Juni 1922: Der Rathenaumord und der Beginn des rechten Terrors in Deutschland* (Cologne: 2022).

Ištok R. – Koziak T., "Międzymorze as a Polish Geopolitical Concept", *Folia Geographica* 14 (2009) 89.

Jackson P., *Beyond the Balance of Power. France and the Politics of National Security in the Era of the First World War* (Cambridge: 2013).

Jasper W., *Lusitania. Kulturgeschichte einer Katastrophe* (Berlin: 2015).

Jaworski R. – Lübke C. – Müller M., *Eine kleine Geschichte Polens* (Frankfurt am Main: Suhrkamp 2000).

Keynes J., *The Economic Consequences of the Peace* (London: 1920).

Kiel M., *The Jews of Częstochowa. The Life and Death of a Community, a Concise History* (Berlin: 2023).

Kleine-Ahlbrandt W., *The Burden of Victory. France, Britain and the Enforcement of the Versailles Peace, 1919–1925* (Lanham: 1995).

Kolb E. –Schumann D., *Die Weimarer Republik* (Berlin: 2022).

Kolb E., *Der Frieden von Versailles* (Munich: 2nd ed. 2011).

Kornat M., "The Victors and the Polish Cause at the End of the Great War. 104th Anniversary of the Polish Independence", available at https://polishhistory.pl/the-victors-and-the-polish-cause-at-the-end-of-the-great-war/ (last accessed on 17 August 2023).

Krüger P., Versailles. *Deutsche Außenpolitik zwischen Revisionismus und Friedenssicherung* (Munich: 1986).

Krumeich G., *Die unbewältigte Niederlage. Das Trauma des Ersten Weltkriegs und die Weimarer Republik* (Freiburg: 2018).

Kusielewicz E., "Paderewski and Wilson's Speech to the Senate, January 22, 1917", *Polish American Studies*, 13 (1956) 65.

Landau R., *Ignace Paderewski. Musician and Statesman* (New York: 1976 [1934]).

Lange F., „Wider das ‚völkerrechtliche Geschwafel' – Hermann Mosler und die praxisorientierte Herangehensweise an das Völkerrecht im Rahmen des Max-Planck-Instituts", *Zeitschrift für ausländisches öffentliches Recht und Völkerrecht* 75 (2015) 307.

Larson E., *Dead Wake. The Last Crossing of the Lusitania* (New York: 2016).

Lehnstaedt S., *Der vergessene Sieg. Der Polnisch-Sowjetische Krieg 1919–1921 und die Entstehung des modernen Osteuropa* (Munich: 2019).

Leinwand A., "Soviet Propaganda and the Independent Polish State", *Studia z Dziejów Rosji i Europy Środkowo-Wschodniej*, (54) 2020, 81, 85.

Macmillan M., *Paris 1919. Six Months That Changed World* (New York: 2003).

Mai G., *Die Weimarer Republik* (Munich: 2009).

Marks S., "Mistakes and Myths: The Allies, Germany, and the Versailles Treaty, 1918–1921", *The Journal of Modern History* 85 (2013) 632.

Marks S., "Smoke and Mirrors: In Some-Filled Rooms and the Galerie des Glaces", in Boemeke M. – Feldman G. – Glaser E. (eds.), *The Treaty of Versailles. A Reassessment after 75 Years* (Cambridge: 1998) 337.

März P., *Nach der Urkatastrophe. Deutschland, Europa und der Erste Weltkrieg* (Cologne: 2014).

Meyer H., "The World Court, Minority Treaties, and Human Rights", *International Journal on World Peace* 14 (1997) 71.

Michael H., *Zwischen den Kriegen. Polens Außenpolitik 1919–1939* (Berlin: 2022).

Miller M., "The Forgotten Pogroms, 1918", *Slavic Review* 78 (2019) 648.

Mommsen W., "Max Weber and the Peace Treaty of Versailles", in Boemeke M. – Feldman G. – Glaser E. (eds.), *The Treaty of Versailles. A Reassessment after 75 Years* (Cambridge: 1998) 535.

Münch I., "Wimbledon-Fall!", in Strupp K. – Schlochauer H.-J. (eds.), *Wörterbuch des Völkerrechts*, vol. 3 (Berlin: 2nd ed. 1962) 850.

N. N., *Der Vertrag von Versailles* (Munich: 1978).

N. N., *Stenographische Berichte über die öffentlichen Verhandlungen des 15. Untersuchungsausschusses der Verfassunggebenden Nationalversammlung nebst Beilagen*, vol. 2 (Berlin: 1920).

Naumann F., *Mitteleuropa* (Berlin: 1915).

Nicolson H., *Peacemaking 1919* (London: 1933).

Nowak A., "Between Imperial Temptation and Anti-Imperial Function in Eastern Politics: Poland from the Eighteenth to Twenty-First Century", in Matsuzato K. (ed.), *Emerging Meso-Areas in the Former Socialist Countries: Histories Revived or Revisited* (Sapporo: Hokkaido University 2005) 247.

Nowak K., *Versailles* (Berlin: 1927).

Orzell L., "A 'Hotly Disputed Issue': Eastern Galicia at the Paris Peace Conference, 1919", *The Polish Review* 25 (1980) 49.

Pauly W., „Das Öffentliche Recht an der Berliner Juristischen Fakultät 1933–1945", in Kloepfer M. – Paulus C. – Schröder R. – Werle G. (eds.), *Festschrift 200 Jahre Juristische Fakultät der Humboldt-Universität zu Berlin. Geschichte, Gegenwart und Zukunft* (Berlin: 2010) 773.

Payk M., *Frieden durch Recht? Der Aufstieg des modernen Völkerrechts und der Friedensschluss nach dem Ersten Weltkrieg* (Berlin: 2018).

Platthaus A., *Der Krieg nach dem Krieg. Deutschland zwischen Revolution und Versailles 1918/19* (Berlin: 2018).

Polsakiewicz M., *Warschau im Ersten Weltkrieg. Deutsche Besatzungspolitik zwischen kultureller Autonomie und wirtschaftlicher Ausbeutung* (Marburg: 2015).

Probst R., „Wir kennen die Wucht des Hasses" (Süddeutsche Zeitung of 28 June 2019).

Protasio J., *The Day the World Was Shocked: The Lusitania Disaster and Its Influence on the Course of World War I* (Havertown: 2011).

Schiff V., *So war es in Versailles ...* (Berlin: 1929).

Seymour C., *The Intimate Papers of Colonel House*, vol. 4 (London: 1928).

Sharp A., *The Versailles Settlement. Peacemaking in Paris, 1919* (London: 1991).

Smith L., *Sovereignty at the Paris Peace Conference of 1919* (Oxford: 2018).

Smogorzewski C., *Poland's Access to the Sea* (London: 1934).

Snyder T., "Federalism and Nationalism in Polish Eastern Policy", *Georgetown Journal of International Affairs* 4 (2003) 111.

Soutou G-H., "The French Peacemakers and Their Home Front", in Boemeke M. – Feldman G. – Glaser E. (eds.), *The Treaty of Versailles. A Reassessment after 75 Years* (Cambridge: 1998) 167.

Steiner Z., *The Lights That Failed. European International History 1919–1933* (Oxford: 2005).

Templin W., *Revolutionär und Staatsgründer. Józef Piłsudski – eine Biographie* (Berlin: 2022).

Thakur-Smolarek K., *Der Erste Weltkrieg und die polnische Frage. Die Interpretation des Kriegsgeschehens durch die zeitgenössischen polnischen Wortführer* (Berlin: 2014).

Toppe A., *Militär und Kriegsvölkerrecht. Rechtsnorm, Fachdiskurs und Kriegspraxis in Deutschland 1899–1940* (Munich: 2008).

Troeltsch E., „Nach der Entscheidung (Juli 1919)", in Hübinger G. (ed.), *Ernst Troeltsch. Spectator-Briefe und Berliner Briefe (1919–1922)* (Berlin: 2015) 125.

Trommler F., "The Lusitania Effect. America's Mobilization against Germany in World War I", *German Studies Review* (32) 2009, 241.

Wagner G., *Deutschland und der Polnisch-Sowjetische Krieg 1920* (Wiesbaden: 1979).

Walicki A., "The Troubling Legacy of Roman Dmowski", *East European Politics and Societies* 14 (2000) 12.

Wandycz P., "Poland's Place in Europe in the Concepts of Piłsudski and Dmowski", *East European Politics and Societies* 4 (1990) 451.

Wandycz P., "The Polish Question", in Boemeke M. – Feldman G. – Glaser E. (eds.), *The Treaty of Versailles. A Reassessment after 75 Years* (Cambridge: 1998) 316.

Weber H., „Die politische Verantwortung der Wissenschaft. Friedrich Berber in den Jahren 1937 bis 1945", in Krause E. – Huber L. – Fischer H. (eds.), *Hochschulalltag im „Dritten Reich". Die Hamburger Universität 1933–1945*, vol. 3 part II (Berlin: 1991) 939.

Wehler H-U., *Deutsche Gesellschaftsgeschichte*, vol. 4 (Munich: 2003).

Winkler H.-A., *Weimar 1918–1933. Die Geschichte der ersten deutschen Demokratie* (Munich: 4th ed. 2005).

Wolff L., *Woodrow Wilson and the Reimagining of Eastern Europe* (Stanford: 2020).

Wolgast E., *Der Wimbledonprozeß* (Berlin: 1926).

Wołos M., "A New Order in Central and Eastern Europe: Polish–Soviet Negotiations and the Peace of Riga (1920–1921)", *Zapiski Historyczne* 86 (2021) 97.

Wüest E., *Der Vertrag von Versailles in Licht und Schatten der Kritik. Die Kontroverse um seine wirtschaftlichen Auswirkungen* (Zurich: 1962).

Wynot E., "The Polish Germans, 1919–1939: National Minority in a Multinational State", *The Polish Review* 17 (1972) 23.

Zamoyski A., *Warsaw 1920. Lenin's Failed Conquest of Europe* (London: 2008).

Zimmermann L., *Deutsche Aussenpolitik in der Ära der Weimarer Republik* (Göttingen: 1958).

CHAPTER 2

Public Interest Litigation *avant la lettre*? Questions of Standing in the *Wimbledon Case*

Christian J. Tams

1 The Hague, 22 July 2022: Clarity at Last

On 22 July 2022, the ICJ finally settled a long-standing question that had occupied commentators for decades. It recognised that certain treaty obligations protecting public interests of the international community could be enforced by each and every State: "any State party to the … Convention may invoke the responsibility of another State party, including through the institution of proceedings before the Court".[1] This holding was made in the context of proceedings in a dramatic dispute involving serious allegations of egregious breaches of international law, namely genocide charges brought against Myanmar concerning the treatment of the Rohingya minority, described by the UN's Secretary-General from 2017 onwards as "a humanitarian and human rights nightmare".[2] These charges, noted the Court (rejecting Myanmar's preliminary objection[3]) could be brought by a State situated around 11,500 km from the site of the atrocities in Rakhine – The Gambia. While determined to "champion an accountability mechanism", The Gambia could not claim to have been affected by "the terrible crimes against the Rohingya Muslims" in a special, personalised, or individual manner.[4] In fact, The Gambia it did not assert any such personal, special or individual injury. Rather, it emphasised the "common interest" of all State parties "in compliance with the obligations under the Genocide Convention"; *like any other State party*, The Gambia considered itself "entitled to invoke the responsibility of [Myanmar]".[5] This claim the Court endorsed,

1 *Application of the Convention on the Prevention and Punishment of the Crime of Genocide* (The Gambia v. Myanmar), Judgment on preliminary objections of 22 July 2022, at para. 112 (at https://www.icj-cij.org/public/files/case-related/178/178-20220722-JUD-01-00-EN.pdf).

2 See 'Rohingya refugee crisis a "human rights nightmare", UN chief tells Security Council', UN News 28 September 2017, at https://news.un.org/en/story/2017/09/567402-rohingya-refugee-crisis-human-rights-nightmare-un-chief-tells-security-council.

3 Judgment of 22 July 2022 (n 1), paras. 93–94.

4 Judgment of 22 July 2022 (n 1), para. 39.

5 Judgment of 22 July 2022 (n 1), para. 100.

 | DOI:10.1163/9789004707979_004

recognising The Gambia's standing to initiate proceedings in defence of a public interest.

This recognition paved the way for something new: for "the first time", in the words of one commentator, "a state has invoked [the ICJ's] jurisdiction to seek redress for alleged genocidal acts committed against the citizens of another state" – the 'opening of a door' in view of supporters,[6] while rather more of an 'opening of floodgates' for critics.[7] But, as commentators were quick to point out, while a 'first' of sorts, the holding did not come out of the blue. Its significance could only be grasped if the judgment of 22 July 2022 was read against the backdrop of a series of ICJ decisions reflecting different approaches to the question of *locus standi,* from *South West Africa* (1962/1966)[8] via *Barcelona Traction* (1970)[9] to *Obligation to Extradite* (2012)[10] and, implicitly, *Whaling in the Antarctic* (2014).[11] The difference between *South West Africa* and the *Rohingya* case is particularly striking: in its 1966 judgment, the Court had considered that "rights or interests [in the enforcement of public interests], in order to exist, must be clearly vested in those who claim them, by some text or instrument, or rule of law".[12] 56 years later, the Court considered the *absence of limiting language* to be sufficient to recognise The Gambia's standing to enforce common interests protected by the Genocide Convention: where

6 See eg Rizwanul Islam, "Not an Overreach of the Court's Jurisdiction, Putting *Erga Omnes* into Motion", *Chinese Journal of International Law* 21 (2022), 611. My own views are set out in Christian J. Tams, "*Erga omnes*-Verpflichtungen vor dem Internationalen Gerichtshof: ein Kontrapunkt", in Donath et al. (eds.), *Der Schutz des Individuums durch das Recht. Festschrift für Rainer Hofmann zum 70. Geburtstag* (Springer 2023), 43; and id., "'Véritables parties' et reconnaissance tardive d'un intérêt à agir en défense d'intérêts collectifs: Remarques sur l'arrêt du 22 juillet 2022 dans l'affaire entre la Gambie et le Myanmar", *Annuaire Français du Droit International* 68 (2022), 285.

7 See eg Xiao Mao, "Public-Interest Litigation before the International Court of Justice: Comment on The Gambia v. Myanmar Case", *Chinese Journal of International Law* 21 (2022), 589 (notably drawing on Judge Xue's dissenting opinion appended to the judgment of 22 July 2022, which notes at § 10: "The bilateral and adversarial structure of the dispute settlement mechanism is reflected in the procedural rules of the Court. Such rules are not suitable to entertain public-interest actions.")

8 *South West Africa* (Ethiopia v. South Africa, Liberia v. South Africa), ICJ Reports 1962, 319 and ICJ Reports 1966, 6.

9 *Barcelona Traction, Light and Power Company, Limited* (Belgium v. Spain) (New Application: 1962), ICJ Reports 1970, 3.

10 *Questions relating to the Obligation to Prosecute or Extradite* (Belgium v. Senegal), ICJ Reports 2012 (II), 422.

11 *Whaling in the Antarctic* (Australia v. Japan: New Zealand intervening), ICJ Reports 2014, 226.

12 *South West Africa* (n 8), ICJ Reports 1966, 6, at para. 44.

a treaty protected an interest of all treaty parties, the Court could be seised unless there were clear indications that such seisin should depend on further conditions – but as the Genocide Convention gave no such clear indications, The Gambia's case could proceed.[13] In his thoughtful Declaration, Judge ad hoc Kress underlined that, if indeed *South West Africa* established a presumption against standing to enforce common interests, then "the present Judgment further consolidates the Court's subsequent departure from the stance it adopted in 1966".[14]

•••

The present contribution does not seek to rehash the many debates about public interests and their protection in and through ICJ proceedings.[15] Nor indeed does it seek to trace in any detail the ICJ's evolving approach to the question of standing, or the Court's long and winding path from *South West Africa* to *Rohingya* case . Instead, the focus is on what might be called a *prequel* to the ICJ's debates. This prequel is set in the 1920s, and more particularly, in the jurisprudence of the PCIJ, beginning with the judgment that is at the heart of this edited collection: the *Wimbledon* case. It is a prequel that lacks the drama of the *South West Africa* and *Rohingya* disputes. But it offers insights into an early approach to what might be called 'public interest litigation': an approach characterised by a degree of healthy pragmatism that would get lost afterwards, and that it is now perhaps possible to reclaim.

---

13 Judgment of 22 July 2022 (n 1), paras. 110–111. That the Genocide Convention had been established to protect interests of all parties, had been recognised decades earlier when the Court described it in the following terms: "In such a convention, the contracting State parties do not have any interests of their own; they merely have, one and all, a common interest" (*Reservations to the Convention on the Prevention and Punishment of the Crime of Genocide,* ICJ Reports 1951, 15, at 23). See also the Declaration of Judge ad hoc Kress (ibid), at para. 15: "Once it has been determined that an obligation has been established in pursuit of a common interest, such as that laid down by the Genocide Convention, there is thus no need to demonstrate, on the basis of additional considerations, the existence of a separate 'individual legal interest' in order to justify standing before the Court. On the contrary, the standing of each contracting State to invoke before the Court a common interest such as that established by the Genocide Convention must be presumed, unless the provisions of the relevant convention indicate otherwise."

14 Judgment of 22 July 2022 (n 1), Declaration of Judge ad hoc Kress, at para. 15.

15 For detailed accounts see notably the treatment in François Voeffray, *Actio popularis ou la défense des interêt collectif devant les juridictions internationales* (Paris, PUF 2004); Santiago Villalpando, *L'émergence de la communauté internationale dans la responsabilité des États* /Paris, PUF 2005); Christian J. Tams, *Enforcing Obligations Erga Omnes in International Law* (Cambridge, CUP 2005).

2 Brunsbüttel, 21 March 1921: a Steamship Is Held Up

It all begins in Brunsbüttel, a small town of then roughly 3000 inhabitants, situated in the Dithmarschen district of Schleswig Holstein, Germany, at the mouth of the Elbe river and the western terminus of the Kiel Canal.[16] On the morning of 21 March 1921, a Monday, a British steamship presents itself at the western entrance of the Canal: the *s.s. 'Wimbledon',* 6200 tons, chartered by a French company and en route from Salonica. Its cargo: 4200 tons of munitions and artillery stores, consigned for the Polish Naval base at Gdansk/Danzig, and meant to support the Polish effort in the Russo–Polish war.

On 21 March 1921, the Wimbledon's progress was interrupted. The German Director of Canal Traffic refuses to allow the *Wimbledon* into the Canal, stating that to do so would violate Germany's neutrality orders, which precluded "[t]he export and transit of arms, munitions, powder and explosives and other articles of war material … in so far as these articles are consigned to the territories of the Polish Republic or of the Federal Socialist Republic of the Russian Soviets".[17] The Wimbledon's advisers intervened, emphasising that Germany, under the terms of Article 380 of the Treaty of Versailles, had to maintain "[t]he Kiel Canal and its approaches … free and open to the vessels of commerce and of war of all nations at peace with Germany on terms of entire equality."[18] But the Canal authorities would not budge. Eleven days, the *Wimbledon* was kept at Brunsbüttel. Then her owners gave in (in the face of Northern German stubbornness), and ordered the Wimbledon to make her way to Gdansk/Danzig by a different route: and so she did, sailing past Skaagen, and further through the Danish straits, as Baltic-bound ships had done for centuries. On 6 April 1921, she reached her destination, with her cargo intact, 13 days later than planned.[19]

16 The following draws on the facts as reported in PCIJ, *The s.s. "Wimbledon",* Ser. A, No. 1, Judgment of 17 August 1923, 18–20; as well as Clemens Feinäugle, *Wimbledon, The,* in Wolfrum R. (ed.), Max Planck Encyclopedia of International Law (Oxford: 2012), online version updated 2013.

17 These are excerpted in the *Wimbledon* judgment (n 16), at 28–29.

18 Further details were set out in Articles 381–385, to which Article 386 added a dispute settlement clause. Articles 380–386 comprised Part XII, section VI, entitled "Clauses related to the Kiel Canal". For details see Rainer Lagoni, "Kiel Canal", in Wolfrum R. (ed.), Max Planck Encyclopedia of International Law (Oxford: 2012), online version updated 2013.

19 See the Applicants' Memorial, PCIJ Ser. C, No. 03/4, at 5 (at https://www.icj-cij.org/sites/default/files/permanent-court-of-international-justice/serie_C/C_03_04/C_03_03_memoire.pdf).

What a difference 13 days make. Where the naive observer might see a short delay, the lawyers saw principles.[20] Could Germany apply its neutrality orders, even though the Treaty of Versailles had opened up and internationalised the Kiel Canal? How did Article 380 of the Treaty affect the status of the Kiel Canal? Could it be construed to require Germany to potentially violate rights of a third State, Soviet Russia? The PCIJ's judgment of 17 August 1923 addressed these (and other) questions of principle, responding to the parties' submissions and those of Poland, which had intervened as a third party.[21] The PCIJ's responses are analysed in various contributions to this volume. The present chapter focuses on a niche question, which the preceding summary has left to a side, but which now needs to be broached – who were the claimant States that brought legal proceedings against Germany? The response appears in the opening lines of the judgment, which list as parties, successively, "The Government of His Britannic Majesty .... The Government of the French Republic ... The Government of His Majesty the King of Italy ... and The Government of His Majesty the Emperor of Japan".[22]

Four claimant States – to defend one small ship's right to enter the Kiel canal? (A well-protected ship the *Wimbledon* was.) The subsequent sections seek to throw light on this niche aspect of the case, and to show that, while the actual disputes prompting the two World Court decisions are worlds apart – 13 days' delay versus 'unspeakable atrocities'[23] –, the *Wimbledon* judgment in some ways foreshadowed the ICJ's eventual recognition, in 2022, of the right of States to initiate proceedings in defence of common interests.

3 Brunsbüttel, Berlin, Paris, The Hague (1921–1923): a Public Interest Case Unfolds

A century later, some aspects of the backstory remain shrouded in mystery. However, the case-file publicly available on the PCIJ section of the ICJ website yields a number of insights. The first is that, perhaps curiously, it was the

20 Admittedly, the Wimbledon incident was not the only one to implicate the principle: A few months earlier, the German authorities had refused access to the Kiel Canal to another ship bound for Danzig, the *Dorrit,* flying a Danish flag: for details see p. 4 of the Applicants' Memorial (n 19).

21 On the intervention before the Court in this case see the Court's judgment of 28 June 1923: *The S.S. "Wimbledon",* (Intervention) PCIJ, Ser. A, No. 1 and contribution by Michał Balcerzak to this volume.

22 *Wimbledon* judgment (n 16), at 15.

23 See n 2.

German government, as future respondent, that suggested, as early as March 1921, to submit the dispute about the proper construction of Article 380 of the Treaty of Versailles to the Permanent Court of International Justice.[24] When making that suggestion, Germany drew attention to Article 386 of the Treaty, which provided that: "In the event of violation of any of the conditions of Articles 380 to 386, or of disputes as to the interpretation of these Articles, any interested Power can appeal to the jurisdiction instituted for the purpose by the League of Nations." Once that 'jurisdiction instituted for the purpose by the League of Nations' (aka the PCIJ) had begun to take shape, Germany reiterated this suggestion in early 1922. Following some further back and forth (and following Germany's refusal to make good the losses caused by the detention of the *Wimbledon* at Brunsbüttel[25]), the four applicants instituted proceedings in January 1923.

The second point clearly emerging from the records concerns the forum for the inter-party discussions preceding the legal proceedings. From April 1921 onwards, the *Wimbledon*'s concern was taken up by the Conference of Ambassadors of the Principal Allied and Associated Powers, an inter-allied organization set up in early 1920, then succeeding the Supreme War Council. Seated in Paris, the Conference brought together the British, Italian and Japanese ambassadors to France, as well as the French foreign minister.[26] During 1921–1922 (and in fact during the earlier *Dorrit* incident of 1920[27]), it was the Conference – as the central coordination group addressing questions arising from the Peace Treaties[28] – that formulated claims on behalf of the *Wimbledon*, and it was to the Conference that Germany submitted its responses. Once it became clear that the matter would be submitted to the PCIJ, the governments of the four Principal Allied and Associated Powers simply continued the path chosen by their ambassadors – and acted jointly (under

24 See Applicants' Memorial (n 19), at 6; as well as the discussion in Germany's Counter-Memorial, PCIJ Ser. C, No. 03/4, at 40–41 (https://www.icj-cij.org/sites/default/files/permanent-court-of-international-justice/serie_C/C_03_04/C_03_04_contre-memoire.pdf).

25 These were put at 174,082.68 French francs: see the *Wimbledon* judgment (n 16), at 17.

26 For background see Edmund Jan Osmańczyk and Anthony Mango, *Encyclopedia of the United Nations and International Agreements* (A-F) (3rd edn., Taylor & Francis 2003), at 434. The US ambassador joined as an observer, as the United States had not ratified the Treaty of Versailles.

27 See the Applicants' Memorial (n 19), at 4.

28 Grown out of the Supreme War Council, the Conference of Ambassadors was tasked to monitor compliance with the post-war settlements, including in relation to the Memel Territory, discussed below, in Section 5.

French leadership). The Memorial explains in rather succinct terms why four States requested the PCIJ to declare Germany to have violated Article 380:

> Cette requête a été présentée au nom des Gouvernements de Sa Majesté britannique, de la République française, de Sa Majesté le Roi d'Italie et de Sa Majesté l'Empereur du Japon. *Ces quatre Gouvernements figurent dans l'instance comme intéressés à l'exacte application des règles sur la liberté de passage dans le canal de Kiel posées par le Traité de Paix de Versailles dont ils sont signataires.*[29]

Not all was done jointly, though: one State was special, asserting a right to damage sustained by its nationals:

> En outre, le Gouvernement français agit pour obtenir la réparation pécuniaire du dommage subi par les 'Affréteurs Réunis', société française ayant son siège social à Paris.[30]

Even from this brief summary, it seems clear that the Wimbledon case could have given rise to protracted debates about the applicants' standing. To begin with, the fact that France took the lead, and asked for compensation, may appear puzzling. The *Wimbledon* flew the British flag after all, not the French. France's interests were economic: the *Wimbledon* had been time-chartered by a French company, which in turn had borne the cost of the delays. From the distance of one century, it is curious to see how lightly the Applicants – and eventually the Court – treated the role of the flag State, subsequently to be strengthened in successive iterations of maritime law-making.[31] But that need not concern us here, as France and the United Kingdom at least could clim to

29 Applicants' Memorial (n 19), at 7 (emphasis added).

30 Applicants' Memorial (n 19), at 7.

31 35 years after the Wimbledon judgment, a then junior scholar would assert that "[n]ational ownership … is the proper basis for the exercise of protection over private shipping", whereas "[t]he flag … [being] primarily only a symbol" was an "unacceptable" basis: see A.D. (later Sir Arthur D.) Watts, "The Protection of Merchant Ships", *British Yearbook of International Law* 33 (1957), 52, at 84. Most authorities have ascribed a much more prominent role to the flag, at least where "[t]here … exists a genuine link between the [flag] State and the ship": see Articles 91–92 UNCLOS, and further *The M/V "SAIGA" (No. 2)* (Saint Vincent and the Grenadines v. Guinea), ITLOS Reports 1999, 10, at para. 180 (noting that in Articles 94, 217, 292 UNCLOS, "the Convention considers a ship as a unit, as regards the obligations of the flag State with respect to the ship and the right of a flag State to seek reparation for loss or damage caused to the ship by acts of other States and to institute proceedings under Article 292 of the Convention. Thus the ship, every thing on

have been affected in some special, individual, personal manner, as the flag State and the state of nationality of the company sustaining losses.

Importantly, Italy and Japan could not make any such claim to special injury: nothing special or individual tied them to the little ship of 6200 tons; neither of them had a particular responsibility vis-à-vis Poland; neither was in any personal way affected by the conduct of the German authorities. And in fact, like The Gambia in the much more dramatic Rohingya case a century onwards, neither Italy not Japan claimed to be acting to pursue individual interests. The brief passage from the Memorial mentions two aspects that they share(d) with dozens of other States: Italy and Japan were interested in the proper application of rules regulation navigation through the Kiel Canal (*intéressés à l'exacte application des règles sur la liberté de passage dans le canal de Kiel*) and they were both parties to the Treaty that had laid down these rules on navigation, viz. the Versailles Peace Treaty (*«le Traité de Paix de Versailles dont ils sont signataires»*).[32] Should this be sufficient for them to initiate legal proceedings before the PCIJ? Germany seemed unconvinced, but unwilling to press the matter. Rather than raising (as would Myanmar, a century later) a preliminary objection for lack of standing, it merely drew attention to the matter:

> Le Gouvernement allemand croit devoir laisser à l'appréciation de la Cour la question de savoir si les Gouvernements des Puissances alliées qui, conjointement avec le Gouvernement français, ont introduit la présente requête, y étaient autorisés.[33]

How would the Court deal with such a lukewarm protest?

---

it, and every person involved or interested in its operations are treated as an entity linked to the flag State. The nationalities of these persons are not relevant.")

32 Applicants' Memorial (n 19), at 7 (emphasis added).

33 Germany's Counter-Memorial (n 24), at 42. Germany only emphasised one aspect: the fact that all four States were members of the Conference of Ambassadors, and that Germany had engaged with them in that forum, did not matter: the Conference possessed no formal competences: "Néanmoins, [le gouvernement allemand] désire faire remarquer que cette autorisation [de porter plainte] ne saurait être fondée sur le fait que l'échange de notes a eu lieu avec la Conférence des Ambassadeurs. La Conférence des Ambassadeurs n'est pas un organe prévu au Traité de Versailles et revêtu de propres compétences. Si, dans ce cas comme dans d'autres, le Gouvernement allemand est entré en échange de vues avec la Conférence des Ambassadeurs, il ne l'a fait que dans l'intérêt d'un règlement objectif du différend et afin de ne soulever aucune difficulté de forme" (ibid.).

4 The Hague, 17 August 1923: a Standing Court Treats 'Standing' Lightly

The Court addressed the matter in its judgment of 17 August 1923, at the outset of its decision, in a dedicated (if brief) section on the admissibility of the application. To begin with the outcome, the Court had "no doubt that it can take cognizance of the application instituting proceedings in the form in which it has been submitted".[34] The reasoning supporting is refreshingly succinct:

> It will suffice to observe for the purposes of this case that each of the four Applicant Powers has a clear interest in the execution of the provisions relating to the Kiel Canal, since they all possess fleets and merchant vessels flying their respective flags. They are therefore, even though they may be unable to adduce a prejudice to any pecuniary interest, covered by the terms of Article 386, Paragraph 1 of which is as follows: 'In the event of violation of any of the conditions of Articles 380 to 386, or of disputes as to the interpretation of these articles, any interested Power can appeal to the jurisdiction instituted for the purpose by the League of Nations'.[35]

While succinct, this passage reflected significant choices made by the Court. Three such choices stand out:

> First, the Court considered a State's standing to institute proceedings under Article 386 to depend on the establishment of an "interest" (rather than a 'right', a 'legal interest', or an 'injury'). This seemed to follow naturally from the language of the provision ("any *interested* power"); the Court's reference to the provision's "terms" as well as the fact that it couched its finding in the same language ("each of the four Applicant Powers has a clear *interest*"), suggests that it considered Article 386 to provide guidance.[36] As in subsequent proceedings before the World Court, the question of standing was approached via the terms of a jurisdictional clause.

Second, the Court took a very broad view of the term "interest". All that was required for Japan and Italy (as well as Great Britain and France) to be

34 *Wimbledon* judgment (n 19), 20.
35 *Wimbledon* judgment (n 19), 20.
36 For brief comment on the matter see Voeffray, *Actio Popularis* (n 15), 46–47; Tams, *Erga Omnes* (n 15), 77–78.

"interested", or even "clearly interested", was that "they all possess[ed] fleets and merchant vessels flying their respective flags".[37] To appreciate the breadth of this test, it is useful to consider what the Court did not require, or did not find necessary to mention: there is nothing in the short passage to suggest that any fleet belonging to the States' flag would have actually had to pass this the Kiel Canal; nothing requiring a large fleet and dependency on maritime trade; no regional link; no interest in the Polish–Russian war, etc. And neither did it seem to matter that Italy and Japan (via the Conference of Ambassadors) had previously taken an interest in the dispute. The language of the *Wimbledon* judgment rather suggests that any seafaring nation that was a party to the Versailles Treaty[38] could invoke its Article 386 and enforce the internationalised regime set out in Articles 380–385. This was indeed (as one observer would note in retrospect) a "generous interpretation of [the terms] 'any interested power'",[39] according to which (as another put it) "un simple intérêt futur ou potentiel" was sufficient.[40]

Third, the short passage hints at a differentiated approach to the question of remedies. While all four powers could initiate the proceedings to seek declaratory relief and to ensure Germany comply with its obligations, only one of them could obtain compensation. This was France, which according to the Court could act on behalf of the 'Affréteurs Réunis', a French company that had suffered economic losses. By contrast, the other powers could not "adduce

37 *Wimbledon* judgment (n 19), 20.

38 In fact, not even that requirement (treaty participation) is certain: Given the objective character of the regime of the Kiel Canal (which after all, had been "permanently dedicated *to the whole world*" [Article 380, emphasis added]), it is tempting to speculate whether States not parties to the Treaty of Versailles would have been entitled to institute proceedings. The Court in the *Wimbledon case* did not have to address this issue – but its statement that the Kiel Canal had "become an international waterway intended to provide under treaty guarantee easier access to the Baltic for the benefit of *all nations of the world*" (*Wimbledon*, 22, emphasis added) suggests that the regime of the canal was not purely a matter for treaty parties. Subsequent codification attempts did recognise a right of non-parties "to invoke the provisions of [an objective] régime" if they (without acceding to the regime-creating treaty) had become bound by it: see draft article 63(3)(b) proposed by Sir Humphrey Waldock as part of his attempt to persuade the ILC to codify the concept of objective regime (in ILC Yearbook 1964, vol. II, 26–27). In the end, the ILC was not persuaded, and no rule on objective regimes features in the Vienna Convention on the Law of Treaties. For more on the matter, see Malgosia Fitzmaurice, Third Parties and the Law of Treaties, *Max Planck Yearbook of United Nations Law* 6 (2002), 37; as well as the briefer discussion in Tams, *Erga Omnes* (n 15), 80–87.

39 Christine D. Gray, *Judicial Remedies in International Law* (Oxford OUP 1987), 211.

40 Voeffray, *Actio Popularis* (n 15), 47–48.

a prejudice to any pecuniary interest": while this did not preclude them from initiating proceedings, it limited the range of remedies available to them.

None of this, to be sure, was developed; for the most part, the Court asserted rather than reasoned in a short passage full of apodictic statements. But it was a remarkable passage that signalled clearly how the newly-established Court would approach the question of standing, that is without undue concern about the dangers of opening its door to States acting in defence of some community interest. Guided by the broad (but obscure) terms of a jurisdictional clause, the Court recognised that all maritime powers had a general interest, sufficient to initiate legal proceedings, in vindicating the international status of the Kiel Canal.[41]

5 Reactions to *Wimbledon*: the *Memel Case*

If the Court was relatively unperturbed by the idea of public interest litigation, then so seemed its clients and readers. As regards the former, Germany's focus may have been on the outcome of the decision: as discussed in other contributions to this volume,[42] Germany eventually paid the required compensation and accepted the decision, at least until it 're-nationalised' the Canal in 1936.[43] The PCIJ's approach to standing did not seem to provoke concerns. Academic commentary also centred on substantive points, which had divided the judges – neutrality, international versus national status, impact on sovereignty. The question of standing was not a major source of concern, but the Court's liberal approach did not go unnoticed either. Two brief reactions are indicative: Salvioli, in his 1926 Hague lectures reviewing the first years of PCIJ jurisprudence, was clearly surprised, but not scandalised: he considered the Court's approach to standing "un peu excessive", but was content merely to note it.[44] In the most-cited German-language discussion of the case, Wolgast

---

41 Voeffray is slightly more cautious, noting that it was "pas encore l'affirmation d'un intérêt général au respect de la légalité conventionnelle, mais on est très proche d'une telle notion": Voeffray, *Actio Popularis* (n 15), 47; but it is not entirely clear what explains the 'pas encore'. Voeffray's other statement – that *Wimbledon* constituted "une reconnaissance embryonnaire" of the *erga omnes* concept (47) – seems more apt.

42 See contributions to this volume by Schäffer, Balcerzak and Kowalski.

43 See the German note of 14 November 1936, by which "the German government unilaterally terminated the internationalized right of passage through the Canal and on certain rivers on German territory": Lagoni, 'Kiel Canal' (n 18), para. 6. The note is reproduced in *Reichsgesetzblatt* 1936, vol. II, 361.

44 Gabriele Salvioli, "'La jurisprudence de la Cour permanente de Justice international'", 12 *Recueil des Cours* (1926 II), 5, at 11–12.

offered a little more, but again, no full-frontal attack. His main point was that the interests of Italy and Japan were not *legal interests* strictly speaking; to consider such non-legal interests sufficient to him seemed incorrect.[45] But again, this stopped short of a full engagement. The overall impression is one of a significant holding on a discrete point – noted by specialists, but not a major bone of contention.

The overall impression is confirmed by a subsequent decision of the PCIJ, which seems animated by the 'spirit' of *Wimbledon* and suggests that it was no one-off, or aberration. The decision was prompted by a dispute set in the very region to which the Kiel Canal was to provided easy access, viz. the Baltic sea. This was the judgment in the *Memel Statute case,*[46] in which the Court was asked to clarify the terms of another post-war regime promoted by the League, the 1924 Convention Concerning the Statute of the Memel Territory – a Convention that had recognised Lithuania's sovereignty over the region (present-day Klaipėda), but protected rights of its German-speaking population through an autonomy statute.[47] The scope of this statute was to be tested when in 1932, the Lithuanian government dismissed the President of the Memel Directorate, elected with support of the 'German' parties, prompting concern among the League Council.[48] Negotiations having led to no avail, the four principal allied powers represented on the Council seised the PCIJ on the basis of Article 17(2) of the 1924 Memel Convention, under which "[T]he Lithuanian Government agree[d] that all disputes [between Lithuania and four powers, pertaining to the scope of the Convention] shall, if the other Party so requests, be referred to the Permanent Court of International Justice". Whereas the scope of Article 386 of the Treaty of Versailles (envisaging claims by "any interested Party"), at stake in the *Wimbledon case,* had been ambiguous, Article 17(2) of the Memel Convention clearly entitled the four powers to do so; the PCIJ was thus on safe grounds to admit their claims.[49] What is significant is that it did so without any qualms, despite the clearest affirmations that this was, in effect, a form of public interest litigation. In the pleadings, the British Agent had noted that "the Applicant Powers are not here [before the

45 Ernst Wolgast, *Der Wimbledonprozeß vor dem Völkergerichtshof* (Berlin 1926), 28–29.

46 See PCIJ Ser. A/B, No. 47 (preliminary objections) and No. 49 (merits); and the summary by Marcelo Kohen, "Memel Territory Statute, Interpretation of, Case", in Wolfrum R. (ed.), *Max Planck Encyclopedia of International Law* (Oxford: 2012), online version updated 2013.

47 29 LNTS 86 (with the Memel Statute added as an Annex). Germany had renounced sovereign rights over the Baltic territories under Article 99 of the Treaty of Versailles.

48 Kohen provides details: see his "Memel Territory Statute" (n 46), paras. 1–2.

49 For commentary see Voeffray, *Actio Popularis* (n 15), 49–52; Tams, *Erga Omnes* (n 15), 75–76.

Court] to defend their particular interests, nor to maintain any rights of their own which they allege to have been infringed. Their only interest is to see that the Convention to which they are Parties is carried out by Lithuania".[50] Italy's agent echoed this almost verbatim, noting that "[a]ucune de ces Puissances n'a d'intérêt particulier à faire valoir contre la Lithuanie".[51] While raising other preliminary objections, Lithuania seemed to accept the applicants' standing. The Court did not mention the matter,[52] but proceeded to examine the claims: finding in favour of Lithuania on the 'Böttcher incident', it saw no problem with entertaining claims aimed at "obtain[ing] an interpretation of the Statute which would serve as a guide to the future". This does not seem to have prompted any reactions among commentators; it was a clear-cut case of four allied powers exercising their rights conferred by treaty – but these were, as Voeffray notes perceptively, rights to act as "guardiennes du respect d'un traité", based on "une conception large de l'intérêt au respect de la légalité conventionnelle", just as in the earlier *Wimbledon case* or the recent *Rohyngia case.*

6 A Prequel and Its Aftermath

As is clear from the preceding sections, the PCIJ approached standing pragmatically. Where it recognised the right of applicants to initiate proceedings in defence of some common interest, it did so on the basis of special treaty provisions and with limited explanation. Looked at in retrospect, the *Wimbledon* and *Memel Statute* decisions are remarkable for the absence of drama: claims by States acting in pursuit of some common interest were admitted without much soul-searching or argument about the character of the underlying rights, or the nature of international litigation. This was no doubt facilitated by the approach adopted by the respective respondent States, which had no major issue with being sued by States that could not conceivably claim to have been individually or personally injured, and instead claimed to act as guardians of treaty provisions. But it remains remarkable because the Court could of course brought up the matter ex officio. Equally remarkable is a look at the rights that were at stake: in the first decade of its existence, the PCIJ not only had admitted public interest claims, but had done so to protect the access to a

50 PCIJ, Ser. C, No. 59, 173.

51 PCIJ, Ser. C, No. 59, 190.

52 According to Voeffray, for the PCIJ, "[a]pparemment, la teneur claire de la clause juridictionnelle lui a paru suffisante pour justifier la qualité pour agir des demandeurs": Voeffray, *Actio Popularis* (n 15), 51.

waterway, and the integrity of a territorial autonomy statute – hardly matters of life and death, or of fundamental importance for the wider international law community.

All this is worth restating because the lessons of the prequel seemed long to be forgotten – and perhaps some remain so to this day. The early jurisprudence of the PCIJ's successor, the ICJ, is chiefly to blame for that; in it, the debate about public interest litigation took an unhelpful turn to the dramatic, and much of the PCIJ's pragmatism was forgotten. The story has been told on numerous occasions, so three brief observations seem sufficient here.

6.1 *South West Africa*

The first concerns *South West Africa,* that unfortunate (and most unfortunately-handled) ICJ case. In it, just as in *Wimbledon,* the question of standing turned on the interpretation of a jurisdictional clause, namely Article 7(2) of the 1922 mandate,[53] which provided for the Court's jurisdiction over "any dispute whatever … between the Mandatory and another Member of the League of Nations relating to the interpretation or the application of the provisions of the Mandate". The Court was divided on the reading of this clause.[54] A narrow majority initially approached it similar to the PCIJ's reading of the terms of Article 386 of the Treaty of Versailles and Article 17(2) of the Memel Statute Convention – pragmatically, one might say, and relying on its express terms. This is what the Court said in its 1962 judgment on preliminary objections:

> The language used [in Article 7(2)] is broad, clear and precise. […] [T]he manifest scope and purport of the provisions of this Article indicate that the Members of the League were understood to have a legal right or interest in the observance by the Mandatory of its obligations both toward the inhabitants of the Mandated Territory, and toward the League of Nations and its Members.[55]

Four years later, and even narrower majority returned (without altering the parties to it who had pleaded the merits at great length) to the matter and reversed course.[56] In its judgment of 18 July 1966, referenced above, the Court

53 Mandate Agreement regarding German South West Africa of 17 December 1920, reproduced at https://www.aalco.int/9thsession/Part%2018.pdf.

54 The discussion in the following draws on Tams, *Erga Omnes* (n 15), 63–69.

55 *South West Africa* (n 8), ICJ Reports 1962, 325, at 343.

56 The Court in 1966 maintained not to have reversed the 1962 judgment. Instead, it argued that there was a distinction between the *locus standi* of applicants – on which it had decided in 1962 – and the legal interest entitling them to a judgment on the merits, see

held that Ethiopia and Liberia as applicants did not have standing to initiate proceedings concerning South Africa's treatment of the population of the mandate territory: the right to control the mandatory's conduct "was vested exclusively in the League, and was exercised through its competent organs".[57] Importantly, the 1966 majority's reading of the jurisdictional clause was heavily influenced by the judges' view of the standard form of international litigation. This standard form was a bilateral dispute about rights and duties individually assigned to the applicant and respondent. President Winiarski put this most emphatically (and categorically); writing at the stage of the preliminary objections judgment, he was adamant that "an interest [has to be] personal and direct"; Article 7(2) could not be construed "in such a way to conflict with general rule of procedure according to which the Applicant Stateri must have the capacity to institute the proceedings, that is to say, a subjective right, a real and existing individual interest which is legally protected".[58] In 1966, this vision was toned down slightly: legal interests, said the 1966 majority, "need not necessarily relate to anything material or 'tangible'"; and States were free to agree on treaty provisions that allowed for standing irrespective of individual injury.[59] But this would have to be done in explicit and unequivocal terms – to reiterate the central passage again, "rights or interests [in the enforcement of public interests], in order to exist, must be clearly vested in those who claim them, by some text or instrument, or rule of law".[60] Article 7(2), despite its use of broad terns ("any dispute whatever", "another Member of the League") was said not to be clear enough.

Given the almost universal condemnation of the 1966 judgment, it is worth noting that this was not an implausible reading of Article 7(2). But offered in 1966, four years after the judgment on preliminary objections, it proved highly problematic. For the Court to re-open the question of standing was clearly a disastrous way of managing a case, and for the new majority to overrule the

---

South West Africa (n 9), ICJ Reports 1966, 6, at paras. 59–61. This distinction has been generally rejected, not the least because the parties to the dispute had assumed that questions of legal interest were no longer at stake: see Rosalyn Higgins, "The International Court and South West Africa: The Implications of the Judgment", *International Affairs* 42/4 (1966), 573, at 577–582.

57 *South West Africa* (n 8), ICJ Reports 1966, 6, at para. 33.

58 *South West Africa* (n 8), Diss. Op. Winiarski, ICJ Reports 1962, at 456 and 455. See also the joint dissent of Judges Spender and Fitzmaurice appended to the 1962 judgment, in which they considered Article 7(2) to refer to "a dispute in the traditional sense of the term" about the parties' "own interests": ICJ Reports 1962, 558–559.

59 *South West Africa* (n 8), ICJ Reports 1966, 6, at para. 44.

60 *South West Africa* (n 8), ICJ Reports 1966, 6, at para. 44.

old one reflected a significant lack of collegiate thinking. As regards the outcome, the 1966 majority, when relying on an alleged bilateralist 'general rule of procedure', showed itself ignorant of the PCIJ's pragmatism. The 1966 majority mentioned neither the *Wimbledon* nor the *Memel Statute* judgments, and perhaps for a reason: could it really be said that Article 386 had clearly vested a right to initiate proceedings in all treaty parties – more clearly than Article 7(2) of the Mandate Agreement (which did not meet the required threshold of clarity)? And if the mandates system was to be 'policed' exclusively by the League and its organs, why did the PCIJ, in the *Memel Statute case,* have so few concerns with scrutinising compliance with another prominent League project, the autonomy of the Memel territory, at the instigation of individual League members? And above all, where did the alleged 'general rule of procedure' and 'traditional understanding' of the notion of the dispute come from that the 1966 majority held so dear – but that seemed not to be known to the PCIJ? The 1966 majority, for all its concern with the historical background to the mandates system, did not care very much about the history of the ICJ's predecessor; its insistence on principle lacked institutional awareness.

6.2 *Barcelona Traction*

As is well known, the victory of the 1966 majority was short-lived; the fallout of the judgment "was severe and deserved".[61] Three months after the *South West Africa* judgment, the General Assembly terminated the mandate.[62] Facing "a storm of indignation",[63] the ICJ had to make amends. Its penitence came in two decisions – in the *Namibia* opinion, the Court ratified the political organs' understanding of the mandate;[64] while in *Barcelona Traction,* it identified a procedural variant of the concept of *erga omnes* obligations. It is this second form of penintence that matters here, i.e. the Court's famous drawing of "an essential distinction" between obligations in the field of diplomatic protection

61 James Crawford, "'Dreamers of the Day': Australia and the International Court of Justice", *Melbourne Journal of International Law* 14 (2013), 1, at 17.

62 See General Assembly Resolution 2145 (XXI). The Security Council recognised this in its Resolutions 264 (1969) and 276 (1970) and "[d]eclare[d] that the continued presence of the South African authorities in Namibia is illegal".

63 Eckart Klein, "South West Africa/Namibia (Advisory Opinions and Judgements)," in Rudolf Bernhard (ed), *Encyclopedia of Public International Law,* vol. IV (2000), 491, at: ebd., S. 260 – 270; EPIL Vol. 4 (2000), 491, at 497.

64 *Legal Consequences for States of the Continued Presence of South Africa in Namibia (South West Africa) notwithstanding Security Council Resolution 276 (1970)* (Advisory Opinion), ICJ Reports 1971, 16.

and "the obligations of a State towards the international community as a whole".[65]

These latter, the Court continued, "[b]y their very nature ... are the concern of all States. In view of the importance of the rights involved, all States can be held to have a legal interest in their protection; they are obligations *erga omnes*".[66]

This was a curious reversal of the 1966 disaster. A reversal it clearly was. 3.5 years earlier, 'community interests' and 'fundamental importance' of rights had been insufficient to found Ethiopia's and Liberia's standing; now a doctrine of public interest standing was built on them; one that was deduced from the character of an obligation, irrespective of an explicit conferral of enforcement powers, let along a "clearly vested one".[67] But it was a curious way to signal that the Cuort had learned its lesson, and most certainly not a return to the pragmatism of old. Under the *Barcelona Traction* logic, standing to enforce obligations *erga omnes* seemed decoupled from treaty clauses; this at least is suggested by a later passage of the judgment in which the Court distinguished *erga omnes* enforcement from treaty-based mechanisms for the protection of human rights which, on the regional level, "entitl[e] each State ... to lodge a complaint against any other contracting State ... irrespective of the nationality of the victim".[68] And it was reserved for obligations protecting dramatically important interests – not access to canals or the finer points of an autonomy statute, but "the outlawing of acts of aggression, and of genocide, as also from the principles and rules concerning the basic rights of the human person, including protection from slavery and racial discrimination".[69] Public interest standing was back, but had become a matter for fundamental concerns.

6.3 *Out of the Long Shadow (1970–2022)*

Looked at from the perspective of the *Wimbledon* and *Rohingya* judgments, it is curious how long it took the ICJ to move out of the shadow of the *South West Africa* and *Barcelona Traction* judgments and to spell out a regime of public interest standing. That process is not complete, but seems now well underway. That it took so long for it to begin is due to several reasons, chiefly the relative unwillingness of States to initiate proceedings in defence of common interests. The fact that, under the *Barcelona Traction* logic, public interest standing came

65 *Barcelona Traction* (n 9) ICJ Reports 1970, 3, para. 33.
66 *Barcelona Traction* (n 9), ICJ Reports 1970, 3, at para. 33.
67 *South West Africa* (n 8), ICJ Reports 1966, 6, at para. 44.
68 *Barcelona Traction* (n 9), ICJ Reports 1970, 3, at para. 91.
69 *Barcelona Traction* (n 9), ICJ Reports 1970, 3, at para. 34.

with such heavy baggage – formulated in the cryptic language of obligations *erga omnes* and implicating the most fundamental rules of international law – may have been a contributing factor. Many reactions since 1970 reflect caution and uncertainty.[70] To illustrate, Judge de Castro early on suggested to take the *Barcelona Traction* dictum "*cum grano salis*";[71] Judge Oda would later seek to turn back time when arguing that, while owed to the international community as a whole, a State's obligation (*erga omnes*) to prevent and punish genocide did not operate "in relation to any specific and particular signatory Contracting Party";[72] and the few States that did raise obligations *erga omnes* before the Court were keen to establish (unlike the applicants in PCIJ proceedings, or The Gambia in the *Rohingya case*) that they also acted in pursuit of a special, individual interest.[73] At the same time, the *erga omnes* concept proved attractive and came to dominate the discourse about common interests, including those under treaty frameworks: to the extent that such treaties protected common interests of treaty communities, they were increasingly said to impose 'obligations *erga omnes partes*', as if only the '*erga omnes*' label could justify a broad approach to standing.

Only in the 21st century would the ICJ begin to leave the caution behind it. Likely aided by the International Law Commission's work on State responsibility, which saw the Commission endorse rights of States to defend common interests protected under treaties as well as under obligations *erga omnes*,[74] the Court took two important steps towards recognising rights of States to initiate public interest proceedings before conclusively settling matters in the *Rohingya* litigation. In *Obligations to Extradite,* it recognised the "[t]he common interest [of all treaty parties] in compliance with the relevant obligations under the Convention against Torture", which "implie[d] the entitlement of

70 For a fuller analysis of the post-1970 jurisprudence see Tams, *Erga Omnes* (n 15), 158–197; Priya Urs, "Obligations *Erga Omnes* and the Question of Standing before the International Court of Justice", *Leiden Journal of International Law* 34 (2021), 505, especially at 509–516.

71 *Nuclear Tests* (Australia v. France), Diss. Op. de Castro, ICJ Reports 1974, 253, at 387.

72 *Application of the Convention on the Prevention and Punishment of the Crimes of Genocide* (Bosnia and Herzegovina v. Federal Republic of Yugoslavia), Declaration Oda, ICJ Reports 1996, 595, 626 (para. 4).

73 This is true e.g. of Australia and New Zealand in *Nuclear Tests* and for Portugal in *East Timor:* see e.g. ICJ Pleadings, *Nuclear Tests*, vol. II, 82; and paras. 8.01–8.17 of the Portuguese Reply in the *East Timor case* (https://www.icj-cij.org/sites/default/files/case-related/84/6838.pdf).

74 See Article 48(1)(a) and (b) ARSIWA, reproduced with commentaries in ILC Yearbook 2001, vol. II/1. As Priya Urs notes, for the ILC, "[c]onceptually, there is no distinction between the two categories" of treaty-based and *erga omnes*-based common interests: see Urs, "Obligations *Erga Omnes*" (n 70), 508.

each State party to the Convention to make a claim concerning the cessation of an alleged breach by another State party"[75] – a clear signal, whose importance may have been affected only by the fact that Belgium as the applicant State had *also* claimed to act in defence of a particular interest.[76] In the *Whaling case,* the Court said nothing on standing – but entertained Australia's claim also insofar as it concerned Japan's whaling on the high seas, a conduct that could have hardly affected any special or individual interests of Australia, and thus "[p]resumably ... accept[ing] the position that Australia had purported to act in the collective interest".[77] This was the backdrop to the judgment of 22 July 2022 in the *Rohingya case,* which now (as noted in the Introduction) clarifies that all State parties have standing to initiate ICJ proceedings against any other State that, in their assessment, violates its obligations *erga omnes partes* under the Genocide Convention. A half-century after *Barcelona Traction,* the ICJ now seems prepared to "put [the] *erga omnes* [concept] into motion".[78]

7 Concluding Thoughts: the Lessons of *Wimbledon*

The recent jurisprudential clarifications are helpful, but they remain closely tied to the thinking of *South West Africa* and *Barcelona Traction.* Adapting Judge *ad hoc* Kress' statement quoted in opening, one could see them as part of "the Court's ... departure from the stance it adopted in 1966";[79] but this is a departure on the terms of *Barcelona Traction*: standing to initiate proceedings in defence of common interests is justified by reference to the *erga omnes* (*partes*) doctrine, which trumps traditional models of bilateral dispute settlement in cases involving personal or individual interests.

All this is an overdue clarification, but perhaps the PCIJ was wiser. In the inter-War jurisprudence, the four Principal Allied Powers did not have to establish that a particular obligation was owed *erga omnes* (*partes*) to initiate proceedings: their standing resulted from the clear terms of a jurisdictional clause; and in the PCIJ's vision, it did not seem all that exceptional for a case to be

75 *Obligation to Extradite* (n 10), ICJ Reports 2012 (II), 422, at para. 68.
76 *Obligation to Extradite* (n 10), ICJ Reports 2012 (II), 422, at para. 65.
77 Urs, "Obligations *Erga Omnes*" (n 70), 514; and for a fuller discussion, see Christian J. Tams, "Roads Not Taken, Opportunities Missed: Procedural and Jurisdictional Questions Sidestepped in the *Whaling* Judgmen"', in M. Fitzmaurice and D. Tamada (eds.), *Whaling in the Antarctic: The Significance and the Implications of the ICJ Judgment* (Brill, 2016), 193.
78 Cf. Islam (n 6), 611.
79 Judgment of 22 July 2022 (n 1), Declaration of Judge ad hoc Kress, at para. 15.

brought by a State that acted as a guardian of some common interest. It is worth restating that the history of World Court litigation began with a public interest suit, in which three of the four applicants challenged Germany's conduct even though it "did not affect their financial, economic, or other 'material', or, say, 'physical' or 'tangible' interests".[80] A century after *Wimbledon*, it is worth remembering that this could be handled pragmatically at the time, without raised eyebrows or cryptic Latin language signalling that only some very special obligation could exceptionally be enforced by all States bound by it. In the history of World Court litigation, the 1966 *South West Africa* judgment is the exception – a case in which general rules of procedure were conjured up to justify the view that inter-State disputes, outside clearly-expressed exceptions, could only be about individual interests. A century of World Court litigation undermines this claim. The PCIJ's approach in fact suggests that public interest litigation can be handled pragmatically, and that it need not be seen as exceptional. From the perspective adopted in this contribution, this is the central lesson of the *Wimbledon* judgment.

Bibliography

Crawford J., "'Dreamers of the Day': Australia and the International Court of Justice", *Melbourne Journal of International Law* 14 (2013), 1.

Feinäugle C., 'Wimbledon, The', in Wolfrum R. (ed.), *Max Planck Encyclopedia of International Law* (Oxford: 2012), online version updated 2013.

Fitzmaurice M., 'Third Parties and the Law of Treaties', *Max Planck Yearbook of United Nations Law* 6 (2002), 37.

Gray Ch.D., *Judicial Remedies in International Law* (Oxford OUP 1987).

Higgins R., "The International Court and South West Africa: The Implications of the Judgment", *International Affairs* 42/4 (1966), 573.

Klein E., "South West Africa/Namibia (Advisory Opinions and Judgements)," in Rudolf Bernhard (ed), *Encyclopedia of Public International Law*, vol. IV (2000), 491.

Kohen M., "Memel Territory Statute, Interpretation of, Case", in Wolfrum R. (ed.), *Max Planck Encyclopedia of International Law* (Oxford: 2012), online version updated 2013.

Lagoni R., "Kiel Canal", in Wolfrum R. (ed.), *Max Planck Encyclopedia of International Law* (Oxford: 2012), online version updated 2013.

80 See *South West Africa* (n 8), Sep. Op. Jessup, ICJ Reports 1962, 325, at 425.

Mao X., "Public-Interest Litigation before the International Court of Justice: Comment on The Gambia v. Myanmar Case", *Chinese Journal of International Law* 21 (2022) 58.

Osmańczyk E.J. – Mango A., *Encyclopedia of the United Nations and International Agreements* (A-F) (3rd ed., Taylor & Francis 2003).

Rizwanul I., "Not an Overreach of the Court's Jurisdiction, Putting *Erga Omnes* into Motion", *Chinese Journal of International Law* 21 (2022), 611.

Salvioli G., "'La jurisprudence de la Cour permanente de Justice international'", 12 *Recueil des Cours* (1926 II), 5.

Tams Ch.J., "'Véritables parties' et reconnaissance tardive d'un intérêt à agir en défense d'intérêts collectifs: Remarques sur l'arrêt du 22 juillet 2022 dans l'affaire entre la Gambie et le Myanmar", *Annuaire Français du Droit International* 68 (2022), 285.

Tams Ch.J., "*Erga omnes*-Verpflichtungen vor dem Internationalen Gerichtshof: ein Kontrapunkt", in Donath et al. (eds.), *Der Schutz des Individuums durch das Recht. Festschrift für Rainer Hofmann zum 70. Geburtstag* (Springer 2023), 43.

Tams Ch.J., "Roads Not Taken, Opportunities Missed: Procedural and Jurisdictional Questions Sidestepped in the *Whaling* Judgment'", in M. Fitzmaurice and D. Tamada (eds.), *Whaling in the Antarctic: The Significance and the Implications of the ICJ Judgment* (Brill, 2016), 193.

Tams Ch.J., *Enforcing Obligations Erga Omnes in International Law* (Cambridge, CUP 2005).

Urs P., "Obligations *Erga Omnes* and the Question of Standing before the International Court of Justice", *Leiden Journal of International Law* 34 (2021), 505.

Villalpando S., *L'émergence de la communauté internationale dans la responsabilité des États* (Paris, PUF 2005).

Voeffray F., *Actio popularis ou la défense des interêt collectif devant les juridictions internationales* (Paris, PUF 2004).

Watts A.D., "The Protection of Merchant Ships", *British Yearbook of International Law* 33 (1957), 52.

Wolgast E., *Der Wimbledonprozeß vor dem Völkergerichtshof* (Berlin 1926).

Judgments and Advisory Opinions

PCIJ

Memel Statute, PCIJ Ser. A/B, No. 47 (preliminary objections) and No. 49 (merits).

The S.S. "Wimbledon", Judgment of 17 August 1923, PCIJ Ser. A, No. 1.

ICJ

Application of the Convention on the Prevention and Punishment of the Crimes of Genocide (Bosnia and Herzegovina v. Federal Republic of Yugoslavia), Declaration of Judge Oda, ICJ Reports 1996, 595.

Application of the Convention on the Prevention and Punishment of the Crime of Genocide (The Gambia v. Myanmar), *Judgment on preliminary objections of 22 July 2022*, (at https://www.icj-cij.org/public/files/case-related/178/178-20220722-JUD-01-00-EN.pdf).

Application of the Convention on the Prevention and Punishment of the Crime of Genocide (The Gambia v. Myanmar), Declaration of Judge ad hoc Kress (at https://www.icj-cij.org/public/files/case-related/178/178-20220722-JUD-01-00-EN.pdf).

Barcelona Traction, Light and Power Company, Limited (Belgium v. Spain) (New Application: 1962), ICJ Reports 1970, 3.

Legal Consequences for States of the Continued Presence of South Africa in Namibia (South West Africa) notwithstanding Security Council Resolution 276 (1970) (Advisory Opinion), ICJ Reports 1971, 16.

Nuclear Tests (Australia v. France), Dissenting Opinion of Judge de Castro, ICJ Reports 1974, 253.

Questions relating to the Obligation to Prosecute or Extradite (Belgium v. Senegal), ICJ Reports 2012 (II) 422.

Reservations to the Convention on the Prevention and Punishment of the Crime of Genocide, Advisory Opinion, ICJ Reports 1951, 15.

South West Africa (Ethiopia v. South Africa, Liberia v. South Africa), ICJ Reports 1962, 319 and ICJ Reports 1966.

South West Africa, Dissenting Opinion of Judge Winiarski, ICJ Reports 1962, 456.

South West Africa, Joint Dissenting Opinion of Judges Spender and Fitzmaurice, ICJ Reports 1962, 558.

South West Africa, Separate Opinion of Judge Jessup, ICJ Reports 1962, 425.

Whaling in the Antarctic (Australia v. Japan: New Zealand intervening), ICJ Reports 2014 226.

Other Cases

The M/V "SAIGA" (No. 2) (Saint Vincent and the Grenadines v. Guinea), ITLOS Reports 1999, 10.

Other Sources

Articles on Responsibility of States for Internationally Wrongful Acts, reproduced with commentaries in ILC Yearbook 2001, vol. II/1.

Convention Concerning the Statute of the Memel Territory of 1924, 29 *LNTS* 86 (with the Memel Statute added as an Annex).

Mandate Agreement regarding German South West Africa of 17 December 1920, reproduced at https://www.aalco.int/9thsession/Part%2018.pdf.

'Rohingya refugee crisis a "human rights nightmare", UN chief tells Security Council', UN News 28 September 2017, at https://news.un.org/en/story/2017/09/567402-rohingya-refugee-crisis-human-rights-nightmare-un-chief-tells-security-council.

CHAPTER 3

From the *s.s. Wimbledon* to the *Allegations of Genocide* Case (Ukraine v. Russia): Third-Party Interventions at the World Court

Michał Balcerzak

Abstract

The chapter discusses the (first-ever) request of Poland to intervene in the *Wimbledon* case, adjudicated by the Permanent Court of International Justice (PCIJ) in 1923. The author explores the origins and context of this request while concurrently addressing a general dilemma regarding the proper legal basis of such an intervention, i.e. Article 62 and/or 63 of the Statute of the PCIJ. It is asserted that the Polish intervention in the Wimbledon case did not establish any firm precedent nor significantly contributed to a better understanding of what an 'interest of a legal nature', as referred to in Article 62 of the Statute, entails. However, the request to intervene in that case, followed by the post-1945 examples of such interventions, paved the way for a more frequent invocation of Articles 62 or 63 of the Statute by intervening states. Almost exactly a century after Wimbledon, in 2022, the International Court of Justice allowed an intervention of no fewer than thirty-two states in the *Allegations of Genocide* case (Ukraine v. Russia). The chapter focuses also on these developments to make the argument that the concept of third-party intervention has come a long way from a relatively modest participation of Poland in the *Wimbledon* case to a substantial presence of numerous states intervening in the broader interest of the international community (as in the *Allegations of Genocide* case).

1 Introduction

In a letter dated May 22nd 1923, the Polish envoy extraordinary and minister plenipotentiary at the Hague, Józef Wierusz-Kowalski, informed the Registrar of the Permanent Court of International Justice (PCIJ), that the Government of Poland had expressed the wish to intervene in the case of *s.s. Wimbledon*,

 | DOI:10.1163/9789004707979_005

invoking Article 62 of the PCIJ's Statute.[1] This request was granted by the PCIJ in a judgment issued on June 28th 1923. Thus in the first contentious case examined by the PCIJ, a state that was neither an applicant nor a respondent participated in the proceedings as an intervenient, and claimed (at least in its original request that was subsequently modified) to have "an interest of a legal nature which may be affected by the decision in the case". Recalling this intervention in the present volume – dedicated to the hundredth anniversary of the Wimbledon judgment – provides an opportunity to take a closer look at third-party interventions that may have contributed to developing the World Court's case law. A pertinent question in this regard is whether some recent cases at the ICJ have opened the door for public- or common-interest litigation, involving multiple interveners.

Almost exactly a century after the PCIJ granted Polish intervention in the *Wimbledon case*, on June 5th 2023, the International Court of Justice (ICJ) allowed the intervention of no less than thirty-two state parties, including Poland, in the case concerning the *Allegations of Genocide under the Convention on the Prevention and Punishment of the Crime of Genocide* (Ukraine v. Russia).[2] It turned out that states are ready to request intervention in order to pursue the interests of the international community as a whole. While it may appear that interventions in *Wimbledon* and the *Allegations of Genocide* cases have little in common, they will be discussed below in a broader context to deduce more general conclusions.

As an introductory point, it is to be recalled that the legal basis for requesting interventions as a third party or declaring intervention in the exercise of a "right to intervene" as a party to a convention being construed in the proceedings at the Court, has been the same in both the Statute of the PCIJ and the ICJ (with minor editorial changes).[3] The relevant provisions stipulated:

1 *Case of the S.S. Wimbledon* [1923] Publ. PCIJ Ser. C, No. 3 ("Acts and Documents Relating to Judgments and Advisory Opinions Given by the Court"), Third Session (June 15th-September 15th 1923), p. 239 (hereinafter as: "The S.S. Wimbledon", Ser. C).

2 See the Order of the ICJ of 5 June 2023, *Allegations of Genocide under the Convention on the Prevention and Punishment of the Crime of Genocide*, available at: https://www.icj-cij.org/sites/default/files/case-related/182/182-20230605-ORD-01-00-EN.pdf.

3 The editorial changes introduced into the Statute of the ICJ consisted in deleting the phrase "as a third party" at the end of first sentence of Article 62. Further, the contents of both articles was split into two numbered sections.

Article 62 (Statute of the PCIJ)
Should a State consider that it has an interest of a legal nature which may be affected by the decision in the case, it may submit a request to the Court to intervene as a third party.It will be for the Court to decide upon this request.

Article 63 (Statute of the PCIJ)
Whenever the construction of a convention to which States other than those concerned in the case are parties is in question, the Registrar shall notify all such States forthwith. Every State so notified has the right to intervene in the proceedings: but if it uses this right, the construction given by the judgment will be equally binding upon it.

2 All Beginnings Are Difficult: the Symbolic Intervention in the *Wimbledon* Case

Let us first discuss the "first ever" Polish intervention of 1923 in the S.S. Wimbledon case. As is known, the cargo of the "S.S. Wimbledon" steamship, whose passage through the Kiel Canal was refused by the German authorities on March 21st 1921, included a large amount of munitions and artillery, consigned to the Polish Naval Base at Gdańsk. The Director of Kiel Canal Traffic refused to allow the steamship's passage based on neutrality Orders issued by Germany "in connection with the Russo–Polish war".[4] Interestingly, three days before the refusal to pass "S.S. Wimbledon" through the Kiel Canal, on March 18th 1921, Poland and the Soviet Union signed a peace treaty in Riga which effectively ended the war between the two states.[5] It is, therefore, highly unlikely that the cargo of "S.S. Wimbledon" would indeed be used in any active hostilities between Poland and the Soviet Union during the spring of 1921.

Whether the Director of Kiel Canal Traffic was privy to the information about the signing of the Treaty of Riga remains a mystery. However, it is plausible to assume that the German authorities in Berlin were well-informed about these pivotal developments. For reasons set out later in the PCIJ judgment,

4 As has been rightly pointed out in the Chapter by M. Kowalski in this volume, the notion of "Russo–Polish war" is actually misleading, as it is more correct to refer to it as a "Polish–Soviet" war (1919–1921).

5 This fact was referred to and broadly discussed by the French agent during the hearing at the PCIJ that took place on 5th July 1923, see "The S.S. Wimbledon", Series C, p. 221 *et seq.*

whether the Polish–Soviet war was still going on March 21st 1921 should not have a bearing on the right of free passage of "s.s. Wimbledon" through the Kiel Canal, in view of Article 380 of the Treaty of Versailles. Nevertheless, even from the perspective of Germany's Orders of 1920, the grounds for halting the steamship and denying its passage were no longer substantiated as of March 21st 1921. Be it as it may, Germany did not change its position, also after the formal request of the French Ambassador at Berlin submitted on March 23rd, 1923. The captain of "s.s. Wimbledon" had to re-direct the vessel via the Danish Straits, and the final destination (Gdańsk/Danzig) was reached on April 6th 1921, almost two weeks later as planned.

It seems that Poland did not undertake any steps about the delayed arrival of the Wimbledon's cargo at any diplomatic or judicial forum, until its request to intervene in the case at the PCIJ. It would probably make little sense to claim compensation in domestic courts for the delay from the French company ("Les Affréteurs réunis") that chartered and operated "s.s. Wimbledon". On the other hand, it would not be unthinkable that Poland has aligned itself with Great Britain, France, Italy and Japan as an applicant, submitting claims against Germany at the PCIJ. Article 386 of the Treaty of Versailles did not differentiate between the Principal Powers (United States, British Empire, France, Italy and Japan) and other signatories.[6] Principal and "other" Powers were referred to as "Allied and Associated Powers". But Poland chose not to do so, and the reasons could be numerous. Shortly after the Polish–Soviet war (and three years after regaining independence in 1918), the new Polish State had plenty on its plate. Engaging itself as an applicant in an international dispute over the right to free passage through the Kiel Canal and Germany's obligation under Article 380 of the Treaty of Versailles probably did not rank among the primary concerns of the Polish government during that particular period. Other factors might have been at play, including a potential absence of incentives from the "principal" applicants who submitted the dispute to the PCIJ. Regardless, Poland formally sought intervention under Article 62 in May 1923, whereas the application by four states initiating the proceedings was lodged with the Registry of the PCIJ on January 16th 1923.

The Polish request to intervene on 22 May 1923 directly invoked Article 62 of the Statute of the PCIJ as well as Articles 58 and 59 of the Rules of Court. It also noted that 'whereas Poland was one of the parties to the Treaty of Peace of

6 According to Article 386(1) of the Treaty of Versailles: 'In the event of violation of any of the conditions of Articles 380 to 386, or of disputes as to the interpretation of these articles, any interested Power can appeal to the jurisdiction instituted for the purpose by the League of Nations'.

Versailles, and that the refusal in question has violated the rights and material interests guaranteed to Poland under the terms of Article 380 of the Treaty of Versailles' the request is submitted 'in agreement with the Government of Great Britain, France, Italy and Japan' and 'on the side of these other States'.[7]

The British government was the only one among the applicant states which commented in writing on the Polish request to intervene in the Wimbledon case under Article 62.[8] The observations started with an assurance that 'the Government of His Britannic Majesty view with sympathy the application made by the Polish Government to intervene in the Wimbledon case, though *they were not aware* of this application until they received a copy of it' (emphasis added).[9] This actually stays in contrast with the assertion of the Polish Government in their request of May 22nd 1923 that the request was submitted 'in agreement' with the applicant Powers. Such an 'agreement' was not necessary anyway. Still, there might have been some miscommunication between Warsaw and London at that time and it seems that the Polish intervention might have been surprising, at least for the British.

Further in their observations, the British government did not doubt that Poland was entitled to intervene as a party to the Treaty of Versailles. However, it has been observed that

> the Polish application is based on Article 62 of the Statute, not on Article 63, and also, that it is not an application for permission to intervene as a third party, as provided in Article 62, but it is an application to be allowed to intervene on the side of the British, French, Italian and Japanese Governments.[10]

Then the observations of the British government become even more intriguing as they express a view that 'Apart from the general Polish interest in the interpretation of the Treaty of Versailles *it is not clear that the Polish Government possess any interest of a legal nature* in matters at issue in the 'Wimbledon' case' (emphasis added). According to the British government, since the Polish

7 The request annexed to the letter of Polish envoy extraordinary and minister plenipotentiary J. Wierusz-Kowalski, dated May 22nd 1923.

8 See 'Observations on the part of the Government of His Britannic Majesty in pursuance of Rule 59 of the Rules of Court on the subject of the Polish application to be allowed to intervene in the 'Wimbledon' case', "The s.s. Wimbledon", Series C, pp. 106–108.

9 Ibid., p. 107. The respondent Government on their part submitted that they 'leave for the consideration of the Court the question whether the participation of Poland meets with objections of principle', see "The s.s. Wimbledon", Series C, p. 252.

10 Ibid.

application to intervene was based 'merely on the injury' which would be suffered if the rights of free passage under Article 380 of the Treaty of Versailles be restricted, a more proper ground to intervene by the Polish government would have been Article 63 of the PCIJ Statute.

Polish diplomats in The Hague seemed concerned by the British position as to Polish intervention even before it was officially lodged at the PCIJ. In a telegram of June 15th 1923 sent from The Hague to the Polish mission in London, J. Wierusz-Kowalski informed about a private conversation of Sir Cecil Hurst (British agent at the PCIJ) with Michał Rostworowski, professor of Jagiellonian University and future judge at the PCIJ, that took place the day before. Sir Cecil shared with Rostworowski (and the latter – apparently – with Wierusz-Kowalski) the position of the British government that acknowledged Poland's right to intervene under Article 63 and not Article 62 of the Statute of the Court. The Polish mission in London was requested to inquire about the reasons why such instructions had been given by HM Government to its agent. The response from Polish diplomats in London came on the same day:

> Hurst, as the government's legal adviser, acts under general instructions which do not bind him in applying an independent legal interpretation in a given case. Therefore, the request [is] impossible; only a direct influence on Hurst can achieve a change of mind.[11]

It does not seem, however, that the Polish mission undertook any steps to 'directly influence' Sir Cecil. It seems even less likely that it would have had any effect on the agent of the British government. Ultimately, any diplomatic 'battle' concerning the British stance on the grounds for Polish intervention would not jeopardize the Polish request to intervene, given that Article 63 of the Statute provided a safe and sufficient basis. However, the fact remains that the British position cast doubt whether Poland possessed any 'interest of legal nature' in the proceedings concerning S.S. Wimbledon, beyond a 'general' one associated with the interpretation of the Treaty of Versailles.

On June 15th 1923 the Registrar of the PCIJ, Åke Hammarskjöld, addressed the Polish envoy at The Hague, inviting the Polish government to appoint an agent in the proceedings.[12] In a separate letter of the same date, the Registrar

11 See *Depesze Poselstwa Rzeczypospolitej Polskiej w Londynie* [Telegrams of the Mission of the Republic of Poland in Londyn], vol. II, marzec 1923 – maj 1926, ed. W. Rojek, J. Łaptos (Kraków: 2019) 53–54 (translation by the author).

12 See "The S.S. Wimbledon", Series C, p. 247. The initial request of Poland under Article 62 included an official authorization for J. Wierusz-Kowalski to submit it on behalf of the Polish Government, signed by the Minister of Foreign Affairs at that time, Aleksander

transmitted to the Polish government the position expressed by the agent of the British government as to the Polish request to intervene. In a letter sent the next day, the Polish envoy at The Hague noted that, while reserving the possibility of submitting subsequent observations, the Polish government considered that 'its special legal interest (*intérêt juridique spécial*) in the Wimbledon case was obvious, since it was the owner of the loading of the vessel in question'. One could interpret it as a defense of Poland's initial request founded on Article 62 of the Statute of the PCIJ. Nevertheless, things were happening fast at that time, leaving little room for extensive elaboration by the Polish mission in The Hague (or in the capital) on what 'special legal interest' actually meant or why it was 'special' in the first place. The correspondence between the PCIJ and Poland reveals that the principal motive of Poland's intervention was actually linked to the ownership of Wimbledon's cargo rather than to a broader legal interest of Poland in upkeeping the *régime* of the Treaty of Versailles as regards free navigation through the Kiel Canal.

The Polish intervention in the Wimbledon case was considered and approved in the judgment of the PCIJ of June 28th, 1923, following a hearing held three days prior. No additional observations by the Polish government were filed with the PCIJ Registry from the day of the request until the hearing. Still, the Polish representative, Mr. Gustaw Olechowski, attended the hearing and delivered a relatively short statement.[13] He referred to Article 62 of the Statute of the PCIJ as the ground for Polish intervention, reiterating that the Polish government, as an owner of the steamship's cargo, 'had *incontestably* a legal interest in the 'Wimbledon' case' (emphasis added). Mr. Olechowski underscored that the delay of S.S. Wimbledon's arrival in Gdańsk resulted in unnecessary waiting of railway cars to unload the vessel. However, he emphasized that the Polish government 'did not intend to ask the German government for special damages for this loss'.[14]

And there came a twist: the Polish representative justified the intervention under Article 62 of the Statute by saying that 'it might be a great advantage [for the Polish Government] to give certain explanations about the interpretation and legal effect of various treaties which may be quoted in this case'.[15] It appeared that Poland wanted to leave some room for the Court to consider

Skrzyński. Yet, the *dossier* of the case indicates that the duties of the Polish agent throughout the proceedings were later executed by a diplomat from the Polish Mission at The Hague, Gustaw Olechowski.

13 See "The S.S. Wimbledon", Series C, p. 116–117.

14 Ibid., p. 117.

15 Ibid.

the request for an intervention on that basis. However, a moment later Mr. Olechowski indicated that because of Poland's status as a signatory of the Treaty of Versailles, the Polish Government intended to avail itself of its right under Article 63 of the Statute and 'did not insist' of its intervention to be considered as one under Article 62.[16] When asked by the President of the Court whether Poland withdraws the request under Article 62, the Polish agent responded negatively, stating that the intervening state simply 'did not insist on the arguments adduced in support of this request'.[17]

As a last point of his intervention, Mr. Olechowski declared that the Polish Government renounced 'the right under Article 31 of the Statute of Court' to appoint a national judge to the bench adjudicating the case.[18] This declaration seems to result from a rather doubtful interpretation that considered an intervening State a 'contesting party' in the meaning of Article 31 of the Statute.[19] It has been, however, not commented upon by either of the other parties or the Court. The French agent, Mr. Jules Basadevant, only noted, though very briefly, the invocation by Poland of Article 63 of the Statute, leaving it to the Court whether allow the intervention exclusively on that basis or also on Article 62.[20] The agent of the British government offered an even more succinct response, stating that he had no further observations apart from those already made in writing.[21] Brief approving statements were also made by Mr. Pilotti, the agent of the Italian government, and Mr. Ito, speaking on behalf of Japan.[22] The agent of the respondent government did not attend the hearing on June 25th, 1923.

The invocation of Article 63 of the Statute in lieu of Article 62 by the Polish government made it relatively easy for the PCIJ to rule in the judgment of June 28th, 1923 that the intervention was accepted.[23] The Court referred to the difference between both Articles, stressing that an intervention under Article 62 should only be admitted if the Court finds that 'the existence of [legal] interest is sufficiently demonstrated'.[24] However, when the issue at stake is the

16 Ibid.

17 See the minutes of the third public sitting of the PCIJ, June 25th 1923, p. 9.

18 Ibid.

19 The relevant part of that Article stipulated: 'If the Court includes upon the Bench no judge of the nationality of the contesting parties, each of these parties may proceed to select a judge as provided in the preceding paragraph'.

20 See "The S.S. Wimbledon", Series C, p. 118–119.

21 Ibid., p. 120.

22 Ibid., p. 120–121.

23 See *Case of the S.S. "Wimbledon". Question of intervention by Poland,* judgment of June 28th 1923, available at: https://www.icj-cij.org/sites/default/files/permanent-court-of-international-justice/serie_A/A_01/01_Wimbledon_Arret_06_1923.pdf.

24 Ibid.

interpretation of an international convention, any of its parties has the right to intervene. Still, in this case, the judgment would be equally binding upon the intervening state as it is upon the original applicant parties. The PCIJ noted the change in the position of the Polish government as regards the ground of intervention and considered that it 'renders it unnecessary for the Court to consider and satisfy itself whether Poland's intervention in the suit before it is justified by an interest of a legal nature, within the meaning of Article 62 of the Statute'.[25] The undisputed status of Poland as a as a contracting party to the Treaty of Versailles has naturally resulted in the approval of Poland's intervention under Article 63 of the Statute.

Following the PCIJ's judgment on the question of intervention, the hearings in the *Wimbledon* case continued between July 5th and July 10th, 1923. After the agents of the applicant states presented their oral statements during the first two days of the public sittings of the Court, on July 7th, 1923 the floor was given to the Polish agent who stated that he 'agreed with the arguments and conclusions of his colleagues, and would not make a special statement on behalf of the Polish government'.[26] This was indeed the last time when a statement of the intervening state appears in the files of the *Wimbledon* case. It can be only seen as regrettable that Poland did not present any observations as to the merits. One could assume that the primary purpose of such an intervention lies in the opportunity to address the factual and legal issues that arose in the case under consideration. For instance, Poland would be in a far better position than any of the other involved states to pronounce on the issue so passionately argued by the French agent (and put into question by the agent of Germany) – notably, whether on March 21st, 1923, three days after signing the Treaty of Riga, the state of war between Poland and the Soviet Union was effectively put to an end.

But there was no reason why Poland could not present its views on other, perhaps more principled, aspects of the case, such as those directly concerning the interpretation of Article 380 of the Treaty of Versailles. Yet, it did not decide to do so, making its presence symbolic rather than meaningful. But as already noted, the first years of reborn Poland were probably not the best time to actively engage in international adjudication. Even though Poland did not participate in any active military conflict as of 1923, the political situation in the country was complicated, to say at least. As many as four different individuals held the office of the minister of foreign affairs in that year.[27] Additionally,

25 Ibid.

26 See the minutes of the seventh public sitting of the PCIJ, July 6th 1923, p. 16.

27 See https://www.gov.pl/web/dyplomacja/ministrowie-spraw-zagranicznych.

Poland entered 1923 in a rather grim atmosphere, following the assassination of President Gabriel Narutowicz on December 16th, 1922. While domestic politics may or may not have been decisive for Poland's willingness to be more active in the *Wimbledon* case, the fact remains that given the "last-minute" decision to request intervention, Poland may have simply lacked the time (and/or human resources) to submit fully-fledged observations as to the merits. Also, other potentially more critical cases of interest for Poland in the context of PCIJ's advisory jurisdiction were already on the horizon, including the case of German settlers[28] or the delimitation of the frontier between Poland and Czechoslovakia in the region known as 'the Spisz district'.[29]

3 The Legacy of the Polish Intervention in *Wimbledon* and Beyond

It would be hard to claim that the Polish intervention in the *Wimbledon* case set any firm precedent or contributed to a better understanding of what 'an interest of a legal nature' referred to in Article 62 of the Statute entails. Neither had the Court explained whether an intervention could be admitted on both grounds when a state simultaneously invokes Article 62 and files a declaration to intervene based on Article 63 of the Statute. We have not learned from the *Wimbledon* judgment if Poland's 'legal interest' in the case could have been regarded as surpassing the 'ordinary interest' of a state party to the Treaty of Versailles. It can be argued that in the early 1920s, it was premature to adopt a more progressive approach towards 'interests of a legal nature', let alone to facilitate states in invoking the legal interests of the international community as a whole. From the enigmatic position of the PCIJ on the interpretation of Article 62 of the Statute it nevertheless transpired, that an intervening state would need to assert *its* legal interest and substantiate it convincingly before the Court.

But as has been pointed out elsewhere in this volume,[30] the approach of the PCIJ to the notion of 'interest' was – perhaps even surprisingly – broad. According to the Court, all it took to have 'clear interest' (and standing) in the proceedings, apart from the status of a state party to the Treaty of Versailles, was to 'possess fleets and merchant vessels flying their respective flags'. It

28 See *Questions relating to Settlers of German Origin in Poland*, Advisory Opinion, (1923) PCIJ Series B no 6, ICGJ 273 (PCIJ 1923), September 10th, 1923.

29 See *Delimitation of the Polish–Czechoslovakian Frontier* (*Question of Jaworzina*), Advisory Opinion, (1923) PCIJ Series B no 8, ICGJ 275 (PCIJ 1923), December 6th, 1923.

30 See Christian Tams' contribution in this volume, Subsection 4.

cannot be perceived as a high threshold at all. These criteria were duly satisfied by Italy and Japan in the *Wimbledon* case, despite their interests not being overwhelming, to say the least. It is thus hard to disagree that the PCIJ, with its pragmatic approach, actually admitted 'public interest claims'[31] and – perhaps inadvertently – sowed a seed that would grow a century later in cases, where vital interests of the international community were at stake. I am referring here to the two cases involving the application of the Convention on the Prevention and Punishment of the Crime of Genocide: The Gambia v. Myanmar[32] and Ukraine v. Russia.[33]

The Polish symbolic intervention in the *Wimbledon* case remains the sole example of this kind in the PCIJ's practice. The first three decades of the ICJ saw only two states invoking Article 63 of the Statute,[34] which led a prominent author to note in the mid-1980s that 'the procedure of third party interventions [...] had been underutilized; as a result, there was scant judicial authority and comparatively little academic discussion'.[35] The situation started to change in the first half of the 1980s when the well-known (failed) request to intervene was submitted by El Salvador in the *Nicaragua* case.[36] Other examples from that period include two cases concerning *Continental Shelf* (both interventions also failed).[37] Subsequent examples encompass: the *Land, Island and*

31 Ibid, Subsection 6, first para.

32 *Application of the Convention on the Prevention and Punishment of the Crime of Genocide* (The Gambia v. Myanmar), instituted on November 11th, 2019, ICJ Judgment of June 22nd, 2022 (Preliminary Objections), ICJ Rep. 2022, p. 477, see: https://www.icj-cij.org/case/178.

33 See note 2.

34 These include: Cuba intervening in the *Haya de la Torre* case (Columbia v. Peru), ICJ judgment of June 13th 1951 (ICJ Reports 1951, p. 830); Fiji intervening in the *Nuclear Tests* (New Zealand v. France), ICJ Judgment of December 20th 1974 (ICJ Rep. 1974, p. 457). The intervention in the first case was not particularly meaningful as it was constrained to submitting a short oral statement. The Fiji's intervention in the second case was more elaborate but the merits of the case was not adjudicated upon by the ICJ so the Fiji's request was considered by the ICJ as lapsed (see the ICJ Order of December 20th 1974, ICJ Rep. 1974, p. 535).

35 See Chinkin, C., "Third Party Intervention before the International Court of Justice", *American Journal of International Law* 80 (1986), 495–531.

36 *Military and Paramilitary Activities in and against Nicaragua* (Nicaragua v. United States), see the Order of the ICJ of October 4th 1984, ICJ Rep. 1984, p. 215. The intervention was considered premature. See Sztucki, J., "Intervention Under Article 63 of the ICJ Statute in the Phase of Preliminary Proceedings: The 'Salvadoran Incident'", *American Journal of International Law* 79 (1985), 1005–1036.

37 The request to intervene came from Malta in the *Case Concerning Continental Shelf* (Tunisia v. Libyan Arab Jamahiriya), ICJ Judgment of April 14th 1981, ICJ Rep. 1981, p. 3; and the second from Italy (Libyan Arab Jamahiriya v. Malta), ICJ Judgment of March 21st 1984, ICJ Rep. 1984, p. 3.

Maritime Frontier Dispute (El Salvador/Honduras: Nicaragua intervening),[38] the *Land and Maritime Boundary between Cameroon and Nigeria* (Cameroon v. Nigeria: Equatorial Guinea intervening);[39] the *Jurisdictional Immunities* case (Germany v. Italy: Greece intervening)[40] or the *Whaling* case (Australia v. Japan: New Zealand intervening).[41] There has also been quite considerable practice of state interventions in advisory proceedings.[42]

The above-mentioned cases and the scholarly attention that inevitably followed,[43] contributed to a better understanding of the function and conditions of third-party interventions at the ICJ. Trying to analyze every instance of invoking Article 62 or 63 of the Court's Statute or summarizing the existing doctrinal understanding of this matter would not be the most efficient use of space in this volume. Instead, I offer a comment on the future of third-party interventions, given that we witness significant – if not groundbreaking – developments that may herald a new era of public-interest litigation at the World Court.

4 The ICJ and Interventions in Public (Common) Interest: a New Beginning?

Let us face it: neither the Polish intervention in the *Wimbledon* case nor the subsequent requests to intervene in pending proceedings at the ICJ under Articles 62 and 63 of the Statute until the 2020s were primarily concerned with

38 See the ICJ judgment of September 13th, 1990, ICJ Rep. 1990, p. 92. The Nicaraguan intervention under Article 62 of the Statute was allowed but the Court carefully "calibrated" its scope.

39 See the ICJ Order of October 21st, 1999, ICJ Rep. 1999, p. 1029. This was an intervention under Article 62 of the Statute.

40 See the ICJ Order of July 4th, 2011, ICJ Rep. 2011, p. 494. Greece intervened under Article 62 of the Statute.

41 See the ICJ Order of Feburary 6th, 2013, ICJ Rep. 2013, p. 3.

42 See Wigard, K., Pomson, O., McIntyre, J., "Keeping score: an empirical analysis of the interventions in *Ukraine v. Russia*", *Journal of International Dispute Settlement* 14(3) (2023) 1–23.

43 See Palchetti, P., "Opening the International Court of Justice to Third States: Intervention and Beyond", *Max Planck Yearbook of United Nations Law* 6 (2002) 139–181; Miron, A., Chinkin, C., "Article 62", "Article 63" in Andreas Zimmermann et al (eds), *The Statute of the International Court of Justice: A Commentary* (3 edn OUP Oxford: 2019) 1686–1740, 1774; Zimmermann, A., Devaney, J., "International Courts and Tribunals, Intervention in Proceedings", in *Max Planck Encyclopedia of International Law* (updated 2019); Barrie, G.N., "Third-party State Intervention in Disputes Before the International Court of Justice: A Reassessment of Articles 62 and 63 of the ICJ Statute", *Comparative and International Law Journal of Southern Africa* 52 (2020) 1–20.

the interests of the international community as a whole. This does not necessarily prove that states have always been selfish and self-oriented; it has been rather the result of the assumption that settlement of international disputes involves two (or more) states, each of which can demonstrate a particular interest of their own. There may have been, however – as observed by Christian Tams in this volume[44] – some small steps taken by the ICJ in *Obligations to Extradite*[45] or the *Whaling case*[46] that paved the way towards a more open-minded approach to initiating proceedings at the ICJ, when obligations *erga omnes partes* have been at stake.[47] It should also be noted that states' submissions in advisory proceedings before the ICJ – such as those in the *Nuclear Weapons* case[48] – can arguably be driven by considerations that account for public interest of the international community.

But it was not until 2020s that the dam really burst: two cases brought under Article IX of the Genocide Convention – The Gambia v. Myanmar and Ukraine v. Russia – were brought to the Court. The former raised legal issues related to particularly grave atrocities committed in Myanmar against Rohingya people; the latter concerned the Russian Federation's attempt to excuse its armed aggression in 2022 by referring to genocide allegedly committed by Ukraine. Both are under consideration; however, on July 22nd 2022 the ICJ found that it had jurisdiction to adjudicate in the case brought by Gambia.[49] And on June 5th 2023 it considered that the thirty-two declarations of interventions under Article 63 of the Statute are admissible already at the preliminary objections stage of the proceedings.[50]

In The Gambia v. Myanmar, Canada and the Netherlands expressed an intention to intervene publicly and on two occasions,[51] finally materializing their

---

44 See Chapter 2 in this volume, Subsection 6.

45 *Questions relating to the Obligation to Prosecute or Extradite* (Belgium v. Senegal), ICJ Judgment of July 20th 2012, ICJ Rep. 2012, p. 422. It is to be noted, however, that this case did not involve third party interventions.

46 See note 41.

47 See in general: Wojcikiewicz Almeida, P., "International Procedural Regulation in the Common Interest: The Role of Third-Party Intervention and Amicus Curiae before the ICJ", *The Law and Practice of International Courts and Tribunals* 18 (2019) 163–188.

48 *Legality of the Threat or Use of Nuclear Weapons*, Advisory Opinion of July 8th 1996. ICJ Rep. 1996, p. 226.

49 See note 32.

50 See note 2.

51 See the statement regarding the intervention by the ministers of foreign affairs of Canada and the Kingdom of the Netherlands: https://www.government.nl/documents/diplomatic-statements/2022/07/22/joint-statement-canada-netherlands-rohingya-genocide-case-between-gambia-and-myanmar. A previous statement on the same issue was made in

plans together with Denmark, France, Germany and the United Kingdom.[52] Regardless of the above and its final outcome, the case initiated by The Gambia takes the public-interest proceedings at the ICJ to the next level. It allows for moderate optimism as to 'keeping *erga omnes* (*partes*) obligations seriously', while using the existing legal tools: jurisdictional clauses in treaties involving such obligations, and the possibility to intervene under Articles 62 and 63 of the Statute.[53] The legal tools mentioned above have their limits and it would be naïve to expect that after The Gambia v. Myanmar case the Court will be overflooded with public-interest-oriented cases, regardless of jurisdictional basis. Yet, it is hard to deny that The Gambia v. Myanmar case should be viewed as a turning point in the Court's approach to public – or common – interest litigation.

Along similar lines, also the case of Ukraine v. Russia can be perceived as groundbreaking, even though it has not yet been examined as to the merits. This time the case was brought by a state directly affected, and further, an unprecedented number of states, i.e. thirty-three (Canada and the Netherlands submitting a joint declaration), requested to intervene under Article 63 of the Statute. It is safe to assume that this is much more than the total number of such requests made since the *Wimbledon* case in 1923. The contents of state interventions in the Ukraine v. Russia case have been thoroughly examined by authors who revealed a remarkable network of citations and overlaps which gave rise to an assumption that many states extensively consulted and co-operated before lodging their declarations.[54] It is actually not surprising, given the level of global outrage in response to the unprovoked aggression by the Russian Federation against Ukraine. The quoted authors observed that 'certain contentions made by the intervenors could be detrimental to Ukraine's case',[55] primarily due to their political flavor and zealousness. This remains to be seen. However, it is unlikely that interventions under Article 63 of the Statute – when declared admissible – would undermine the proper administration of justice at the Court.

2020 but apparently both states waited until the preliminary objections were adjudicated upon in 2022.

52 See the joint declaration of intervention of Canada, Denmark, France, Germany, the Netherlands and the United Kingdom, registered on November 15th, 2023. On the same day the ICJ also registered the declaration of intervention of Maledives. Both declarations invoked Article 63(2) of the Statute.

53 For an extensive analysis see McGarry, B. "Obligations *Erga Omnes* (*Partes*) and the Participation of Third States in Inter-State Litigation", *The Law and Practice of International Courts and Tribunals* 22 (2023) 273–300.

54 See Wigard, K., Pomson, O., McIntyre, J., "Keeping score" at 15 *et seq*.

55 Ibid., at 23.

In the Order of June 5th 2023[56] the ICJ examined a plethora of objections raised by the Russian Federation with respect to all the declarations of intervention. The objections concerned, *inter alia*, the 'genuine character' and/or 'hidden intentions' of the requesting states, the infringement of the equality of the parties and the good administration of justice (in view of the number of interventions), alleged abuse of process, and the fact that the declarations had been submitted at the preliminary objections stage. The respondent claimed further that the declarations of intervention presuppose the Court's jurisdiction and the admissibility of Ukraine's application and argued that interventions cannot concern the construction of compromissory clauses such as the one invoked by Ukraine (i.e. Article IX of the Geneva Convention). Additionally, Russia maintained that the declarations of intervention go beyond the construction of the Genocide Convention and undermined the admissibility of joint declarations (such as the one filed by Canada and the Netherlands). The final objection concerned the admissibility of the declaration of the United States, given the reservation filed by the US with respect to Article IX of the Convention. Only the latter was upheld though the Court found the US declaration inadmissible 'in so far as it concerns the preliminary objections stage of the proceedings', so it is not excluded that the intervention will prove possible later. The Order was adopted by a 14 to 1 majority, with judge Xue dissenting. In the judgment delivered on February 2nd, 2024, the Court rejected a vast majority of preliminary objections raised by the respondent.[57]

5 Instead of a Conclusion: Is This "Just a Beginning"?

It would be premature to assess the impact of interventions under Article 63 in the Ukraine v. Russia case, given that at the time of writing, the Court has not yet pronounced on the merits of the case. But it is safe to argue that the interventions of over thirty states in that case, as well as the public-interest-oriented litigation in The Gambia v. Myanmar proceedings, have a chance of influencing international law and contributing to its development. It is not excluded that the relatively broad and open-minded interpretations of '(legal) interests' offered by the PCIJ have impacted modern trends in public- or

56 See note 2.

57 See the *Allegations of Genocide under the Convention on the Prevention and Punishment of the Crime of* Genocide (*Ukraine v. Russian Federation: 32 States intervening*), Judgment of 2 February 2024 (preliminary objections).

common-interest litigation at the ICJ.[58] By it as it may, one must admit that the concept of third-party intervention has come a long way from the humble and somewhat symbolic presence of Poland in the *Wimbledon* case to the robust engagement of thirty-three states as expressed in their declarations to intervene in the Ukraine v. Russia proceedings.

There are two more points I wish to make. My first point is that litigations in public or common interest at the ICJ may become increasingly prevalent. This assumption is well illustrated by the proceedings instituted jointly by Canada and the Netherlands against Syria under the Convention Against Torture and Other Cruel, Inhuman or Degrading Treatment or Punishment (CAT)[59] on June 8th 2023.[60] It appears that the applicant states took much effort to satisfy the criteria provided in Article 30 of CAT to establish the jurisdiction of the Court.[61] It remains to be seen if they had done so and what will be the outcome of the case. But even at this very initial stage, it is noteworthy that both states decided to invoke CAT and the undeniably crucial norm of international law prohibiting torture, to initiate proceedings against Syria at the ICJ.

The point about increased prevalence of 'public interest litigation' at the World Court can be further illustrated by two more proceedings brought to the ICJ under Article IX of the Genocide Convention in late 2023 and early 2024: South Africa v. Israel[62] and the Republic of Nicaragua v. Federal Republic of Germany.[63] The first case concern's Israel's acts undertaken after the attacks by Hamas of October 7th, 2023. In the second one Nicaragua argues that Germany breached the Genocide Convention, along with the Geneva Convention of 1949 and their Additional Protocols, by providing political, financial and military support to Israel and by defunding the United Nations Relief and Works Agency for Palestine Refugees in the Near East (UNRWA). It

58 See also: Farnelli, G.M., Sardu, A., "Third-party participation in international adjudication: recent trends and ongoing issues", *Questions of International Law. Zoom-in*, 100 (2023), 1–3; and in the same volume: McGarry, B., "A Rush to Judgment? The Wobbly Bridge from Judicial Standing to Intervention in ICJ Proceedings", 5–18.

59 *Convention Against Torture and Other Cruel, Inhuman or Degrading Treatment or Punishment*, 10 December 1984, 1465 UNTS, 85.

60 *Application of the Convention against Torture and Other Cruel, Inhuman or Degrading Treatment or Punishment* (Canada and the Netherlands v. Syrian Arab Republic), see: https://www.icj-cij.org/case/188.

61 See paras. 8–24 of the joint application instituting proceedings, available at: https://www.icj-cij.org/sites/default/files/case-related/188/188-20230608-APP-01-00-EN.pdf.

62 *Application of the Convention on the Prevention and Punishment of the Crime of Genocide in the Gaza Strip* (South Africa v. Israel), 29 December 2023.

63 *Proceedings instituted by the Republic of Nicaragua against the Federal Republic of Germany* on 1 March 2024.

remains to be seen how the ICJ will approach both cases. However, it is very likely that there will be states interested in intervening under Article 62 of the ICJ Statute.[64]

My second point is that Article IX of the Genocide Convention and Article 30 of CAT do not exhaust the potential legal bases of the ICJ's jurisdiction in public-interest litigation. As is well known to those familiar with the Court's docket, there have been at least several cases brought under the International Convention on the Elimination of All Forms of Racial Discrimination (ICERD),[65] starting with the Georgia v. Russia case instituted in 2008.[66] The same convention was invoked by Ukraine v. Russia in 2017,[67] Qatar v. United Arab Emirates in 2018,[68] as well as (mutually) by Armenia and Azerbaijan in 2021.[69] While these cases do not illustrate litigation in the common interest, the fact remains that Article 22 of ICERD (jurisdictional clause)[70] may also serve as a basis for litigation of that character. Suffice it to recall that the prohibition of racial discrimination, which includes distinction, exclusion, restriction or preference based on race, colour, descent, or national or ethnic origin (Article 1 of ICERD), is a norm of a peremptory character and creates obligations *erga omnes*.

64 On 23 January 2024 Nicaragua filed an application for permission to intervene in the South Africa v. Israel case.

65 International Convention on the Elimination of All Forms of Racial Discrimination, 21 December 1965, 660 UNTS, 195.

66 *Application of the International Convention on the Elimination of All Forms of Racial Discrimination* (Georgia v. Russia), ICJ Judgment of April 1st, 2011 (Preliminary Objections), ICJ Rep. 2011, p. 70.

67 *Application of the International Convention for the Suppression of the Financing of Terrorism and of the International Convention on the Elimination of All Forms of Racial Discrimination* (Ukraine v. Russia), ICJ Judgment of November 8th, 2019 (Preliminary Objections), ICJ Rep. 2019, p. 558.

68 *Application of the International Convention on the Elimination of All Forms of Racial Discrimination* (Qatar v. United Arab Emirates), ICJ Judgment of February 4th, 2021 (Merits), ICJ Rep. 2021, p. 71.

69 *Application of the International Convention on the Elimination of All Forms of Racial Discrimination* (Armenia v. Azerbaijan), see https://www.icj-cij.org/case/180, and the mutual case instituted by Azerbaijan v. Armenia: see https://www.icj-cij.org/case/181.

70 Article 22 of ICERD stipulates: *Any dispute between two or more States Parties with respect to the interpretation or application of this Convention, which is not settled by negotiation or by the procedures expressly provided for in this Convention, shall, at the request of any of the parties to the dispute, be referred to the International Court of Justice for decision, unless the disputants agree to another mode of settlement.*

What might have seemed unthinkable in 1923 when the PCIJ adjudicated its first contentious case with the intervention of a 'third state', i.e., litigation in the interest of the international community, has become a reality in 2023.

5.1 *Postscriptum*

The ICJ's experience with numerous interventions submitted in the Ukraine v. Russia case likely prompted a reflection within the Court on the practical and procedural implications of this trend. On February 28th, 2024, the ICJ introduced amendments to its Rules of Court which provide for a stricter time-limits to file an application for an intervention under Articles 62 or 63 of the Statute ('as soon as possible, and not later than the date fixed for the filing of the Counter-Memorial').[71] Precise rules have been established regarding deadlines for declarations of intervention if the Court has authorized further written pleadings or if a counter-claim has been made, as well as when a declaration concerns preliminary objections. An important amendment concerns also Article 86 of the Rules of Court, which in its current version reads:

> **Article 86**
> 1. If an intervention under Article 63 of the Statute is admitted, the intervening State shall be furnished with copies of the pleadings and documents annexed, and shall be entitled, within a time-limit to be fixed by the Court, or by the President if the Court is not sitting, to submit its written observations on the subject-matter of the intervention.
> 2. These observations shall be communicated to the Parties and to any other State admitted to intervene. The intervening State may also submit its observations with respect to the subject-matter of the intervention in the course of the oral proceedings, unless the Court decides otherwise.

The previous text of this provision entitled intervening states to submit their observations in the oral proceedings, whereas the current version entrusts the Court with the authority to ultimately decide if the interveners will be granted such an opportunity. The amendments to the Rules of Court may play a role in ensuring that proceedings at the ICJ are not unnecessarily prolonged by a large number of intervening states reiterating the same arguments. It is unlikely, however, that the new procedural rules would discourage states from

71 See Articles 81 (1) and 82 (1) of the Rules of Court.

submitting declarations of intervention 'in the public interest', or as they perceive it to be.

Bibliography

Barrie, G.N., "Third-party State Intervention in Disputes Before the International Court of Justice: A Reassessment of Articles 62 and 63 of the ICJ Statute", *Comparative and International Law Journal of Southern Africa* 52 (2020).

Chinkin, C., "Third Party Intervention Before the International Court of Justice", *American Journal of International Law* 80 (1986).

Farnelli, G.M., Sardu, A., "Third-party participation in international adjudication: recent trends and ongoing issues", *Questions of International Law. Zoom-in*, 100 (2023).

McGarry, B. "Obligations *Erga Omnes* (*Partes*) and the Participation of Third States in Inter-State Litigation", *The Law and Practice of International Courts and Tribunals* 22 (2023).

McGarry, B., "A Rush to Judgment? The Wobbly Bridge from Judicial Standing to Intervention in ICJ Proceedings", *Questions of International Law. Zoom-in*, 100 (2023).

Miron, A., Chinkin, C., "Article 62", "Article 63" in Andreas Zimmermann et al (eds), *The Statute of the International Court of Justice: A Commentary* (3rd ed. OUP Oxford: 2019).

Palchetti, P., "Opening the International Court of Justice to Third States: Intervention and Beyond", *Max Planck Yearbook of United Nations Law* 6 (2002).

Rojek, W., Łaptos J., (eds), " Depesze Poselstwa Rzeczypospolitej Polskiej w Londynie" [Telegrams of the Mission of the Republic of Poland in Londyn], vol. II, marzec 1923 – maj 1926, (Kraków: 2019).

Sztucki, J., "Intervention Under Article 63 of the ICJ Statute in the Phase of Preliminary Proceedings: The 'Salvadoran Incident'", *American Journal of International Law* 79 (1985).

Wigard, K., Pomson, O., McIntyre, J., "Keeping score: an empirical analysis of the interventions in *Ukraine v. Russia*", *Journal of International Dispute Settlement* 14(3) (2023).

Wojcikiewicz Almeida, P., "International Procedural Regulation in the Common Interest: The Role of Third-Party Intervention and Amicus Curiae before the ICJ", *The Law and Practice of International Courts and Tribunals* 18 (2019).

Zimmermann, A., Devaney, J., "International Courts and Tribunals, Intervention in Proceedings", in *Max Planck Encyclopedia of International Law* (Oxford: 2019).

Judgments and Advisory Opinions

Allegations of Genocide under the Convention on the Prevention and Punishment of the Crime of Genocide, Order of the ICJ of 5 June 2023.

Allegations of Genocide under the Convention on the Prevention and Punishment of the Crime of Genocide (*Ukraine v. Russian Federation:32 States intervening*), ICJ Judgment of February 2nd, 2024 (Preliminary Objections).

Application of the Convention on the Prevention and Punishment of the Crime of Genocide (The Gambia v. Myanmar), instituted on November 11th, 2019, ICJ Judgment of June 22nd, 2022 (Preliminary Objections), ICJ Rep. 2022, p. 477.

Application of the International Convention for the Suppression of the Financing of Terrorism and of the International Convention on the Elimination of All Forms of Racial Discrimination (Ukraine v. Russia), ICJ Judgment of November 8th, 2019 (Preliminary Objections), ICJ Rep. 2019, p. 558.

Application of the International Convention on the Elimination of All Forms of Racial Discrimination (Qatar v. United Arab Emirates), ICJ Judgment of February 4th, 2021 (Merits), ICJ Rep. 2021, p. 71.

Case Concerning Continental Shelf (Libyan Arab Jamahiriya v. Malta), ICJ Judgment of March 21st 1984, ICJ Rep. 1984, p. 3.

Case Concerning Continental Shelf (Tunisia v. Libyan Arab Jamahiriya), ICJ Judgment of April 14th 1981, ICJ Rep. 1981, p. 3.

Case of the S.S. "Wimbledon" [*1923*], Judgment of the PCIJ of June 28th, 1923 (Question of Intervention by Poland), Judgment of the PCIJ of August 17th, 1923 (Merits), Publ. PCIJ Ser A No 1.

Delimitation of the Polish–Czechoslovakian Frontier (*Question of Jaworzina*), Advisory Opinion, (1923) PCIJ Series B no 8, ICGJ 275 (PCIJ 1923), December 6th, 1923.

Haya de la Torre case (Columbia v. Peru), ICJ Judgment of June 13th, 1951, ICJ Rep. 1951, p. 830.

Jurisdictional Immunities of the State (Germany v. Italy: Greece intervening) ICJ Order of July 4th, 2011, ICJ Rep. 2011, p. 494.

Land and Maritime Boundary between Cameroon and Nigeria (Cameroon v. Nigeria: Equatorial Guinea intervening) *Cameroon and Nigeria*, ICJ Order of October 21st, 1999, ICJ Rep. 1999, p. 1029.

Land, Island and Maritime Frontier Dispute (El Salvador/Honduras: Nicaragua intervening) ICJ Order of October 21st, 1999, ICJ Rep. 1999, p. 1029.

Legality of the Threat or Use of Nuclear Weapons, Advisory Opinion of July 8th 1996, ICJ Rep. 1996, p. 226.

Military and Paramilitary Activities in and against Nicaragua (Nicaragua v. United States), see the Order of the ICJ of October 4th 1984, ICJ Rep. 1984, p. 215.

Nuclear Tests (New Zealand v. France), ICJ Judgment of December 20th, 1974 (ICJ Rep. 1974, p. 457).

Questions relating to Settlers of German Origin in Poland, Advisory Opinion, (1923) PCIJ Series B no 6, ICGJ 273 (PCIJ 1923), September 10th, 1923.

Questions relating to the Obligation to Prosecute or Extradite (Belgium v. Senegal), ICJ Judgment of July 20th 2012, ICJ Rep. 2012, p. 422.

Whaling in the Antarctic (Australia v. Japan: New Zealand intervening), ICJ Order of February 6th, 2013, ICJ Rep. 2013, p. 3.

Cases Pending at the ICJ

Alleged Breaches of Certain International Obligations in respect of the Occupied Palestinian Territory (Nicaragua v. Germany).

Application of the Convention against Torture and Other Cruel, Inhuman or Degrading Treatment or Punishment (Canada and the Netherlands v. Syrian Arab Republic).

Application of the International Convention on the Elimination of All Forms of Racial Discrimination (Armenia v. Azerbaijan).

Application of the International Convention on the Elimination of All Forms of Racial Discrimination (Azerbaijan v. Armenia).

Treaties

Convention Against Torture and Other Cruel, Inhuman or Degrading Treatment or Punishment, 10 December 1984, 1465 UNTS, 85.

International Convention on the Elimination of All Forms of Racial Discrimination, 21 December 1965, 660 UNTS, 195.

Treaty of Versailles, 28 June 1919, 34 LNTS.

CHAPTER 4

The *s.s. Wimbledon* Judgment

General International Law, 'Objective Regimes', 'Self-Contained Regimes' and Fragmentation of International Law: Then and Now

Malgosia Fitzmaurice and Agnes Rydberg

Abstract

Under Article 380 of the Treaty of Versailles, 'the Kiel Canal and its approaches shall be maintained free and open to the vessels of commerce and of war of all nations at peace with Germany on terms of entire equality'. In the *s.s. Wimbledon* judgment, the Permanent Court of International Justice (PCIJ) held that Article 380 established an objective legal regime of the Kiel Canal and changed its legal status. The Kiel Canal ceased to be an internal and national waterway and became an international waterway for the 'benefit of all nations of the world'. According to the Court, the provisions of Article 380 which established this 'international and objective regime' were 'self-contained'; most likely the first time this term was introduced into the international legal vocabulary.

This chapter addresses the following four questions: 1) has the *s.s. Wimbledon* judgment been a first clear sign of a phenomenon known as 'fragmentation of international law'; 2) what is the relationship between 'international objective regimes' and 'self-contained regimes'; 3) what is the relationship between these regimes and general international law; and 4) do the forementioned issues have a different legal expression and dimension today than they had 100 years ago?

1 Introduction

The *s.s. Wimbledon* – the first ever judgment by the Permanent Court of International Justice (PCIJ) – raised many and complex issues of international law, some of which do not find a straightforward answer today; a century after

 | DOI:10.1163/9789004707979_006

the delivery of the judgment.[1] Soon after the end of World War I (WWI), Russia and Poland were at war over certain disputed territories. Germany had declared its neutrality in the war. The United Kingdom (UK) and France, together with certain other States, had expressed support for Poland.

On 21 March 1921, the steamship S.S. Wimbledon was refused permission by Germany to pass through the Kiel Canal, which runs through Germany and links the Baltic and North Seas. The Wimbledon was an English steamship, chartered by the French company *Les Affréteurs réunis*, which carried 4,200 tons of munitions and artillery consigned to the Polish Naval Base at Danzig. Germany's refusal was based on two neutrality orders of 25 and 30 July 1920, issued in connection with the Russo–Polish war. Those neutrality orders prohibited the transit of cargoes of munitions and artillery destined for Poland or Russia.[2] The applicants – the UK, France, Italy and Japan, with Poland intervening – were all the Parties to the 1919 Treaty of Versailles and brought a claim arguing that Germany's refusal was incompatible with Article 380 of the Treaty of Versailles. Under Article 380, the 'Kiel Canal and its approaches shall be maintained free and open to the vessels of commerce and of war of all nations at peace with Germany on terms of entire equality'. Thus, according to the applicants, since the Wimbledon belonged to a nation that – at that moment – was at peace with Germany, it was entitled to free passage through the Canal.

The Court upheld this claim by stating that the terms of Article 380 were categorical and gave rise to no doubt. It followed that:

> the canal had ceased to be an internal and national navigable waterway, the use of which by the vessels of States other than the riparian State is left entirely to the discretion of that State, and that it has become an international waterway intended to provide under treaty guarantee easier access to the Baltic for the benefit of all nations of the world. Accordingly, … under its new régime, the Kiel Canal must be open, on a footing of equality, to all vessels, without making any distinction between war vessels and vessels of commerce, but on one express condition, namely, that these vessels must belong to nations at peace with Germany.[3]

1 *S.S. Wimbledon* (*United Kingdom, France, Italy & Japan v. Germany*) (Poland intervening), 1923 PCIJ Ser A, No. 1 (Aug. 17).

2 The relevant neutrality order of Germany stated in Article 1: 'The export and transit of arms, munitions, powder and explosives and other articles of war material is prohibited in so far as these articles are consigned to the territories of the Polish Republic or of the Federal Socialist Republic of the Russian Soviets' (*Wimbledon* (n 1) 28–29.

3 Ibid 22.

Thus, the intention of the authors was to facilitate access to the Baltic by establishing an international regime, and consequently to keep the canal open at all times to foreign vessels of every kind.[4]

Furthermore, although the Kiel Canal, having been constructed by Germany in German territory, was, until 1919, an internal waterway, the Treaty ensured that the Kiel Canal was not assimilated with other internal navigable waterways in Germany. A special section had been created in the treaty, which laid down rules exclusively designed for the Kiel Canal.[5] For the Kiel Canal, access was open to the war vessels and transit traffic of all nations at peace with Germany, whereas free access to the other German navigable waterways was limited to the Allied and Associated Powers only. This led the Court to conclude that the provisions relating to the Kiel Canal were self-contained; if they had to be supplemented and interpreted by the aid of those referring to the inland navigable waterways of Germany in other sections of the treaty, they would lose their very *raison d'être*.[6]

In order to dispute the right of the Wimbledon to free passage under the terms of Article 380, the argument was urged upon the Court that this right was a servitude by international law resting upon Germany and which had to be construed as restrictively as possible, especially in the sense that it should not be allowed to affect the rights consequent upon neutrality in an armed conflict.[7] The Court however held that it was not

> called upon to take a definite attitude with regard to the question, which is moreover of a very controversial nature, whether in the domain of international law, there really exist servitudes analogous to the servitudes of private law. Whether the German Government is bound by virtue of a servitude or by virtue of a contractual obligation undertaken towards the Powers entitled to benefit by the terms of the Treaty of Versailles, to allow free access to the Kiel Canal in time of war as in time of peace to the vessels of all nations, the fact remains that Germany has to submit to an important limitation of the exercise of the sovereign rights which no one disputes that she possesses over the Kiel Canal. This fact constitutes a sufficient reason for the restrictive interpretation, in case of doubt, of the clause which produces such a limitation. But the Court feels obliged to stop at the point where the so-called restrictive interpretation would

4 Ibid 29–30.

5 Ibid 31.

6 Ibid 32.

7 Ibid 34.

> be contrary to the plain terms of the article and would destroy what has been clearly granted.[8]

The Court also examined the position of Germany as a neutral State towards Russia, and whether the general grant of passage to vessels of all nationalities through the Kiel Canal would deprive Germany of the exercise of its rights as a neutral State in time of war. The Court held that it would not. It turned to other relevant precedent, such as the Suez Canal and Panama Canal, under whose regimes ships carrying contraband had been permitted in many different circumstances to pass freely through the Canals; such passage had never been regarded by anyone as violating the rules of neutrality.[9] Accordingly, the Court found that that Germany's neutrality would not have been imperilled if its authorities had allowed the passage of the Wimbledon through the Kiel Canal. Germany was therefore wrong in refusing access to the Kiel Canal to the Wimbledon.[10]

2 Objective Regimes

2.1 *General Remarks*

In the judgment, it appears that the PCIJ acknowledged that the Treaty of Versailles granted the Kiel Canal a 'new regime' of a permanent character, the main objective of which was to be applied objectively in the interest of international navigation.[11] As such, the Court admitted the existence of a certain objective and permanent regime of the Kiel Canal based on the explicit language of Article 380 of the Treaty of Versailles. However, the Court did not specify the nature of free passage through the canal for third States, and whether this was a right or benefit upon such States.[12]

The idea and notion of objective regimes in international law has not been uncontroversial. In broad brushstrokes, treaties establishing objective regimes are international agreements setting up 'objective rules' with *erga omnes* effect, regardless of the number of contracting States to the treaty.[13] The concept is

8 Ibid.

9 Ibid.

10 Ibid.

11 See further Malgosia Fitzmaurice, 'Third Parties and the Law of Treaties' (2002) 6 Max Planck Yearbook of United Nations Law 37, 86.

12 Ibid.

13 Francesco Salerno, 'Treaties Establishing Objective Regimes' in Enzo Cannizzaro (ed), *The Law of Treaties Beyond the Vienna Convention* (OUP 2011) 225. On objective regimes,

therefore counterintuitive to the principle *pacta tertiis nec nocent nec prosunt*, according to which treaties may only create rights and obligations binding on the parties to the treaty.[14] Thus, a treaty is *res inter alios acta* for non-parties – i.e. third States – to the treaty. *Pacta tertiis* stems of the notion of sovereign equality of all States in international law and is given expression to in Article 34 of the Vienna Convention on the Law of Treaties (VCLT),[15] stipulating that '[a] treaty does not create either obligations or rights for a third State without its consent'.

Objective regimes with regard to treaties can also be analysed within the context of rules of law deviating from general international law (i.e. the phenomenon of *lex specialis*). This specific rule, in case of objective regimes, claims autonomy in relation to various aspects of international law from general rules, such as secondary rules on State responsibility, rules on dispute resolution and rules deriving from other institutions of international law.[16] The rationale of *lex specialis* can be a result of a practical approach with regulate the matter at hand more effectively than general rules. However, *lex specialis* and general international law may lead to conflicting interpretations, also within the judicial context. Such conflicting interpretations create problems in international law, such as diminishing legal security and putting legal subjects in an unequal position *vis-à-vis* each other. For example, in relation to the Kiel Canal, the majority of judges overcame the problems of neutrality in war by referring to an 'objective' change of the status of the Kiel Canal.

It has been argued that given the existence of the *pacta tertiis* principle as embodied in Article 34 VCLT, 'it would appear that the concept of objective

---

see further Hans Kelsen, 'Contribution à la théorie du traité international', Revue internationale de la théorie du droit (1936); Arnold McNair, *The Law of Treaties* (OUP 1961); J.F. *Prevost, Les eff ets des traités conclus entre Etats à l'égard des Etats tiers, thèse doctorale* (Paris 1973); H. Mosler, 'The international society as a legal community', 140 Recueil des Cours (1974) 234; P. Cahier, 'Le problème des eff ets des traités à l'égard des États tiers', 143 Recueil des Cours (1974); S. Bastid, Les traités dans la vie internationale. Conclusion et eff ets (Paris: Economica, 1985); P. Subedi, 'The Doctrine of Objective Regimes in International Law and the Competence of the United Nations to Impose Territorial or Peace Settlements on States' (1994) 37 GYIL 174.

14 Richard Barnes, 'Objective Regimes Revisited' (2004) 9 Asian Yearbook of International Law 97.

15 Vienna Convention on the Law of Treaties (VCLT) (adopted 22 May 1969, entered into force 27 January 1980) 1155 UNTS 331.

16 International Law Commission Study Group on 'Fragmentation of international law: difficulties arising from the diversification and expansion of international law', Official Records of the General Assembly, Fifty-seventh Session, Supplement No. 10 (A/57/10), paras. 492–494.

regimes is redundant'.[17] However, there are – perusal – certain acknowledged exceptions to the general expression of the *pacta tertiis* rule. The first exception is found in Article 35 VCLT, relating to treaties providing for obligations for third parties. According to Article 35, '[a]n obligation arises for a third State from a provision of a treaty if the parties to the treaty intend the provision to be the means of establishing the obligation and the third State expressly accepts that obligation in writing'.[18] Two conditions must be satisfied: 1) it must have been the intention of the parties to the treaties to create the obligation(s) in question; and 2) consent to the obligation must be expressed in writing, whereby conduct consistent with the obligation or implicit consent appear insufficient.

The second exception is outlined in Article 36 VCLT. The provision stipulates that:

> 1. A right arises for a third State from a provision of a treaty if the parties to the treaty intend the provision to accord that right either to the third State, or to a group of States to which it belongs, or to all States, and the third State assents thereto. Its assent shall be presumed so long as the contrary is not indicated, unless the treaty otherwise provides.
> 2. A State exercising a right in accordance with paragraph 1 shall comply with the conditions for its exercise provided for in the treaty or established in conformity with the treaty.

Thus, the parties to the treaty much have intended to create a right for the third State and the third State must assent thereto. Assent to a right – in contrast to consent to an obligation – is always presumed if there is no contrary indication or unless the treaty otherwise provides.

The question of how objective regimes are situated within the wider concept of the *pacta tertiis* principle and the effect of treaties on third States is not clear. It can be said that the notion of objectives regimes 'derives from the absence of an objective form of law making capable of developing and prescribing the international public interest'.[19] As McNair has outlined,

> [w]hen it is remembered that international society has at present no legislature, the treaty is the only instrument available for doing many of the

17 Barnes (n 14) 98.

18 Article 35 VCLT. See further *Free Zones of Upper Savoy and the District of Gex* (*France v Switzerland*) (Judgment of 7 June 1932) PCIJ Series A/B No 46.

19 Barnes (n 14) 99.

> things which an individual State would do by means of its legislature; and the making of rules of law is not the only function of a legislature. It is therefore not surprising that from time to time groups of States should have assumed the responsibility of leadership and used the instrument of a treaty to make certain territorial or other arrangements required, or which they consider to be required, in the interest of this or that particular part of the world.[20]

Thus, objective regimes can be viewed as performing a 'surrogate legislative role' in the absence of any formal institutionalised process, effectively circumventing the *pacta tertiis* rule.[21] This proposition particularly holds true against the background of the growing corpus of international law, which is moving away from a purely reciprocal conception of the international legal system towards one that can accommodate a wider range of community and global interests, including human rights law and environmental protection.[22] Objective regimes accordingly stand at odds with *the pacta tertiis* rule, which derives from a 'strong bilateral model based on an anachronistic conception of sovereignty'.[23] The departure from bilateralism has been part of the ongoing process of reconceptualising international law and the notion of State sovereignty,[24] and a restrictive understanding of sovereignty today appears conformable with case-law of the International Court of Justice (ICJ).[25] Furthermore, as stated by Judge Anzilotti back in 1931, '[t]he sovereignty of the State consists of its competence as defined and limited by international law and is not a discretionary power which overrides the law'.[26]

Objective regimes thus operate to serve wider community interests on the international level. Simma has defined universal community interests as 'a consensus according to which the respect for certain fundamental values is not to be left to the free disposition of States individually or *inter se* but is

---

20 McNair (n 13) 259.

21 Barnes (n 14) 100.

22 Ibid. See also B. Simma, 'From Bilateralism to Community Interest' (1994 – VI) 250 RdC 217.

23 Barnes (n 14) 101.

24 Ibid 102.

25 *Corfu Channel* case (Merits), ICJ Rep. 1949, 4 at 29–30.

26 *Austro-German Customs Union* case, 1931 PCIJ Ser. A/B, No. 41, 3. Likewise, Lauterpacht has noted that '[t]here is no room in a developing international society for a rigid application of the principle according to which the rights and duties of a State can never be determined by a will other than its own', see Hersch Lauterpacht, *The Development of International Law by the International Court* (1958) 180–81.

recognized and sanctioned by international law as a matter of concern to all States'.[27] Community interests are characterised by the fact that they transcend the interests of States and rather 'correspond to the needs, hopes and fears of all human beings, and attempt to cope with problems the solution of which may be decisive for the survival of entire humankind'.[28] Examples of such community interests include questions of maintenance of peace and security, environmental protection, and protection of human rights.[29] Thus, the international legal system is growing into a 'more socially conscious legal order', increasingly reflective of 'community interests' and – resultingly – narrower interests of States.[30]

The question of objective regimes is not given explicit referral to in the text of the VCLT. That said, the International Law Commission (ILC), when drafting the VCLT, discussed the matter at great length. It was Special Rapporteur Fitzmaurice who introduced the subject in 1960.[31] In his draft Article 18, subject to certain conditions:

> All States are under a duty to recognize and respect situations of law or of fact established by lawful and valid treaties tending by their nature to have effect *erga omnes*. The following are amongst the more important types of treaties producing effects of this kind: (a) Peace treaties, and other treaties containing political or territorial settlements; (b) Treaties creating a general regime or status of neutralization, or demilitarization, for particular territories or localities; (c) Treaties of a dispositive character, such as treaties of cession, frontier demarcation, or treaties creating a servitude.[32]

Later on, subsequent Special Rapporteur Waldock's draft Article 63(1) stipulated that:

27 B Simma, 'From Bilateralism to Community Interest in International Law' (1994) 250 Recueil des Cours de l'Académie de Droit International 217, 233.

28 Ibid 234.

29 Ibid 244.

30 Ibid. See also Fastenrath, Ulrich and others (eds), *From Bilateralism to Community Interest: Essays in Honour of Bruno Simma* (OUP 2011); Christian Tomuschat, 'Obligations Arising for States Without or Against Their Will' (1993) 241 Recueil des Cours 195, 211, 219–20; James Crawford, 'Multilateral Rights and Obligations in International Law (Volume 319) Collected Courses of the Hague Academy of International Law'.

31 See Yearbook of the International Law Commission (YBILC), vol. II, 1960, 72 et seq.

32 Ibid.

> A treaty establishes an objective regime when it appears from its terms and from the circumstances of its conclusion that the intention of the parties is to create in the general interest general obligations and rights relating to a particular region, State, territory, locality, river, waterway, or to a particular area of sea, sea-bed, or air-space; provided that the parties include among their number any State having territorial competence with reference to the subject-matter of the treaty, or that any such State has consented to the provision in question.[33]

Whereas their respective proposals were discussed in detail by members of the ILC, the subject was eventually set aside as being outside the scope of the draft Convention.[34] Among the reasons given for deleting proposed draft Article 63 was that this article 'might be unlikely to meet with general acceptance'.[35] Some members of the ILC were indeed concerned with the imposition by the 'Great Powers' of their will on other less powerful States. For instance, de Luna argued that 'it was to be feared that States might regard such an article as approval of *de facto* legislation or of government of the world by the Great Powers; for "objective regimes" had in fact been used to impose certain conditions on small States at a time when the sovereign equality of States had not been much respected'.[36] Nevertheless, it appears from the discussion within the ILC that it did not reject the idea of objective regimes in its entirety, but – to reiterate – it was rather removed from the ILC agenda for being outside the scope of the VCLT.

The question of objective regimes was eventually discussed by the ILC when drafting the 1978 Vienna Convention on Succession of States in Respect of Treaties (VCST),[37] where the ILC finally acknowledged the existence of a category of treaties creating objective regimes.[38] In particular, Special Rapporteur Waldock was of the view that the 'weight both of opinion and practice seems clearly to be in favour of the view that boundaries established by treaties remain untouched by the mere fact of succession'.[39] He drafted a provision

33 YBILC, vol. II, 1964, 26.

34 See ILC commentary to draft Article 34, YBILC, vol. II, 1964.

35 Ibid.

36 YBILC, vol. 1, 1964, 99–100. Similarly, Jimenez de Arechaga (Uruguay) was of the view that 'certain groups of States might acquire a sort of legislative power over the rest of the world' and that power 'would be exercised mainly by the Great Powers, as in the case of the so-called "international settlements"', see YBILC, vol. 1, 1964 100–101.

37 Vienna Convention on Succession of States in Respect of Treaties (adopted 23 August 1978, entered into force 6 November 1996) 1946 UNTS 3.

38 YBILC, vol. II, 1974, 204.

39 YBILC, vol. II, 1968, 92–93 (footnotes omitted).

adopted as Article 11 VCST to this effect.[40] The provision stipulates that '[a] succession of States does not as such affect: (a) a boundary established by a treaty; or (b) obligations and rights established by a treaty and relating to the regime of a boundary'. Because of their sensitivity in international relations, boundary treaties have long been considered an archetypical example of objective regimes and was the main point of issue in *Free Zones of Upper Savoy and the District of Gex*.[41]

The question of treaties creating other territorial regimes (for instance 'dispositive' or 'localised' treaties) than those establishing boundaries was however less straightforward when drafting the VCST. The underlying issue in this regard was the concern of several States that imposing territorial treaties other than boundary treaties on a successor State was difficult to reconcile with the principles of self-determination and the sovereign equality of States.[42] However, the ILC eventually took the view that not only treaties establishing a boundary, but also other territorial treaties remain unaffected by State succession. This view was incorporated in Article 12 VCST, which provides that:

> 1. A succession of States does not as such affect: (a) obligations relating to the use of any territory, or to restrictions upon its use, established by a treaty for the benefit of any territory of a foreign State and considered as attaching to the territories in question; (b) rights established by a treaty for the benefit of any territory and relating to the use, or to restrictions upon the use, of any territory of a foreign State and considered as attaching to the territories in question.
> 2. A succession of States does not as such affect: (a) obligations relating to the use of any territory, or to restrictions upon its use, established by a treaty for the benefit of a group of States or of all States and considered as attaching to that territory; (b) rights established by a treaty for the benefit of a group of States or of all States and relating to the use of any territory, or to restrictions upon its use, and considered as attaching to that territory.

40 UN Doc. A/CONF.80 / 15 from 22 June 1977 and UN Doc. A/CONF.80 / 31 from 27 October 1978.

41 PCIJ, Ser. A / B, No. 24 and Ser. A / B No. 46, 1932. The PCIJ made the well-known categorical statement concerning the lack of effects of treaties upon third States: '[I]t is certain that, in any case the Treaty of Versailles is not binding upon Switzerland, who is not a Party to that Treaty, except to the extent to which that country accepted it'. As Switzerland had never accepted the treaty, France could not enforce it against Switzerland.

42 Examples include Zambia, Romania, Afghanistan, Swaziland, and Syria, see UN Doc. A/CONF.80 / 5 from 4 March 1977, 139, 143, 149, 170–71; YBILC, vol. II, 1969, 76, 75.

In its commentary, the ILC stated that with respect to the rules concerning succession of States in respect of treaties,

> there are cases where the treaty intended to establish an objective regime would not be binding upon a successor State, unless such a treaty were considered to fall under a special rule to that effect. Equally, if the succession of States occurs in relation to a treaty establishing an objective regime, under the general law of treaties and the law of succession the successor State would not necessarily be entitled to claim the rights enjoyed by its predecessor State, unless the treaty were considered to fall under such a special rule. That such a special rule exists is, in the opinion of the Commission, established by a number of convincing precedents.[43]

Thus, a successor State is precluded from relying on the *pacta tertiis* principle. The rights and obligations established under the regimes of Articles 11 and 12 VCST would not be affected by a succession of States in respect to the territory concerned. The ILC observed, however, that due to the 'legal nexus which existed between the treaty and the territory prior to the date of succession of States', the successor State 'is not properly speaking a "third State" in relation to the treaty' and 'it is not open to the successor State simply to invoke article 35 of the Vienna Convention under which a treaty cannot impose obligations upon third States without its consent'.[44] The VCST is not widely ratified; nonetheless, it is broadly accepted that Articles 11–12 have acquired the status of norms of international customary law.[45]

Articles 11 and 12 VCST formed part of arguments both by Hungary and Slovakia in the *Case Concerning the Gabcikovo-Nagymaros Project*.[46] In 1977, Hungary and Czechoslovakia signed a Treaty for the construction of dams and other projects along the Danube River that bordered both nations (1977 Treaty on the Construction and Operation of the Gabcikovo-Nagymaros Barrage System, hereinafter 'the 1977 Treaty'). Czechoslovakia began work on damming the river in its territory when Hungary stopped working on the project. Negotiation could not resolve the matter, which led Hungary to terminate the Treaty. Hungary based its action on the fact that the damming of the river had been agreed to only on the ground of a joint operation and sharing of benefits

43 YBILC, vol. II, 1974, 204.

44 YBILC 1974, Part Two, 204, at para 30.

45 Fitzmaurice (n 11) 78.

46 *Gabcikovo-Nagymaros Case* (*Hungary v Slovakia*) ICJ Reports 1997, 7 et seq., (70–71 paras 119–123).

associated with the project, to which Czechoslovakia had unlawfully unilaterally assumed control of a shared resource.

Hungary claimed that there was no rule of succession that would be applicable in this case. It submitted that the 1977 Treaty did not create 'obligations and rights ... relating to the regime of boundary' within the meaning of Article 11 VCST.[47] It observed that the existing course of the boundary was unaffected by the Treaty. It also negated that the Treaty was a 'localised' treaty; or that it created rights 'considered as attaching to [the] territory' within the meaning of Article 12, which, as such, are unaffected by a succession of states'.[48] The 1977 Treaty was, according to Hungary, nothing more than a joint investment. Therefore, Hungary concluded that there was no basis on which the Treaty could have survived the disappearance of Czechoslovakia so as to be binding as between itself and Slovakia.[49]

According to Slovakia, the 1977 Treaty, which was not lawfully terminated by Hungary's notification in May 1992, remained in force between itself, as a successor State, and Hungary. Slovakia argued, *inter alia,* that Treaty was one 'attaching to the territory' within the meaning of Article 12 VCST, and that it contained provisions relating to a boundary. The 1977 Treaty was said to fall within its scope because of its 'specific characteristics ... which place it in the category of treaties of a localised or territorial regime' which operates in the interest of all Danube riparian States, and as a 'dispositive treaty, creating rights in rem, independently of the legal personality of its original signatories'.[50] Slovakia relied on the recognition by the ILC of the existence of a rule of succession of treaties whereby treaties intend to establish an objective regime which must be considered as binding on the successor State. In the view of Slovakia, the 1977 Treaty was not one that could have been terminated through the disappearance of the original parties.[51]

The Court indeed acknowledged that the 1977 Treaty confirmed that, aside from its undoubted nature as a joint investment, its major elements were the proposed construction and joint operation of a large, integrated and indivisible complex of structures on specific parts of the respective territories of Hungary and Czechoslovakia. The Treaty also established the navigational rights for an important sector of an international waterway, in particular the relocation of the main international shipping lane to the bypass canal. In doing so, it

47 Ibid.
48 Ibid.
49 Ibid.
50 Ibid.
51 Ibid.

inescapably created a situation in which interests of other users of the Danube were affected.[52]

The Court further observed that according to Article 12 VCST, the rights and obligations of a territorial character established by a treaty are unaffected by the succession of States. The Court thus found that the content of the 1977 Treaty indicated that it must have been regarded as establishing a territorial regime within the meaning of Article 12 of the Vienna Convention. It created rights and obligations 'attaching to' the parts of the Danube to which it relates; thus the Treaty itself could not be affected by a succession of States, and continued to be binding on both Hungary and Slovakia, although Slovakia had not originally been a party to the treaty. In other words, Slovakia could not rely on an argument of *pacta tertiis* or trying to prove its status as a third State but was bound to respect the 1977 Treaty as it constituted an objective regime.[53]

The findings of the Court have been the subject of some criticism. Klabbers, for instance, submitted that the Court never referred to the text of Article 12 directly, only to preparatory works, the reason being, in his view, that Article 12 had no direct bearing on the situation at hand. According to him, the provision really only referred to servitudes, but not to rivers or dams etc. In order to circumvent the issue, the Court had no option but to fall back on preparatory work. The appropriateness of this can be questioned as the precedents submitted by the ILC when drafting Article 12 VCST dealt only with such aspects of the rights and obligations in relation to the water rights as fishing, irrigation or supply of water. Accordingly, the Court made 'something of a stretch in its attempt to bring the Gabcikovo project within the scope of article 12'.[54]

The above interpretation is however a rather limited understanding of the applicability of Article 12 in relation to the rights and obligations flowing from territorial regimes.[55] When drafting the provision, the ILC in particular submitted that '[t]he characteristic of the treaties in question is that they attach obligations to a particular territory, river, canal, etc., for the benefit either of a group of states (e.g., riparian states of a particular river) or all states generally. They include treaties for the neutralisation or demilitarisation of a particular territory, treaties according freedom of navigation, waterway or rivers, treaties for the equitable use of the water resources of an international river basin and the like'.[56] This formulation clearly indicates that the list of possible rights

52 Ibid.

53 Ibid.

54 Jan Klabbers, 'Cat on Hot Tin Roof: The World Court, State Succession, and the *Gabcikovo-Nagymaros* case' (1998) 11 LJIL 345, 353.

55 See further Fitzmaurice (n 11).

56 YBILC 1974, Vol. II, Part One, paras 30, 204.

and obligations that may be governed by Article 12 is broader than the narrow interpretation as favoured by Klabbers.[57]

Today, the legal status of objective regimes is not entirely clear, although they are often viewed as providing for an exception to the *pacta tertiis* rule. Special Rapporteur Fitzmaurice, for instance, argued that such regimes 'constitute in the aggregate a considerable gloss on the *pacta tertiis* rule'.[58] State practice in support of the existence of certain objective regimes include: i) international settlements (including neutrality and demilitarisation);[59] ii) boundary agreements;[60] and iii) internationalised territories.[61] With respect to the first category of international settlements, Barnes gives the example of the Kiel Canal and the Panama Canal as regulated by treaties providing for objective regimes.[62] This question is further discussed below.

The demilitarisation of the Iraqi territory along the border with Kuwait after the recent Gulf War under United Nations Security Council Resolution (UNSC) 687 (1991) and the demarcation of the boundary between Iraq and Kuwait under UNSC Resolution 833 (1993) are likewise examples of international settlements forming objective regimes valid *erga omnes*. However, as Subedi points out:

> these settlements are significant and different from previous settlements in that they were not concluded by the major Powers or by the victorious Powers acting individually. This time they were concluded collectively under the United Nations. These settlements under the Security

57 Klabbers (n 54) 354.

58 [1960] YBILC, vol. II, 73. See also Subedi (n 13).

59 Examples include: the 1713 Treaty of Utrecht in respect of certain territories including Gibraltar, the Congress of Vienna, establishing the permanent neutrality of Switzerland, the Treaty of Versailles 1919, in respect of Germany, and the 1856 the Aaland Islands Convention, in which France, Great Britain and Russia agreed that 'the Aaland Islands shall not be fortified, and that no military or naval base shall be maintained or created there', see BFSP (1855–1856), London 1865, 24. Furthermore, the demilitarisation of certain Iraqi territory under Security Council Resolution 687 (1991) may be regarded as a recent example of an international settlement. See further Subedi (n 13) 174–75.

60 Articles 11 and 12 of the Vienna Convention on Succession of States in Respect of Treaties reaffirms this by maintaining the legitimacy of boundary agreements *vis à vis* a succession of States.

61 See generally, the mandate system as established under the League of Nations. The objective character of such regimes was reaffirmed in the International Status of *South West Africa Advisory Opinion*, ICJ Rep. 1950, 132. In particular, see McNair's separate opinion at 153–55.

62 Article 2 of the Panama Canal Treaty provides for the Canal being 'open to peaceful transit by the vessels of all nations' ((1977) 16 ILM 1022); Barnes (n 14) 129.

> Council's resolutions can be regarded as objective regimes established by the United Nations.[63]

There is, as of yet, no straightforward definable criteria for the existence of objective regimes. Barnes, in his comprehensive study on objective regimes, identifies the following factors on the basis of State practice, scholarship and case-law: i) there must be an intention by the parties to create an objective regime; ii) the regime must be territorial; iii) the parties must have a competence in respect of the territory or an interest in the creation of the regime; and iv) the regime must be in the general interest of the international community.[64] These factors correspond with the two-element definition advanced by Special Rapporteur Waldock during the drafting history of the VCLT: '(i) the intention of the parties must be to create general rights and obligations in the general interest relating to a particular region, State, territory etc., and (ii) the parties must include among their number the State or States having territorial competence with reference to the subject-matter of the treaty or at least, that State or States must have expressly assented to the provisions creating the regime'.[65]

The intention of the parties is imperative in establishing an exception to the *pacta tertiis* rule (as also recognised in Articles 35–36 VCLT) and serve as a reminder of the sovereign equality of States. Barnes identifies a number of factors, 'including the actual language and emphasis of the agreement, the practice of the parties, and the object and purpose of the agreement' to be taken into consideration when elucidating the intention of the parties.[66] The 'result of such investigation must reveal a clear and unambiguous intention to create a regime that has *erga omnes* effect and also that is in the general interest'.[67] Furthermore, Subedi argues that it is the intention of the parties to create legal

63 Subedi (n 13) 179. Indeed, in *Reparation for Injuries Suffered in the Service In the United Nations*, the Court held that the United Nations possessed international personality and that personality was of an objective character not limited to the parties to the Charter of the United Nations. The Court stated that '[f]ifty States, representing the vast majority of the members of the international community, had the power, in conformity with international law, to bring into being an entity possessing objective international personality and not merely personality recognized by them alone, together with capacity to bring international claims', ICJ Reports 1949, 185.

64 Barnes (n 14) 131. See also H. Mosler, 'The International Society as a Legal Community' (1974-IV) 150 RdC 11, 235.

65 [1964] YILC, vol. II, 26ff.

66 Barnes (n 14) 132.

67 Ibid.

relations, rather than the form in which such intention is expressed, which is important. If such 'intention can be established, no matter what form may be adopted in expressing that intention, the form used can be regarded as being capable of creating legal relations between States'.[68]

Moreover, for an objective regime to be effective, the parties must demonstrate that they are competent to act in the subject matter area. Competence to act can be understood in terms of strict territorial competence.[69] It can also be understood through the lens of the 'Great Powers' theory, which mandates competence to a group of influential and powerful States to impose their will on other States in the interests of all nations.[70] In order to establish competence on the basis of strict territorial competence, it is necessary that State parties have a territorial competence with regards to the subject matter of the treaty that non-party States do not have.[71] Strict territorial competence has thus far been most commonly relied on to in order to establish competence to create an objective regime.[72]

The second avenue of demonstrating competence to act – the 'Great Powers' theory – is supported by early State practice, including the Peace of Westphalia, the Treaty of Utrecht, and the Treaty of Versailles.[73] The 'Great Powers' theory was discussed by McNair in his separate opinion in the *South West Africa Advisory Opinion*, where he recognised that:

> [f]rom time to time it happens that a group of great Powers, or a large number of States both great and small, assume a power to create by a multi-partite treaty some new international regime or status, which soon acquires a degree of acceptance and durability extending beyond the limits of the actual contracting parties, and giving it an objective existence. This power is used when some public interest is involved, and its exercise often occurs in the course of the peace settlement at the end of a great war.[74]

68 Subedi (n 13) 194–95.

69 Barnes (n 14) 135.

70 Ibid. There is also 'the liberal approach to competence, which turns on the manifestation of actual State interest rather than the formalistic requirement of territorial competence'.

71 Eckart Klein, 'Self -Contained Regime, Oxford Public International Law, https://opil.ouplaw.com/display/10.1093/law:epil/9780199231690/law-9780199231690-e1467?prd=EPIL 21.

72 Barnes (n 14) 135–37.

73 Ibid 136.

74 ICJ Rep. 1950, 132.

For example, through three treaties of 19 April 1839 (one between the UK, Austria, France, Prussia, and Russia on the one hand and the Netherlands on the other, a second between the same five 'Great Powers' and Belgium, and the third between the Netherlands and Belgium), it was agreed that 'Belgium ... shall form an Independent and perpetually Neutral State. It shall be bound to observe such neutrality towards all other States'.[75] A similar provision was incorporated in Article 2 of the 1867 Treaty of London, concluded between the UK, Austria, Belgium, France, Italy, the Netherlands, Prussia, and Russia on the neutralisation of Luxembourg. Under the terms of the treaty, Luxembourg – a non-State party – was bound to observe its neutrality 'towards all other States'.[76] Those are all examples of regimes created by the 'Great Powers' imposing the objective regime as valid *erga omnes* on a third State.[77]

There are, however, some drawbacks with the 'Great Powers' theory. Barnes correctly points out that it 'appears only to pertain to periods of great upheaval, such as the aftermath of a war when the need for political stability is paramount, and so does not properly account for other instances of objective regimes during peace time'.[78] The theory has also not been relied on to 'explain State practice in the period since the end of World War II, suggesting that it may be obsolete'.[79] More concerning, however, is the incompatibility of the theory with the sovereign equality of States. Today, in post-World War II (WWII) time, the 'modern analogy' to the 'Great Powers' theory might rest with the United Nations Security Council (UNSC), which can impose legally binding measures on UN member States on matters of international peace and security, even if a certain State voted against the decision, or abstained from voting.[80]

Lastly, with respect to the last requirement, the 'decisive criterion' for whether an objective regime valid *erga omnes* exists is whether or not a general interest is served.[81] Examples of those general interests include international peace and security, the prohibition on the unlawful use of force,[82] and political

75 For the original analysis, see Subedi (n 13).

76 Edward Hertslet, *Map of Europe by Treaty*, vol. III, (1864–1875).

77 Subedi (n 13) 177.

78 Barnes (n 14) 137.

79 Ibid.

80 As advanced by Subedi (n 13). See UN Charter Articles 25.

81 Klein (n 71) 352.

82 Barnes (n 14) 142. As Barnes recognises, this has 'underpinned numerous demilitarisation and neutrality regimes'. He gives the example of the Committee of Jurists, which 'reasoned that the Treaty of Paris 1856, which placed the Aaland Islands under a regime of permanent neutrality was laid down in European interests. They constituted a special international status, relating to military considerations, for the Aaland Islands. It follows

stability.[83] Furthermore, in *Wimbledon*, the PCIJ seemed to have recognised that rights of navigation, transit and innocent passage meet the criteria of 'general interests'.[84]

In light of the above, it deserves emphasising that objective regimes are different from the rules on treaties providing for rights and/or obligations of third States under the law of treaties and within the broader framework of general public international law. The former are more conventional means of establishing exceptions to the *pacta tertiis* rule in the sense that the consensual paradigm is never departed from; when either establishing an obligation under Article 35 VCLT or a right under Article 36 VCLT, the relevant State's consent and/or assent – respectively – is needed. In contrast, a treaty with *erga omnes* effect, creating an objective regime, can impose duties and obligations on third States even in the absence of their individual consent and without the same obligation parallelly existing under the *corpus* of customary international law. That said, for the very reason that obligations *erga omnes* are 'obligations of a State towards the international community as a whole' which are 'the concern of all States' and for whose protection all states have a 'legal interest',[85] a third State may be viewed as generally agreeing with objective of the *erga omnes* rule in question, but it does not resolve the fact the State has not consented to the third party effects of the treaty in question.

2.2 *The* S.S. **Wimbledon** *and Objective Regimes*

As outlined above, the PCIJ rejected the contention of Germany that it was obliged to deny access to the Kiel Canal owing to its duties towards Russia as

that until these provisions are duly replaced by others, every State has the right to insist upon compliance with them. It also follows that any State in possession of the Islands must conform to the obligations binding upon it, arising out of the system of demilitarisation established by these provisions', see Barnes (n 14) 142.

83 *Certain Phosphate Lands in Nauru* (*Nauru v Australia*) (Preliminary Objection), ICJ Rep. 1992, 240, 251–253.

84 The PCIJ stated that the 'canal has ceased to be an internal and national navigable waterway, the use of which by the vessels of States other than the riparian State is left entirely to the discretion of that State, and that it has become an international waterway intended to provide under treaty guarantee easier access to the Baltic for the benefit of all nations of the world' see *Wimbledon* at 22.

85 *Barcelona Traction, Light and Power Company, Limited* (*Belgium v Spain*) (New Application: 1962) Preliminary Objections (second Phase) (1970) paras 33–34; *Questions relating to the Obligation to Prosecute or Extradite* (*Belgium v Senegal*) (Judgment) ICJ Rep 2012 p. 422; *Application of the Convention on the Prevention and Punishment of the Crime of Genocide* (*The Gambia v Myanmar*) Order of Provisional Measures, 23 January 2020, para 69.

a neutral State in the war. The Court held that the terms of Article 380 were categorical: the Kiel Canal had ceased to be an internal navigable waterway to become an international waterway intended to provide under treaty guarantee easier access to the Baltic for the benefit of all nations of the world. Thus, the Court acknowledged the creation of an objective regime by the authors of the Treaty of Versailles for the benefit of *all* States. Whilst Russia was not a party to the Treaty, the Court treated Article 380 as having effects *erga omnes* and prevailing over German neutrality *vis-a-vis* Russia.[86] The Court also argued that the grant of passage to Wimbledon through the Kiel Canal would not deprive Germany of the exercise of its rights as a neutral State. In this regard, the Court draw parallels to the Suez Canal and Panama Canal, under whose regimes ships carrying contraband had been permitted in many different circumstances to pass freely through the Canals. Such passage had never been regarded by anyone as violating the rules of neutrality.

There are certain limitations to the Court's assessment of the issues involved. Those were recognised and discussed by the dissenting judges. Judge Schücking argued that the right of free passage through the Kiel Canal was a servitude that had to be interpreted restrictively.[87] According to a purely literal construction of Article 380, the servitude was excluded from application only in cases where ships were concerned which belong to nations themselves at war with Germany. Serious doubts, however, arose as to whether Germany, in order to safeguard its interests when placed in the position of a belligerent or neutral, should in fact lose the right to take special measures as regards the Canal as against ships belonging to States other than its enemies.[88]

In this regard, it may indeed be questioned whether the Kiel Canal had been neutralised in the same unambiguous manner as the Suez and Panama Canals. If the Kiel Canal had not been neutralised, it is doubtful whether it constituted an objective regime in the form of an international settlement. To elaborate, according to Article 2 of the 1977 Protocol concerning the Permanent Neutrality and Operation of the Panama Canal provides that the Canal 'shall remain ... open to peaceful transit by the vessels of *all nations on terms of entire equality*'.[89] Article 1 of this Protocol declared the permanent neutralisation of the Canal.

By the Convention of Constantinople of 1888, the relevant States declared that the Suez Canal should 'always be free and open, *in time of war as in time of*

86 Subedi (n 13) 187–88.

87 Dissenting Opinion of Judge Schücking 87.

88 Ibid 89.

89 ILM, vol. 16, 1977, 1022 (emphasis added).

peace, to every vessel of *commerce or of war* without distinction of flag' including even the vessels of countries at war with Turkey, the territorial sovereign (emphasis added). The essential words which were used to provide for the neutralisation of the Suez Canal – to remain open in time of *war as in time of peace* – did not appear in Article 380 of the Treaty of Versailles. Thus, the legal situation of the Suez and Panama Canals is entirely different from that of the Kiel Canal, in that, as regards the former Canals, neutralisation has taken place, whereas such a neutralisation is not established by Article 380 as regards the Kiel Canal.[90]

As Judge Schücking argued, the Canal had therefore been internationalised rather than neutralised.[91] The right to take special measures in times of war or neutrality had not been *expressly* renounced (the provision is to be interpreted restrictively), and such renunciation could not be inferred from the fact that the Canal was to be 'maintained free and open'.[92] Whereas such a restrictive interpretation of the treaty – establishing a servitude – may infringe on the strict literal reading of Article 380, the vital interests of Germany under its servitude should in all circumstances be respected, and the benefiting State must under certain circumstances accept that its rights are temporarily impaired.[93]

Furthermore, some of the defining elements of objective regimes ought to be discussed. As noted above, in order for an objective regime to validly exist, there must be: i) an intention by the parties to create an objective regime; ii) the regime must be territorial; iii) the parties must have a competence in respect of the territory or an interest in the creation of the regime; and iv) the regime must be in the general interest of the international community. Whereas the regime in Article 380 as relating to the Kiel Canal was no doubt territorial, Judge Schücking pointed out that it could not have been the intention underlying the Versailles Peace Treaty to create an objective regime and bind Germany to commit offences against third States like belligerent Russia, which had not participated in that treaty and could thus still expect Germany to fulfil her duties as a neutral towards Russia.[94]

Moreover, whereas the Treaty of Versailles served a general interest of protecting peace and security, the competence of the parties to act can be questioned, at least in light of contemporary international law. The applicants of the *Wimbledon* case could not rely on the strict territorial competence to establish

90 Dissenting Opinion of Judge Schücking 89.
91 Ibid.
92 Ibid.
93 Ibid.
94 Ibid 91.

the objective regime as the Kiel Canal passes through Germany territory only. They did, undoubtedly, act as the 'Great Powers' in drawing up the treaty in the sense that they imposed the regime in a general interest benefitting all States. However, as also noted above, there has been virtually no resort to the 'Great Powers' theory since the end of WWII. As the case took place in the aftermath of WWI, this might at the time have been sufficient to demonstrate their competence to act in the subject matter. Today, however, the practice of the 'Great Powers' appears to be out of use.[95] Instead, the UNSC may be able to play the nineteenth-century role of the 'Great Powers' to impose a territorial settlement in the interests of international peace and security regardless of the consent of the State concerned – Germany in this case – hence creating objective regimes with *erga omnes* effect.[96]

3 Fragmentation of International Law

3.1 *General Remarks*

Fragmentation of international law refers to the process and result of separate legal norms and institutions developing (predominately) independently from one another. It is often instigated in response to specific functional issues by non-identical groupings of States. Furthermore, the proliferation of international and regional courts and tribunals has increased the potential for fragmentation and diversification of international law. This has been accompanied by the emergence of specialised and autonomous rules, legal institutions, and spheres of legal practice on both international and regional levels.

In fact, 'general international law' has now become a system for a multiplicity of specialist areas, such as 'trade law', 'human rights law', 'environmental law', the 'law of the sea', 'European law', 'international criminal law, or 'international refugee law' etc., each possessing its own principles and institutions.[97] The problem involved is that specialised law-making within various institutions tend to ignore developments taking place under the purview of other specialised systems. The result is potential 'conflicts between rules or rule systems, deviating institutional practices and, possibly, the loss of an overall perspective on the law'.[98] Conflict may also take the form of overlapping

95 See further above.
96 On this issue, see generally Subedi (n 13).
97 See further Gerhard Hafner, 'Pros and Cons Ensuing from Fragmentation of International Law' (2004) 25 Michigan Journal of International Law 849.
98 See further S.E. Merry, 'Legal pluralism' (1988) 22(5) Law and Society Review 869.

jurisdiction, triggering questions such as *who* should decide a given dispute in a certain area.[99] Thus, fragmentation:

> engenders losses of legal certainty which is in turn an element of the (global) rule of law. The insecurity is both procedural (relating to jurisdiction and admissibility of complaints) and substantive. Law-users may exploit the fragmentation (and the diverse institutional outlooks going with it) through forum-shopping and regime-shifting, based on the strategic consideration which forum and regime will respond best to their claims based on their parochial interest.[100]

The perhaps most well-known example often cited in support of demonstrating the problems with diversification (and ensuing fragmentation) of international law is the judgment of the Appeals Chamber of the International Criminal Tribunal for Yugoslavia (ICTY) in *Tadić*. The ICTY seemingly interpretated the term 'control' in Article 8 of the ILC Articles on State Responsibility inconsistently with previous case-law of the ICJ. While the *Tadić* tribunal had satisfied itself with an 'overall control' in 1999,[101] the ICJ asked, more exactingly, for 'effective control' in 1986.[102]

If legal principles that emerge in certain fields may be inapplicable in others, the crucial question will be to determine under which regime they should be decided. For instance, as Koskenniemi asks, should the importation of hormone meat 'be understood principally as a trade question, or an environmental (health) question'?[103] In the *Beef Hormones* case, the Appellate Body of the World Trade Organization (WTO) assessed the status of the precautionary principle under treaties covered by the WTO, concluding that irrespective of

99 See Martti Koskenniemi, The Fate of Public International Law: Between Technique and Politics' (2007) 70(1) Modern Law Review 1.

100 Anne Peters, 'The refinement of international law: From fragmentation to regime interaction and politicization' (2017) 15(3) ICON 671, 679.

101 *Prosecutor v Duško Tadić*, Appeals Chamber, Case No. IT-94-1-A (Merits) para 117 (ICTY 15 July 1999).

102 *Case Concerning Military and Paramilitary Activities in and against Nicaragua* (Nicaragua v USA) (Merits) 1986 ICJ Rep. 14 at paras109 and 115 (June 27, 1986); *Case Concerning the Application of the Convention on the Prevention and Punishment of the Crime of Genocide (Bosnia and Herzegovina v Serbia and Montenegro)*, (Judgment) ICJ Rep 2007 p. 43, para 406.

103 Koskenniemi (n 99) 5.

the status of the precautionary principle 'under international environmental law', it was not yet binding for the WTO.[104]

Furthermore, in the *Legality of the Threat or Use of Nuclear Weapons* case, the ICJ recognised that both human rights law[105] and the laws of armed conflict applied 'in times of war'. When making a determination of what legal framework to apply in the context of applying Article 6 of the International Covenant on Civil and Political Rights (prohibiting the arbitrary deprivation of life), this was 'to be determined by the applicable *lex specialis*, namely the law applicable to armed conflict'.[106] The Court was thus reluctant to afford priority to any of the legal regimes, but rather wanted to emphasise that they were equally applicable; only in the case of conflict between them was it necessary to apply the more specific regime.[107] The various reasons informing and impacting the choice of one among equally applicable legal regimes as made between different courts and tribunals has been described by Koskenniemi:

> [t]he choice of one among several applicable legal regimes refers back to what is understood as significant in a problem. And the question of significance refers back to what the relevant institution understands as its mission, its structural bias. If the WTO Appellate Body dealt with hormone beef as a trade (instead of a health) issue, this follows from the fact that it was constitutionally mandated to treat it in that way.[108]

Moreover, the problems caused by fragmentation do not necessarily need to be overstated. For instance, Webb – in her study of the case-law of four courts (the ICJ, the International Criminal Court (ICC), the ICTY, and the International Criminal Tribunal for Rwanda (ICTR)) – identified both areas of divergence and convergence, and ultimately concluded that 'there are few instances of genuine fragmentation in the areas examined. The overall picture is one of genuine integration'.[109] Indeed, courts and tribunals have made used of various interpretative techniques to avoid conflict by harmonising the multiplicity of international rules stemming from different systems and regimes.

104 *Measures Concerning Meat and Meat Products* (Hormones), 13 February 1998, WT/DS26/AB/R,WT/DS48/AB/R, at 123–25.

105 In particular the International Covenant on Civil and Political Rights (ICCPR).

106 *Legality of the Threat or Use of Nuclear Weapons* (Advisory opinion) ICJ Reports 1996, 240, at 25.

107 Ibid.

108 Koskenniemi (n 99) 6.

109 Philippa Webb, *International Judicial Integration and Fragmentation* (OUP 2016) 203.

One example of such interpretive technique is the one of presumption of law-abidingness.[110] The ICJ has for instance recognised that '[i]t is a rule of interpretation that a text emanating from a Government must, in principle, be interpreted as producing and as intended to produce effects in accordance with existing law and not in violation of it'.[111]

Likewise, in *Al-Jedda*, the European Court of Human Rights (ECtHR) established a presumption which leads to the avoidance of any conflict between a State party's obligations under the ECHR and obligations under UNSC Resolutions:

> the Court considers that, in interpreting its resolutions, there must be a presumption that the Security Council does not intend to impose any obligation on Member States to breach fundamental principles of human rights. In the event of any ambiguity in the terms of a Security Council Resolution, the Court must therefore choose the interpretation which is most in harmony with the requirements of the Convention and which avoids any conflict of obligations.[112]

Thus, the ECtHR must presume that a UNSC decision allows member States to implement the decision in a way that is compatible with the ECHR. This presumption is significant in that it entails the inapplicability of Article 103 of the UN Charter,[113] which otherwise stipulates that 'in the event of a conflict between the obligations of the Members of the United Nations under the present Charter and their obligations under any other international agreement, their obligations under the present Charter shall prevail'. As the Grand Chamber of the ECtHR stated in *Al-Dulimi*, the Court 'will in principle conclude that there is no conflict of obligations capable of engaging the primacy rule in Article 103 of the UN Charter'.[114]

Fragmentation may even have some 'positive effects on the rule of law in international relations, and can contribute to inducing States to comply more strictly with international law; States would be more inclined to comply with norms of a regional nature that better reflect the particular political situation of the States in that region'.[115] Peters likewise bids 'farewell to fragmentation' and

---

110 Peters (n 100) 690.

111 *Right of Passage over Indian Territory* (*Portugal v India*) (Preliminary Objections) ICJ Rep 1957, p. 125, 142 For the original analysis, see Peters (n 100) 690–91.

112 *Al-Jedda v UK*, Appl. No. 27021/08 (7 July 2011) para 102.

113 Peters (n 100) 690–92.

114 *Al-Dulimi v Switzerland*, Appl. No. 5809/08 (21 June 2016) para 140; Peters (n 100) 691.

115 Hafner (n 97) 850–51.

concentrates on the positive contribution of the new techniques which courts, tribunals, and other actors have developed in order to coordinate the various subfields of international law.[116] In her view, fragmentation is 'an adequate reaction to modernity and modern complexity of life. Complexity requires differentiated norms and specialised law-appliers who divide labour'.[117] A related benefit is the competitive pressure exercised by fragmentation:

> competition between regimes, organisations, courts, and any other institutions may promote productive exploration and experimentation, enhances creativity, allows for correcting mistakes, reduces the risk of failure of one single institution, and thus overall leads to improved performance, notably to better law-making and law-application. The number of decision-makers, their multiplicity, and their competition and rivalry will normally lead to a denser body of law, which also includes more sophistication, and a further elucidation of fundamental principles underpinning the order.[118]

3.2 *The Work of the International Law Commission*

In 2006, the ILC concluded its work on the question of fragmentation and diversification of international law. Its conclusions made important contributions to the issue of coherency of international law as a *legal system* and the various questions raised by the increasing specialisation and diversification of international law.[119] The ILC concluded that the rules and principles of international law should be interpreted against the background of other rules and principles as there are meaningful relationships between them. Thus, in applying international law, it is often necessary to determine the precise relationship

116 Anne Peters, 'The refinement of international law: From fragmentation to regime interaction and politicization' (2017) 15(3) ICON 671.

117 Ibid 680.

118 Ibid. See also Colin Murray and Aoife O'Donoghue, 'A Path Already Travelled in Domestic Orders? From Fragmentation to Constitutionalisation in the Global Legal Order' (2017) 13 Int'l J.L. Context 1, 4.

119 ILC, *Fragmentation of International Law: Difficulties arising from the Diversification and Expansion of International Law* (2006), adopted by the International Law Commission at its Fifty-eighth session, in 2006, and submitted to the General Assembly as a part of the Commission's report covering the work of that session (A/61/10, para. 251). The report appears in Yearbook of the International Law Commission, 2006, vol. II, Part Two. See also Bruno Simma, Universality of International Law from the Perspective of a Practitioner, 20 EUR. J. Int'L L. 265, 272 (2009).

between two or more rules and principles that are both valid and applicable in respect of a situation.[120]

The Report identified four types of 'collision rules' or relationships that promote harmonisation. The first one is relationships between special and general law. The maxim *lex specialis derogat legi generali* is a generally accepted technique of interpretation and conflict resolution in international law. It suggests that whenever two or more norms deal with the same subject matter, priority should be given to the norm that is more specific. The principle may be applicable in several contexts: between provisions within a single treaty, between provisions within two or more treaties, between a treaty and a non-treaty standard, as well as between two non-treaty standards. The source of the norm (whether treaty, custom or general principle of law) is not decisive for the determination of the more specific standard.[121] A group of rules and principles concerned with a particular subject matter may form a special regime ('self-contained regime') and be applicable as *lex specialis* (this is further addressed below).

The second relationship is between prior and subsequent law, often expressed as the principle of *lex posterior derogate lege priori*. This later-in-time rule cannot claim absolute priority in application, but context remains important. In particular, problems arise when considering the divergences that arise when there is discordance in membership of States to overlapping multilateral treaty regimes.[122] According to Article 30 VCLT, when all the parties to a treaty are also parties to an earlier treaty on the same subject, and the earlier treaty is not suspended or terminated, then it applies only to the extent its provisions are compatible with those of the later treaty. This is an expression of the principle according to which 'later law supersedes earlier law'. The applicability of the *lex posterior* principle is, however, limited. It cannot be automatically extended to the case where the parties to the subsequent treaty are not identical to the parties of the earlier treaty (also recognised in Article 30(4) VCLT).[123]

The third one is the principle of systemic integration. Article 31(3)(c) VCLT provides one means within the framework of the VCLT, requiring the interpreter of a treaty to take into account 'any relevant rules of international law applicable in relations between the parties'.[124] Article 31(3)(c) VCLT thus gives

120 ILC Report (n 119) paras 1–2.

121 Ibid para 5.

122 Ibid para 25.

123 Ibid para 25.

124 For an in-depth analysis and assessment of Article 31(3)(c) VCLT, see Panos Merkouris, *Article 31(3)(c) VCLT and the Principle of Systemic Integration* (Brill Nijhoff 2015).

expression to the principle of 'systemic integration' and deals with the case where material sources external to the treaty are relevant in its interpretation. These may include other treaties, customary rules or general principles of law.[125] In explaining the rationale of the existence of the principle of systemic integration, the Report recognised that all treaty provisions receive their force and validity from general law and set up rights and obligations that exist alongside rights and obligations established by other treaty provisions and rules of customary international law. None of such rights or obligations has any intrinsic priority against the others. The question of their relationship can only be approached through a process of reasoning that makes them appear as parts of some coherent and meaningful whole.[126]

Peters argues that systemic interpretation of international norms is currently the most discussed 'de-fragmentation' technique. In fact, international law-applying bodies have often practiced harmonious interpretation, sometimes without explicit reliance on Article 31(3)(c) VCLT.[127] In the *Oil Platforms* case, the ICJ interpreted Article XX of a bilateral treaty on friendship between the United States (US) and Iran in light of general international law. This led the Court to conclude that the 'measures' referred to in the treaty precluded an unlawful use of force by one party against the other.[128] In *Hassan*, the European Court of Human Rights (ECtHR) 'harmonised' the European Convention on Human Rights (ECHR) with the rules of international humanitarian law in the context of deprivation of liberty in armed conflict. In interpreting Article 5 ECHR in harmony with other rules of international law, the ECtHR concluded that a person may be detained even in the absence of a particular ground permitting deprivation of liberty (although such a specific ground is required by the wording of Article 5 ECHR) under the circumstances allowed for by international humanitarian law.[129]

The fourth and last relationship is rooted in hierarchical relations between norms of international law. The main sources of international law are not in a hierarchical relationship *inter se*. Nevertheless, some rules of international law are more important than other rules and for this reason enjoy a superior

---

125 ILC Report (n 119) paras 17–18.

126 International Law Commission, Fragmentation of International Law: Difficulties Arising from the Diversification and Expansion of International Law – Report of the Study Group of the International Law Commission UN Doc. A/CN.4/L.682 (Apr. 13, 2006), as corrected UN Doc. A/CN.4/L.682/Corr.1 (Aug. 11, 2006) (finalized by Martti Koskenniemi) 208.

127 Peters (n 100) 692.

128 *Case Concerning Oil Platforms (Islamic Republic Iran v US)* (Judgment) ICJ Rep 2003 p. 161 at para 41.

129 *Hassan v UK*, App no 29750/092014 (ECtHR) at para 77.

position or special status in the international legal system. This is sometimes expressed by the designation of some norms as 'fundamental' or as expressive of 'elementary considerations of humanity'. Hierarchical relation may also be recognised by the substance of the rules; a rule of international law may be superior to other rules on account of the importance of its content as well as the universal acceptance of its superiority. This is the case of norms *ius cogens*, which are 'accepted and recognized by the international community of States as a whole from which no derogation is permitted'.[130] Likewise, the concept of *erga omnes* obligations has also been used to refer to treaty obligations that a State owes to all other States parties (obligations *erga omnes partes*) or to non-party States as third-party beneficiaries.[131]

3.3 S.S. Wimbledon*: a First Sign of Fragmentation?*

The *Wimbledon* judgment was issued at a time when the term 'fragmentation' had not yet entered the international legal arena. The PCIJ in its judgment gave significant weight to the explicit wording of Article 380 of the Treaty of Versailles; in fact, too much weight according to the joint dissenting opinion of judges Anzilotti and Huber. They argued that:

> the question to be decided was not whether Germany was in a position to advance, in justification of its refusal to allow the passage through the Kiel Canal of the Wimbledon, a neutral duty taking precedence over the contractual obligation in favour of the shipping of States at peace with Germany, but rather whether the clauses of the Treaty of Versailles relating to the Kiel Canal also applied in the event, of Germany's neutrality, or whether they only contemplated normal circumstances, that is to say, a state of peace, without affecting the rights and duties of neutrality.[132]

At the time when the steamship Wimbledon was refused the right of passage, Poland and Russia were still in a state of war. Germany was therefore still in the position of a neutral.[133] Furthermore, for the purposes of the interpretation of treaties, consideration had to be given to the complexity of interstate relations and the fact that the contracting parties are independent political entities. Though it is true that

130 Conclusions (n 126) paras 32–34; Article 53 VCLT.

131 Ibid para 39.

132 *Wimbledon* (n 1) 66.

133 Ibid 67.

> when the wording of a treaty is clear its literal meaning must be accepted as it stands, without limitation or extension, it is equally true that the words have no value except in so far as they express an idea; but it must not be presumed that the intention was to express an idea which leads to contradictory or impossible consequences or which, in the circumstances, must be regarded as going beyond the intention of the parties.[134]

In this respect, it must be remembered that treaties are generally concluded having regard to normal peace conditions. If, as the result of a war, a neutral or belligerent State is faced with the necessity of taking extraordinary measures temporarily affecting the application of a given treaty in order to protect its neutrality or for the purposes of national defence, it is entitled to do so even if no express reservations are made in the convention.[135] The right of a State to adopt the course which it considers best suited to the exigencies of its security and to the maintenance of its integrity, is so essential a right that treaty stipulations cannot be interpreted as limiting it.[136]

The words 'nations at peace with Germany' by no means necessarily meant that States which were not at war with Germany were entitled to avail themselves in all possible circumstances of the provision of Article 380; it rather meant that a state of peace was the condition upon which the application of these provisions was dependent.[137] The legal status of the Kiel Canal, therefore, resembled that of the internal navigable waterways of international concern. If Germany itself had admitted an obligation to allow the men-of-war of belligerents to pass through the Canal, in spite of its neutrality, it would consequently fail to comply with an essential obligation of every neutral State, namely the duty of prohibiting the passage of belligerent forces through its territory.[138]

There is no question that the phenomenon of fragmentation as we understand it today did not exist at the time of the judgment. Obviously, this part is not a critique of the judgment as in 1923, the phenomenon of fragmentation and systematic integration had not yet developed. A speculative question is whether PCIJ put in motion a first point of development of the phenomenon of fragmentation of international law; undeniably, it interpreted Article 380 of the Treaty of Versailles in a vacuum, distinct and separate from the broader

134 Ibid 68.
135 Ibid 69.
136 Ibid 72.
137 Ibid 76.
138 Ibid 82.

international legal framework, and in particular the rules of neutrality in situations of war. Analysing the judgment from a present-day perspective, the Court could have had recourse to Article 31(3)(c) VCLT and the principle of systemic integration to seek to harmonise the wording of Article 380 of the Treaty of Versailles with the rules of neutrality in international law. However, it may be said that the judges of the PCIJ made an effort to conceptualise neutrality in war by referring to objective regimes.

The present-day approach, i.e. recourse to systemic integration, would have allowed the Court to take material sources external to the Treaty of Versailles and the broader normative environment into consideration when interpreting its provisions so that Article 380 and the Treaty of Versailles could have remained integrated within the legal system as a whole. If having done so, the resulting interpretation – as recognised by dissenting judges Anzilotti and Huber – would be that Germany, in times of peace, would have to allow for passage of all vessels at peace with itself. In times of war, however, Germany ought to have the right to take measures to protect its interests and fulfil its duties as a neutral in the war.

At the same time, the PCIJ also sought to harmonise the meaning and effect of Article 380 with that of other 'neutralisation' provisions in other treaties, such as the provision neutralising the Suez and Panama Canals. That said, as noted above, there are substantial and significant differences between the wording of the treaties laying down objective regimes for the Suez and Panama Canals and Article 380 of the Treaty of Versailles as pertaining to the Kiel Canal. It is questionable whether the Kiel Canal had been neutralised as such, but the more convincing point of view appears to be the one of the internationalisation of the Kiel Canal. Thus, since the Kiel Canal was internationalised rather than neutralised, it could not have been the intention of the drafters of the Treaty of Versailles to deprive Germany of the possibility to fulfil its obligations as a neutral State in the war between Russia and Poland. It therefore appears that the attempted 'harmonisation' between the three regimes of the Kiel, Panama and Suez Canals was unsatisfactory and inherently difficult; the regimes were clearly construed entirely differently, whereby differentiation – 'fragmentation' of 'neutralisation' provisions if one wants – was not only appropriate but also legally convincing.

4 The Question of Self-Contained Regimes

The question of legal nature of self-contained regimes, including their architecture, characteristics and the position in general international law, has been a subject of an in-depth analysis and debate by the ILC and international law scholars.[139] The authors of this chapter will not endeavour to engage in a detailed debate on well-known general questions concerning self-contained regimes, but rather focus on the PCIJ's approach to self-contained regime in the *Wimbledon* case and the journey of this notion from the past to the present. A short analysis will be presented concerning general questions of self-contained regimes, as a background and the scene setting for the approach adopted in the *Wimbledon* case. In this case for the first time in international law the term 'self-contained' regime was used.

The Applicants had challenged the German authorities' right of the refusal of the access to the Kiel Canal and argued that a right to free access is bestowed by Article 380 of Treaty of Versailles Treaty regarding international waterways. In this respect, the PCIJ has made the following statement:

> the provisions relating to the Kiel Canal in the Treaty of Versailles are therefore self-contained; if they had to be supplemented and interpreted by the aid of those referring to the inland navigable waterways of Germany in the previous Sections of Part XII, they would lose their '*raison d'être*' … The idea which underlies Article 380 and the following articles of the Treaty is not to be sought by drawing an analogy from these provisions but rather by arguing *a contrario*, a method of argument which excludes them.[140]

In this case, the Court applied the notion of 'self-contained regimes' to settle the problem of treaty interpretation between two sets of primary international obligations;[141] or in other words 'to determine the relationship between conflicting treaty provisions, ie to resolve clash of primary obligations'.[142]

The Court interpreted the provisions of the of the Treaty of Versailles and in order to analyse the legal obligations of Germany in relation to navigational

139 See e.g. Bruno Simma, 'Self-Contained Regimes' (1985) XVI *The Netherlands Yearbook of International Law* 111; *ibid* with Dirk Pulkowski, 'Of Planets and the Universe: Self - Contained Regimes in International Law', (2006) 17 *EJIL* 483; Anja Lindroos and Michael Mehling, 'Dispelling the Chimera of "Self-Contained Regimes" in International Law and the WTO (2005) 16 *EJIL* 857; Fragmentation of International Law: Difficulties Arising from the Diversification and Expansion of International Law. Report of the Study Group of the International Commission, Finalised by Martti Koskenniemi, Erik Castrén Institute of International Law and Human Rights, 2007; Klein (n 71).

140 *Wimbledon* case (n 1) p. 8.

141 Simma and Pulkowski (n 139) 491.

142 Klein (n 71) para. 4.

rights through the Kiel Canal. The main points of reasoning of the Court were as follows. The Court held that that Article 380 of the Treaty has intentionally deprived the Kiel Canal of the status of internal waters in relation to navigational rights of ships of all States which are not in a belligerent position *vis-à-vis* Germany. The Court reasoned that:

> the terms of article 380 are categorical and give rise to no doubt. It follows that the canal has ceased to be an internaı and national navigable waterway, the use of which by the vessels of states other than the riparian state is left entirely to the discretion of that state, and that it has become an international waterway intended to provide under treaty guarantee easier access to the Baltic for the benefit of alı nations of the world. Under its new régime, the Kiel Canal must be open, on a footing of equality, to alı vessels, without making any distinction between war vessels and vessels of commerce, but on one express condition, namely, that these vessels must belong to nations at peace with Germany.[143]

The Court thus acknowledged that Article 380 of the Treaty of Versailles was a provision limiting Germany's exercise of sovereign rights in respect to Canal, which is a sufficient reason to apply restrictive interpretation, in case of doubt, due to the clause which incorporates such a limitation. The Court stated that it 'felt obliged to stop at the point where the so-called restrictive interpretation would be contrary to the plain terms of the article and would destroy what has been clearly granted'.[144]

The oral argument presented by Germany interpreting the language of Article 380 in a narrower way was not addressed by the Judgment.[145] The Court's interpretation of the rights and duties of Germany regarding the Kiel Canal was hinged on the following reasoning: i) that no obligation of Germany as a neutral would have been compromised by allowing the Wimbledon to have access to the Kiel Canal; and ii) that the German Government at the time of the Wimbledon incident its right to close the Canal to war ships of belligerents at peace with Germany.[146] The reasoning of the Court was subject to robust critique by Judges Anzilotti and Huber in their Dissenting Opinions. The gist of their dissent is based on the premise that regulation of the navigation through

143 *Wimbledon* case (n 1) p.22. See also Charles Cheney Hyde, 'The Interpretation of Treaties by the Permanent Court of International Justice' (1930) 24 *AJIL* 1.

144 *Wimbledon* case (n 1) 24–25.

145 Hyde (n 143) 2.

146 Ibid.

the Kiel Canal, as set out in Article 380, should be interested as relating to the situation of normal circumstances, which is the state of peace, without affecting the rules of neutrality.[147] Treaty interpretation requires that complex relations between the States must be accounted for and the most importantly they have argued that the textual interpretation is very valid and should be accepted as it stands, it is equally important to emphasise that words have no value, except when they reflect an idea,

> but it must not be presumed that the intention was to express an idea which leads to contradictory or impossible consequences or which, in the circumstances, must be regarded as going beyond the intention of the parties. The purely grammatical interpretation of every contract, and more especially of international treaties, must stop at this point.[148]

The Dissenting Judges expressed the view that in case of engagements affecting the rights of States 'could never be assumed' and that such an essential right should not be interpreted in a limitative manner, even if such an interpretation would not be in conflict with the textual interpretation.[149] They compared the legal status of the Suez and Panama Canals, which leave open a maritime waterway in time of war, they had taken care to ensure respect for it during that period as being a matter of supreme importance.[150] The view contesting a limitative interpretation of Article 380 was also expressed by Judge Schücking.[151] He argued that the right to free passage through the Kiel Canal undoubtedly assumes the form of a servitude. Treaties concerning servitudes must be interpreted restrictively as an exceptional right set out upon the territory of a foreign State and should limit as little as possible the sovereignty of that State. He had doubts as to whether Germany, in order to safeguard its interests, when placed in the position of a belligerent or neutral, should in fact, under Article 380, lose the right to take special measures as regards the canal, not provided for under Article 381, paragraph 2, also as against ships belonging to States other than her enemies.[152]

In the view of Judges Anzilotti and Huber, the omission of such a provision in relation to the Kiel Canal further proved that the Treaty of Versailles was not

147 Ibid and Dissenting Opinion of Judges Anzilotti and Huber, p. 35.
148 Dissenting Opinion, p. 36.
149 Ibid p. 38.
150 Ibid p. 40.
151 Judge Schücking, Dissenting Opinion, p. 44.
152 Ibid 44.

intended to institute a regime similar to that established by the conventions relating to the Suez and Panama Canals. Thus, the status of the Kiel Canal was rather to resemble 'that of internal navigable waterways of international concern'.[153] In conclusion it may be said that both Dissenting Judges, in contrast to the majority, were of the view that the plain meaning of the Article 380 (which they did not contest) should be subordinated to particular circumstances of the case. Hyde has summed up this debate as follows:

> The latter [the Dissenting Judges] felt it to be inconceivable that the contracting parties would have agreed to establish a war-time regime for the Kiel Canal restricting the freedom of the territorial sovereign without specific provisions declaratory of such an understanding. The majority was, however, of opinion that the language of the text pointe to such a design which should not, therefore, be frustrated by an argument based upon the scope and nature of the sacrifice which full respect for the language would entail.[154]

It may be noted that in the case of *Exchange of Turkish and Greek Population,* the PCIJ held that in order to interpret certain notions used in a treaty, it was not mandatory to refer to external sources. It said as follows: '[e]verything therefore seems to indicate that, in regard to this point, the Convention is self-contained'. The Court further stated, similar to the *Wimbledon* case, that the natural meaning of words should be relied on.[155]

The contemporary analysis of the notion of the self-contained regimes by the PCIJ in the *Wimbledon* case is hinged on the premise of the Court applying this concept in order to resolve treaty interpretation concerning the relationship between two sets of primary international obligations.[156] Further it was observed that the first 'classical' notion of self-contained regimes, was defined as 'a set of treaty rules, which cannot be complemented by the way of other rules by analogy'.[157] The legal journey of the notion of the self-contained regimes has departed from its formulation and understanding by the PCIJ. The main focus of this section is on the work of the ILC in relation to this subject. The relevant case-law has been analysed in many publications

153 Dissenting Judges Anzilotti and Huber p. 40.

154 Hyde (n 143) 4.

155 *Exchange of Turkish and Greek Population,* Advisory Opinion, PCIJ Series B, No. 10 (1925), p. 20.

156 Simma and Pulkowski (n 139) 491.

157 Ibid 492.

and largely conforms to and confirms the ILC approach. It suffices to say that the *Hostages* case stoked a renewed interest in autonomous regimes of international law.[158]

Firstly, the main and most fundamental difference in the analytical approaches to self- contained regimes between the *Wimbledon* case and its contemporary notion is that, in broad brushstrokes, at present self-contained regimes belong to the paradigm of secondary rules of international law, i.e., that of State responsibility, as contrasted with their PCIJ's understanding as a method of resolving conflict between two sets of primary rules.

The work of the ILC on the topic of self-contained regimes and in this context the fragmentation of international law is very well documented. We present the main legal contours of the debate. It must be said from the outset that the ILC's approach to self-contained regimes within the realm of State responsibility is far from clear and rather complex. There are at present several questions, which are not entirely resolved; or approach to which lacks the uniformity in the scholarship of international law, such e.g., as the relationship between self-contained regimes and general international law; 'the of the *lex specialis* maxim as a tool for networking "traditional" international law and "new" subsystems of international law'.[159]

As succinctly stated by Simma and Pulkowski on the approaches of the ILC to self-contained regimes:

> The International Law Commission's stand with regard to the existence of so-called self-contained regimes concerning state responsibility has varied with each special rapporteur taking up the subject of legal consequences of internationally wrongful acts. In a nutshell, the ILC first appeared to embrace the concept of self-contained subsystems (Riphagen), then became highly critical of the systematic feasibility of such isolation from state responsibility (Arangio-Ruiz), and finally adopted the position of pragmatic 'maybe' (Crawford).[160]

The approach of the Special Rapporteur Riphagen was based on a premise that international law is not constituted by one system but consists of a variety of the nexus of interrelated subsystems, in which there is a close nexus of primary

158 *United States Diplomatic and Consular Staff in Tehran, ICJ Reports 1980* p. 3, at 38.
159 Simma and Pulkowski (n 139) 485.
160 Ibid p. 493.

and secondary norms.[161] Riphagen's concept of subsystems was very complex and not always unambiguous. In broad brushstrokes a system consisted of a comprehensive set of various rules which constituted a close regime in a separate area of factual relationships. The subsystems are concepts which are not characterised by the same degree of singularity as systems. One of the most complex tenets of Riphagen's theory was an interrelationship between systems and subsystems and between subsystems.[162]

Special Rapporteur Arangio-Ruiz analysed the question of the applicability of countermeasures within the context of self-contained regimes under general international law. He was of the view in principle the resort to countermeasures in the situation of closed subsystems is possible but should be an exception and subject to the condition of the proportionality.[163] Finally, last Special Rapporteur James Crawford passed the question of self-contained regimes onto the Working Group on Fragmentation of International Law. However, the ILC introduced Article 55 of the ILC 2001 Articles on State Responsibility (ASR).[164] Article 55 (*Lex specialis*) reads as follows: 'These articles do not apply where and to the extent that the conditions for the existence of an internationally wrongful act or the content or implementation of the international responsibility of a State are governed by special rules of international law'. According to the ILC Commentary to Article 55, it refers to both 'strong' form of *lex specialis*, including self-contained regimes, as well as 'weaker' form i.e., specific treaty provisions on a single point, for example, such as excluding restitution.[165] Article 55 has been a subject of an analysis by Simma and Pulkowski in relation to a debate concerning international law as a unified legal system and to a certain degree a hierarchical legal order.[166]

In view of the present authors, the most interesting contribution of the Working Group (WG) to the understanding of self-contained regimes was its analysis of the relationship between them and general international law, an approach which is broader than approaching them within the paradigm of

161 Willem Riphagen, 'Third Report on the Content, Forms and Degrees of International Responsibility (Part 2 of the Draft Articles) by Special Rapporteur (1982) vol II, part I *YBILC*, 28.

162 Draft Articles by the Special Rapporteur (1982) vol I *YBILC* 202.

163 Gaetano Arangio-Ruiz,' Fourth Report on State Responsibility' *YBILC* (1992) vol II, part One, pp. 76–77.

164 Draft articles on Responsibility of States for Internationally Wrongful Acts, with commentaries, Text adopted by the International Law Commission at its fifty-third session, in2001, and submitted to the General Assembly (A/56/10).

165 Ibid, p. 140.

166 Simma and Pulkowski (n 139) 495 *et seq.*

State responsibility. The WG identified three instances of limitations (apart from the norms of *ius cogens*), which should be considered:

(i) The regime may not deviate from the law for benefits of third parties (including individuals and non-state entities);
(ii) It may not deviate from general international law if the obligation has an integral or interdependent nature, is of a character of the *erga omens* nature or there are legitimate expectations of non-derogation established in practice;
(iii) The regime may not derogate from treaties of a public law nature or are a constituent instrument of an international organisation.[167]

The WG reached the following general conclusions. The rationale behind self-contained regimes is the same as of *lex specialis*, i.e. they a better suited to reflect singularities of a particular regime than general international law (with an exception of *ius cogens* norms). However, there is no absolutely isolated self-contained regime. General international law has at least two fundamental functions in relation to these regimes. It provides a normative background in case of the lack of relevant mechanism in a self-contained regime and; it operates as a rescue mechanism in case of a failure of a regime to function properly. Finally, the term of a self-contained regime is, according to a WG a misnomer. There is no legal regime exiting in absolute isolation from general international law. A regime can only receive legally binding force (or the lack thereof) only by reference to valid and binding rules outside it.[168]

In conclusion of the section, may be said that the notion of self-contained regimes used by the PCIJ in the *Wimbledon* case is different from the contemporary usage. It was limited to an interpretation of conventional rules (primary rules), which had a priority over any external ones and at the same time serving as a tool of conflict resolution. The work of the ILC, the relevant case-law and the scholarly input have contributed linking of these regimes to State responsibility and analysing their relationship with general international law. However, we also should note that it was the *Wimbledon* case, which introduced this institution to international law and provided a fertile ground for its further development.

167 Working Group report (n 139) p. 83.
168 Ibid, pp. 99–100.

5 Conclusion

It may be said that the PCIJ in *Wimbledon* case in the areas analysed in this Chapter was a precursor or even a visionary in setting up the scene for the further development and the consolidation of international law. By the introduction of ideas of the objective regimes, it has paved the way for the emergence of international law institutions which are of an *erga omnes* character. The objective regimes have become a fertile ground for the debate on the differences between them and the rule *pacta tertiies*. As is above illustrated, problems of objective regimes and self -contained regimes (and their relation to general international law) have retained their importance for a contemporary and robust discussion by international law scholars.

The fragmentation of international law is a current phenomenon, and it would perhaps be an exaggeration to imply that the Judges of the PCIJ were already aware of it. However, it may be noted that the PCIJ has taken into consideration a broader normative environment into consideration when interpreting provisions of Article 380 of the Treaty of Versailles. It can thus be inferred that this case may have given rise to the development of international law, in particular of the so-called principle of systemic integration, which is codified in Article 3(1) (c) of the 1969 VCLT and which has played a pivotal role in the debate on fragmentation of international law within the ILC. Obviously, some institutions from this period are only of historical (nostalgic) value such as so -called 'Great Powers'. However, the overall conclusion is that it is difficult to overstate the continuing importance and inspiration of the *Wimbledon* case, which is clearly illustrated by this chapter.

CHAPTER 5

The *Wimbledon* Statement on State Sovereignty, and the Relationships between International and National Law: Then and Now

Władysław Czapliński

1 Introduction

The facts of the case decided by the World Court in its first judgment are well known and we only quote those that are directly relevant to our contribution. In March 1921, the vessel S.S. *Wimbledon* was chartered by a French shipowner. *Wimbledon*, with its cargo of ammunition and other military equipment, was not allowed to pass through the Canal by the German administration of the Kiel Canal. The basis for the refusal was the German declaration of neutrality and the implementing regulations of 25 July and 30 July 1920 on neutrality in the Polish–Soviet war, which prohibited the transit of military materials. According to the German government, Article 380 of the Peace Treaty, relating to freedom of passage through the Canal, could not constitute an obstacle to the application of the regulations to the Kiel Canal. The stance of the German authorities led to a transport delay of 13 days. The Court declared the lawsuit of four States (France, Great Britain, Italy and Japan) against Germany admissible.

From a substantive point of view, the key issue was whether Germany could invoke the declaration of neutrality in the Polish–Soviet war and the corresponding domestic acts to justify the failure to fulfill Germany's obligations under the Treaty of Versailles. The question posed in this way required the PCIJ to consider the importance of State sovereignty for the State's international obligations. In the early years of the Court's operation, the issue of sovereignty appeared in subsequent judgments, starting with the advisory opinions on the *Nationality decrees in Tunisia and Morocco*, and in *ILO* cases. The *Wimbledon* judgment had in fact a creative impact on the *Nationality decrees* opinion. Advisory Opinion No. 4 of 23 February 1923 on the decrees regulating nationality in Tunisia and Morocco, concerned the power of France to extend French nationality to all persons falling within the personal scope of the decrees issued in the protectorates of Tunisia and Morocco. Great Britain protested against the granting of French nationality to British subjects. The French government argued that the legal regulation of citizenship was an exclusive

 | DOI:10.1163/9789004707979_007

internal competence of the State, and therefore France allegedly enjoyed an unrestricted freedom of action in this matter. The Court emphasized that in its view the expression 'solely within the domestic jurisdiction', *'d'ordre intérieur'* and *'à la compétence exclusive'* had to be regarded in this case as having the same meaning.[1] In fact these terminological issues were of secondary importance and the substance of the case was decisive for the resolution.

As to the scope of State sovereignty (or exclusive regulatory competence of the State), the Court stated[2] that it is neither absolute nor unlimited, and its limits are defined by international law. It pointed out *expressis verbis* that international law must be understood as both general customary law and special treaty law. We shall not go here into terminological issues, especially the meaning of the concept of general international law, even though it seems to be important from the point of view of the Respondent's constitutional law. We will only assume that a State's freedom of action is limited by its international obligations under international law. As emphasized by the PCIJ, it is up to each State to assess whether a specific matter falls within its exclusive internal competence. This principle is still valid today. In accordance with the arbitral award in the *Air service agreement of 27 March 1946 between the USA and France* case,[3] in the absence of centralized agencies with mandatory jurisdiction in international relations, each State assesses its own legal situation and takes such actions as it considers appropriate to protect its rights. The Court's view is fully justified. The Hague judges also emphasized that the scope of domestic jurisdiction of a State is an essentially relative question; it depends upon the development of international relations. The freedom of action by the State (including the domestic law-making) depends on the obligations undertaken by the State in relation to other international subjects.

In the advisory opinion No. 2, the PCIJ, commenting on the ILO's competence to deal with agricultural workers, recalled that even if the organization's powers derive from the sovereign power of the Member States and therefore cannot be extended through interpretation, such an approach is secondary to the ILO Constitution, the wording of which must be treated as decisive.[4]

1 The PCIJ stated: 'The Court is, however, of opinion that these differences are of no juridical importance', *Nationality Decrees in Tunisia and Morocco*, Advisory Opinion, PCIJ Publ., [1923] Series B, No.4, at 22.

2 Ibid, at 23.

3 *Air service agreement of 27 March 1946 between the USA and France*, 9 December 1978, RIAA vol.18, at 417.

4 *Competence of the ILO in regard to International Regulation of the Conditions of the Labour of Persons Employed in Agriculture*, Advisory Opinion, PCIJ Publ., [1923] Series B, No. 2, at 23.

2 State Sovereignty and the *Wimbledon* Judgment

In the context of the *Wimbledon* case, the Court was given the opportunity to comment on the concept of State sovereignty in a contentious proceeding, which is of higher authority than an advisory one. The culmination of the deliberations was, of course, the subsequent judgment in the *Lotus* case. In fact, all considerations of the World Court came down to resolving the so-called sovereignty dilemma. This question concerns the mutual relationship between sovereignty as a certain status of the State, meaning that the State is not subject to any restrictions in its actions, and the international obligations of that State, which could in some way impose restrictions on the State's actions in relations with other subjects of international law.

The discussed judgment deals with two aspects of State sovereignty, which the Court seemed to deliberately not differentiate. On the one hand, it refers to political sovereignty, which can be considered as one of the four elements of the definition of a state formulated in the 1933 Montevideo Convention on Rights and Duties of States.[5] On the other hand, there arises the problem of territorial sovereignty, i.e. an exclusive regulatory competence of legal relations within the State territory. In the *Wimbledon* case, there is an additional aspect of territorial sovereignty, namely, whether and to what extent the obligations arising from the Treaty of Versailles influenced the legal status of the Kiel Canal and, in particular, imposed restrictions on the freedom of German legislation.

Sovereignty was reflected in one of the most frequently cited passages of the judgment, according to which the conclusion of an international agreement cannot be treated as a limitation of State sovereignty, but on the contrary – it is an expression of this sovereignty. Therefore, the right of entering into international engagements is, according to the Court, an attribute of State sovereignty. Was this position innovative under international law of that time?[6]

5 *1933 Convention on Rights and Duties of States*, 165 *LNTS* 19.

6 We disagree with the view proposed by Jan Klabbers, 'Clinching the Concept of Sovereignty: the Wimbledon Redux', *Austrian Review of International and European Law* 3 (1998) 345, at 356, that on the eve of the *Wimbledon* judgment, the concept of absolute sovereignty dominated, especially since even in the short practice of the Court (opinion on nationality decrees) the view of limiting the freedom of states to make treaties was expressed. The passage of the judgement concerning the right to conclude treaties as a consequence of state sovereignty was confirmed in judicial practice, including the advisory opinion on *Exchange of Greek and Turkish Populations* (PCIJ, Series B, No. 14, p. 36 [1923]) and arbitral award in *Krouprius Gustaf Adolf* case (arbitrator E. Borel, 18 July 1932, RIAA, vol. 2, s. 1254). The said opinion read in para 55 that [T]he principal reason why the Turkish Delegation has maintained the theory of an implicit reference to local legislation appears to be that, in their opinion, a contrary

To respond this question, the starting point for our discussion is to address meanings of the concept of State sovereignty in the time when the *Wimbledon* judgment was issued. Majority[7] of learned writers raised the issue of sovereignty in the context of the concept of the State (contrasting sovereign States as full members of the international community with entities close to States or non-sovereign or partially sovereign States) and the rights and obligations of States. E.g. J. Bluntschli[8] defined sovereignty as the independence of a State from any foreign State. It consists of the freedom to adopt or issue of acts of will in relations with other States and – in domestic relations – the right to adopt a constitution. Bluntschli accepted the concept of international servitudes, but did not consider them as limitations on sovereignty, although they limited the competences of the State.

F.L. Oppenheim[9] when defining the State, started from the concept of legal personality under the law of nations. Every State that recognizes the binding force of this law belongs to the category of civilized States, is a member of the Family of Nations, and has an international personality. Only sovereign States are entities, although they can be full and not-full sovereign States. According to him, the State must meet four conditions. There must, first, be a *people*, secondly, a *country* in which the people has settled down, thirdly, a *government,* and fourthly and lastly, a *Government should be Sovereign*. Sovereignty is supreme authority which is independent of any other earthly authority. Sovereignty in the strict and narrowest sense of the term includes, therefore, independence within and outside the borders of the State. Probably no other international legal concept is more controversial There can be no limitation or restriction of independence, for it is a recognized principle that independence must be absolute and inalienable. As Oppenheim argued, every State

solution would involve consequences affecting Turkey's sovereign rights. But, as the Court has already had occasion to point out in its judgment in the case of the Wimbledon, "the right of entering into international engagements is an attribute of State sovereignty . In the present case, moreover, the obligations of the contracting States are absolutely equal and reciprocal. It is therefore impossible to admit that a convention which creates obligations of this kind, construed according to its natural meaning, infringes the sovereign rights of the High Contracting Parties. It therefore referred directly to the Wimbledon case. The award quoted above stated that [t]he very existence of the [said] provisions is a manifestation of the sovereign will of the Powers which have deemed it convenient to stipulate the said provisions and to accept them as governing their mutual relations. We are unable to identify a corresponding reasoning in the juydicial practice preceding the Wimbledon judgement.

7 Though Dioniso Anzilotti in his *Cours de droit international*, translated by G. Gidel, Paris 1929, never referred in his manual to the notion of sovereignty.

8 J. Bluntschli, *Droit international codifié*, translated by C. Lardy, Paris 1874, at 85.

9 L. Oppenheim, *International Law. A Treatise*, vol.1 *Peace*, 2nd ed., London 1912, para 64, at 109.

voluntarily accepts either formally by treaty or tacitly by practice, many conditions which restrain it in the exercise of its powers. The independence of the State is not thereby violated, since the restraint is exercised by the State itself, and is not an act of external control. The number of these restraints which States voluntarily assume is continually increasing, owing to the closer relations of humanity. The exercise of the right of independence involves the privilege of making treaties, alliances, contracts, and municipal laws, so far as these do not violate international law or the right of independence as possessed by other States. The international rights of a State are in general closely related to the right of independence. The right of independence is strictly connected with the correlative obligation of non-intervention, *i.e.* of refraining from all acts that would forcibly limit the freedom of another State. The freedom of treaty-making by the sovereign State is restricted by 'immoral obligations and illegal obligations', i.e. obligations which are contrary to universally recognised principles of international law.[10] These restrictions are of customary nature.

W.E. Hall[11] also believed that State sovereignty means the freedom of action, but it is limited by the rights and obligations of other States. Moreover, international agreements inconsistent with the fundamental principles of international law, agreements on the division of the State or the appropriation of the high sea can be invalidated. Treaties are not binding if they are incompatible with the general obligations of States, if there is a change in undisputed law or if they are immoral. A State may enter into agreements on a limitation of its independence or on merger with another State, but such waiver must be express. The limit of treaty-making freedom is self-preservation.

G. Grafton Wilson and G. Fox Tucker[12] defined a State as an unity, which, first, must be political (i.e., organized for public ends as understood in the family of nations and not for private ends as in the case of a commercial company, a band of pirates, or a religious organization), and, second, must possess sovereignty, i.e., supreme political power beyond and above which there is no political power. It is not inconsistent with sovereignty, that a State should voluntarily take upon itself obligations to other States, even though the obligations be assumed under stress of war, or fear of evil. The most fundamental right of a State is the right to exist as a sovereign political unity. General rights of independence, equality, jurisdiction, property, and intercourse are based on that right, and they imply also certain obligations connected with the exercise of these rights. Independence from the point of view of international law is a

10 Ibid, paras 505–506, at 550.

11 W.E. Hall, *International Law. A Treatise*, Oxford 1890, at 50.

12 G.G. Wilson and G. Fox Tucker, *International Law*, New York-Boston-Chicago 1901, at 31.

crucial element of statehood, and it should be understood as a freedom from external political control. While not all States possessing such freedom may be admitted to the family of States, yet in order that a State may be admitted, it is essential that it must be considered as independent. The recognition of a State implies the recognition of its independence. It is a recognized principle that independence must be absolute and inalienable. In fact, every State voluntarily accepts either formally by treaty or tacitly by practice, many conditions which restrict the exercise of its powers. The independence of the State is not thereby violated, since the restraint is exercised by the State itself, and is not an act of external control. The exercise of the right of independence involves the privilege of making treaties, alliances, contracts, and municipal laws, so far as these do not violate international law or the right of independence as possessed by other States.

T.J. Lawrence and P.H. Winfield[13] considered sovereignty from the point of view of a State, which possesses not only internal sovereignty, or the power of dealing with domestic affairs, but also external sovereignty, or the power of dealing with foreign affairs. The fundamental aspect of sovereignty is non-intervention and an important discussion was devoted to different forms of intervention. Effects of independence are defined as the right of a State to manage all its affairs, whether external or internal, without control from other States. According to Lawrence and Winfield, this right of independent action is the natural result of sovereignty. When a State is entirely its own master, it is sovereign from its own perspective, and independent from the point of view of the others. Independence is, therefore, predicated by modern international law of all the sovereign States who are its subjects. Even in the case of fully sovereign States, and in regard to the conduct of the most powerful among them, restrictions upon unlimited freedom of action are imposed temporarily by events and circumstances; but since they are not permanent legal incidents of the political existence of the communities subjected to them, but are in the main necessary conditions of social life imposed by the good sense of the powers concerned, they do not detract from the independence and sovereignty of the States that live under them. They often spring from treaty stipulations entered into voluntarily by governments to avoid difficulties in their future intercourse. Another source of self-imposed restrictions upon the freedom of action granted by the right of independence is to be found in consideration for the corresponding right of other States. Just as in the society formed by

13 T.J. Lawrence and P.H. Winfield, *The Principles of International Law*, London 1927, at 48, 115ff.

individuals, friendly intercourse would be impossible, if each insisted upon using the full freedom secured to him by law without regard to the feelings and convenience of his neighbors, so in the society of nations a similar abstinence is necessary, if peace and harmony are to be preserved. Mutual concession is the price paid for social life. Sometimes an independent State finds itself obliged to submit for a while to restraints imposed upon it by superior force. Such limited and temporary restraints upon the freedom of action of a State are not held to derogate from its independence.

According to C. Calvo,[14] sovereignty is defined separately for every independent State. If the State renounces its treaty-making power, it cannot be considered sovereign and it is not a member of the Great Family of Nations (*grande famille des nations*).

The most characteristic statement on the relationship between sovereignty and international obligations of the State can be probably found in a treatise by H. Bonfils, as edited by P. Fauchille:[15]

> Le droit à l'indépendance est en lui-même inaliénable. Sa dispartition complète entrainerait l'extinction de l'Etat, la suppression de sa personalité. La disparition partielle ou l'amoindrissement ferait de l'Etat, précédemment souverain, un vassal ou un protégé. Mais si le droit à l'indépendance est inaliénable, son exercise peut se produire sous de formes variées, qui, pour un oeuil inattentif, ont l'apparence de restrictions. Toute communauté implique des concessions faites par chacun des membres dans l'intérêt commun. Plus la communauté se resserre et se fortifie, plus les concessions réciproque croissent, et en nombre, et en intensité. L'indépendance des Etats paraît ainsi restreinte sur des points spéciaux, dont le nombre va sans cesse s'acroissant par les traités, qui créent entre les Etats des obligations. Mais ne nous y trompons pas. L'indépendance de l'Etat, restreinte ainsi en certaines applications, n'est pas atteinte in se: tout au contraire. Elle s'affirme par la conclusion même des traités. La manifestation de volonté, contenue dans un traité, est l'application la plus formelle du droit à l'indépendance.

Similar idea was proposed by Lassa Oppenheim. According to him, there can be no limitation or restriction of independence, for it is a recognized principle that independence must be absolute and inalienable. In fact, every State

14 C. Calvo *Le droit international théorique et pratique*, t.1, Patris 1880, at 264.

15 H. Bonfils, *Manuel de droit international public* (*droit de gens*), 4th ed., edited by P. Fauchille, Paris 1905, para 269, at 140.

voluntarily accepts either formally by treaty or tacitly by practice, many conditions which restrain it in the exercise of its powers. The independence of the State is not thereby violated, since the restraint is exercised by the State itself, and is not an act of external control. Oppenheim clearly linked the treaty making power of the State with sovereignty. He claimed that

> [t]he so-called right of making treaties is not a right of a State in the technical meaning of the term, but a mere competence attaching to sovereignty. A State possesses, therefore, treating-making power only so far as it is sovereign. Full-Sovereign States may become parties to treaties of all kinds, being regularly competent to make treaties on whatever matters they please. Not-full Sovereign States, however, can become parties to such treaties only according to their competence to conclude. It is impossible to lay down a hard-and-fast rule concerning such competence of all not-full Sovereign States. Everything depends upon the special case.[16]

Anticipating the case law of the PCIJ, we can conclude that a well-established principle arising from international law is *obligationes sunt servandae*, which requires the performance of international obligations in good faith.[17] This principle is, of course, also valid in the context of contemporary international law, even if the *Vienna Convention on the Law of Treaties* contains only two provisions regarding the implementation of international agreements, which should be superior to constitutional regulations. They usually concern two things: the way of introducing international law into domestic law, and the place of law international in the system of sources of domestic law. In the context of the *Wimbledon* proceedings it is necessary to present a position of international law in the German constitutional order.

3 International Law and the German Legal Order

One of the basic arguments put forward by the applicants in the proceedings before the Hague Court was Germany's reference to acts of municipal law of relatively low rank, regulating the position of the German State and the rights and obligations of individuals. This claim was raised in their memorial by the States initiating proceedings before the Court. They indicated that Germany

16 Oppenheim (n 9) para. 494, at 544–5.

17 This principle appeared in the subsequent PCIJ's case law, although it was actually initiated by the *Wimbledon* judgment.

subordinated its international obligations to low-level regulations: the orders 25 and 30 July 1920, which determined the conduct of the German government (state) in the Russian–Polish armed conflict.[18] The Court therefore asked whether Germany could have invoked the regulations of July 1920 in order to prevent the S.S. *Wimbledon* from entering the Kiel Canal, despite the clear and categorical wording of Article 380 of the Treaty of Versailles.

Our considerations deal mostly with international law, but we should also present regulations concerning a relationship between international law and the German law. Determining the principles of binding a State to international law, and in particular the procedures for binding a state to international law and the place of international law in the legal order of a State, is the matter of constitutional law. The latter issue is of secondary importance in the context of the *Wimbledon* case; we concentrate upon rules of application of international law in the German legal order.

Contrary to the Constitution of the German Reich of 1871, the Constitution of the Weimar Republic of 11 August 1919 regulated the relationship between international law and municipal law. According to Article 4, *allgemein anerkannten Regeln des Völkerrechts* constituted a part of German law (*Reichsrecht*). A corresponding provision can be found in Article 25 of the Basic Law currently binding in Germany,[19] provided, however, that while under federal law generally recognized principles of international law have priority over statutes and can create rights and obligations for citizens, under Weimar law a statute inconsistent with the universal rules of international law excluded the possibility of applying these rules.[20] The interpretation of the concept of generally recognized principles of international law is not clear, but according to the legal writing and contemporary jurisprudence of German courts it refers to universal customary law, i.e. norms recognized and accepted by all States (which, however, would exclude particular or regional customary law in a sense other than territorial).[21] Additional problems arise when defining, for the purposes of Article 25 of the Basic Law, the relationship between customary law, general

18 Memoire PCIJ Publ., Series C, at 11.

19 Basic Law, Translated by Professor Christian Tomuschat, Professor David P. Currie, Professor Donald P. Kommers and Raymond Kerr, in cooperation with the Language Service of the German Bundestag, Article 25 [Primacy of international law]: *The general rules of international law shall be an integral part of federal law. They shall take precedence over the laws and directly create rights and duties for the inhabitants of the federal territory.* https://www.gesetze-im-internet.de/englisch_gg/englisch_gg.html.

20 G. Dahm, J. Delbrück, R. Wolfrum, *Völkerrecht*, Band I/1, Berlin-New York 1989, at 117.

21 Ph. Kunig, R. Uerpmann-Witzack, 'Völkerrecht und staatliches Recht', in: W. Graf Vitzthum, A. Proelss (ed.), *Völkerrecht*, 8 ed., de Gruyter, Berlin-Boston 2019, at 138.

principles of law and treaty norms reflecting or repeating customary norms. However, it seems that reducing the general rules to customary law exhausts the content of this concept, but also gives direction to the interpretation of Article 4 of the Constitution of the Weimar Republic (*Weimarer Reichsverfassung*). From the perspective of the topic of this text, it can be assumed that the basic norms of customary law regarding neutrality were in force in the German legal system under the constitutional provision cited here. We do not analyze here the possibility of direct application of customary norms regulating neutrality towards individuals. The problem was *prima facie* solved by the adoption of regulations specifying the trade and transport of military materials, weapons and ammunition. On the basis of the constitutional regulation, it can therefore be stated that the German State was bound by customary law, especially since the rules regarding neutrality should – in our opinion – be included in the generally accepted principles of international law.

German notification concerning neutrality in the Polish–Soviet war, signed by President F. Ebert,[22] provided that Germany was not at war with any of the belligerents and respected and would continue to respect impartiality. All German citizens at home and abroad were obliged to observe neutrality. At the same time, an order was announced banning the export and transit of military materials, ammunition, gunpowder and explosives from Germany to the belligerent countries (Poland and the Soviet Russia).[23] The governmental regulations were intended to clarify Germany's obligations under international law. The basis for the regulations was the clearly declared neutrality of Germany in the war between Poland and the Soviet Russia. Therefore, the argument presented in the applicants' memorial that the acts of the German government had no basis in international law was not entirely correct. The German government could not release itself from the international obligations assumed by the treaty by defining a given line of conduct by State authorities under municipal law. The complainants pointed out that the export ban contained in the regulations did not apply to transit (flow) through the Kiel Canal because it referred to German territory, which in turn was not covered by the provisions of Article 380 of the Treaty of Versailles. In any case, the neutrality regulations could not take precedence over the Treaty. It is therefore not surprising that the PCIJ concluded that Germany had full freedom to regulate its neutrality in the Polish–Soviet armed conflict. However, German government had to take into account their treaty obligations, including those concluded on 28

22 Reichsanzeiger of 21 July 1920, at 1.

23 Reichsgesetzblatt 1920, No. 158, Item 7685.

June 1919 in Versailles. These obligations obligated Germany to consent to S.S. Wimbledon's passage through the Kiel Canal, and the neutrality obligations did not require Germany to prohibit the passage. During the hearing before the Court, German government argued that the right to remain neutral in the armed conflict was an important element of sovereignty. This was a higher-ranking obligation than the restrictions imposed on Germany in the Treaty of Versailles. Therefore, the universal granting of the right to pass through the Kiel Canal to ships of all flags (resulting from Article 380 of the Treaty of Versailles) could deprive Germany of the ability to exercise the rights arising from war neutrality and require it to give preference to one of the belligerents. Moreover, Article 380 had to be interpreted in the light of the principle of neutrality, even if this would not result from the wording of the Treaty. The right resulting from the proclamation of neutrality is closely related to the legal personality of the State and its sovereignty, and it cannot be predicted in advance how and in relation to whom it will be exercised.

The arguments presented by the claimants are not convincing. The basic argument of the German government was to maintain legal neutrality.[24] Therefore, the dispute over consent to the passage of the Wimbledon ship was not really about a conflict between international law and domestic law, but about a conflict between two norms of international law.[25] One of them is the customary norm regarding neutrality in an armed conflict, and the other is the treaty obligation contained in the Treaty of Versailles. We may additionally wonder whether the conflict did not arise between a unilateral act: the declaration of neutrality, triggering obligations arising from neutrality, regulated by customary law and codified in the Fifth Hague Convention on Neutrality of 1907, and the treaty regulation of Article 380 of the treaty of Versailles.

The Tribunal drew attention to the fact that regardless of the basis of the obligation, that is, whether as an international servitude following from customary rule of international law, or as a treaty obligation arising from the Treaty of Versailles, the substance of which is to allow the use of the Kiel Canal by all vessels notwithstanding their origin, Germany must subordinate the exercise of its sovereign right over the Canal to important restrictions. The adoption of such a formula therefore implies that the legal basis for the restriction is

24 From a political perspective, the German government was not interested in the Polish victory in the war against Soviet Russia.

25 On conflicting international legal norms see W. Czaplinski, G. Danilenko, 'Conflict of Norms in International Law', *NethYBIL* 21(1990), p.3 ff. Cf also Chapters 6 by Roman Kwiecien and 7 by Michal Kowalski in the present volume.

irrelevant and is always treated in the same way, notwithstanding the origin of the obligation.

In fact, maintaining neutrality is an essential element of State sovereignty. This institution is the subject of a separate study in the present volume.[26] It is not our task to discuss in this contribution the detailed rights and obligations arising from it. We have to emphasize only that neutrality means equal treatment of both belligerents. Thus, Germany could hypothetically prohibit all vessels from passing through the canal, but it would equally have to ensure the freedom of passage for ships carrying supplies for the Red Army. However, the Court did not go into a detailed analysis of the context of Article 380, limiting itself to a grammatical interpretation of the statement that the letter of the treaty is unambiguous and leaves no doubt as to the nature of the restrictions imposed on Germany under the Treaty of Versailles. The Court pointed out that the German argument regarding the possibility of invoking neutrality was 'in conflicts with general considerations of the highest order' (whatever it meant) and was 'gainsaid by consistent international practice'. However, these statements are unclear, and the Hague judges did not consider them sufficiently to explain them convincingly. Moreover, the Court emphasized that the textual interpretation implied that Germany was obliged to ensure freedom of transit through the canal in times of peace and war[27] without any discrimination, and restrictions could be imposed exclusively because of requirements arising out of police, customs, sanitary, emigration or immigration regulations and those relating to the import or export of prohibited goods. Such a possibility, based directly upon Article 381 of the Versailles Treaty, proves that Germany's territorial sovereignty had not been questioned and the Kiel Canal had not been internationalized.

It remains unclear whether the priority of application granted to the treaty norm at the interface with the customary norm, proposed by PCIJ in the *S.S. Wimbledon* case, is of universal application. The variant of applying a more specific or detailed norm (either conventional or customary) is based on the formula of Article 38 of the Statute of the Court, but the writers agree that there is no hierarchy among the formal sources of international law. The State decides for itself how to resolve the conflict, bearing in mind, however, the international responsibility for violations of the law. The above-mentioned references to international practice, which, according to the Court, exclude the possibility of invoking neutrality, seem to concern the Suez and Panama

26 See Chapter 7 by Michał Kowalski in this volume.

27 Article 380 did not distinguish between both situations.

Canal regime. The solutions in the two cases are different. They also have a treaty basis and it would be difficult to demonstrate the creation of a customary norm regulating the behavior of the riparian sovereign in the matter of war neutrality. The Court limited itself to stating that such waterway is assimilated to natural straits in the sense that even the passage of a belligerent man-of-war does not compromise the neutrality of the sovereign State under whose jurisdiction the waters in question lie. In their joint dissenting opinion, judges Max Huber and Dionisio Anzilotti proposed a different solution to the conflict between the norms regulating the conduct of neutral States and the provisions of the Treaty of Versailles. They pointed out the need to interpret Article 380 *et seq.* in the light of the purpose and context of this provision.[28] They referred to the fact that Article 380, like the entire Treaty of Versailles, was imposed on Germany and, consequently, should be interpreted restrictively. Therefore, it would be justified to refer to the requirement to remain neutral in an armed conflict. Moreover, they emphasized that if Germany could control the movement of ships through the canal in times of peace, it should be even more capable of doing so in times of war in order to ensure neutrality.

Judge Schücking, on the other hand, following the argumentation of the German government, preferred to consider the situation of the Kiel Canal as an international servitude, which 'should limit as little as possible the sovereignty' of the riparian state or states.[29] Judge Schücking reminded that Russia, one of the belligerents, was not a party to the Versailles Treaty; therefore, under general international law, Germany was obliged to fulfil her duties of neutrality towards Russia, which in turn implied that Germany could not be expected to grant passage to a vessel carrying military supplies for Poland. The judges' opinion ignores one important element: the very construction of servitude in international law is controversial and was so in the interwar period. However, as indicated above, granting the right to transit through German territory did not violate Germany's sovereignty.

Klabbers[30] pointed out one more problem related to the duty to fulfill the obligations arising from the Treaty of Versailles. At the hearing before the Tribunal, the agent of Germany pointed out, en passant, without formulating – apparently for political reasons – an explicit objection, that the Treaty of Versailles was imposed on Germany by the victorious Entente States, and

28 PCIJ Publ. [1923] Series A, No.1, at 36.

29 Ibid, at 43.

30 Klabbers (n 6) at 359. See also in the context of the Treaty of Versailles, S.S. Malawer, 'Imposed Treaties and International Law', 7 *California Western International Law Journal* (1977) 62, at 81.

therefore the question arose whether could it actually be said that Germany, a sovereign State, freely and wittingly expressed its consent to be bound by the Versailles Treaty? Neither the majority of the judges voting in favour of the judgment, nor dissenting judges Huber and Anzilotti questioned the lawfulness and binding force of the imposed peace treaty. They also disagreed with the German view that Germany's obligations under the Treaty should be interpreted restrictively. This would be inconsistent with the clear and unambiguous wording of Article 380. It should be noted, however, that a request for a restrictive interpretation going in the same direction was taken up by the World Court in its advisory opinion on *German Settlers in Poland*.[31]

The argument about so-called 'Dictate of Versailles' was often put forward in political discussions, pointing to such elements as war reparations imposed on Germany, territorial losses, and above all, forcing Germany to acknowledge its sole responsibility for the outbreak of the war or holding Kaiser Wilhelm and higher officers responsible for the crimes committed during the war. The opinion that the treaty was unfair was common in Weimar Germany and widespread among all political circles.[32] In fact, similar doubts can be raised about most peace treaties, especially those concluded shortly after the cessation of hostilities. Peace treaties were and are still concluded between the victor and the defeated.[33] In fact, they were an example of unequal treaties, based on the imbalance of the parties. They serve a dual purpose: compensation for the damage suffered by the victor and protection against the outbreak of war again. Hence, typical clauses are: provisions regarding the cession of territory, demilitarization and contributions. In this way, they fit into the law on the international responsibility of States, providing for the cessation of violations of law, a guarantee of non-repetition and reparations. Peace treaties were and are concluded for a long time; in reality, however, they rarely survive for long. One of the reasons for this state of affairs is the tendency to question peace treaties as being concluded under the influence of compulsion. This concept, however, is different from coercion, which is a premise for the invalidity of treaties, for example under the *Vienna Convention on the Law of Treaties* of

31 PCIJ Publ. [1923] Series B, No.6, at 43.

32 See Chapter 1 by Raphael Schäfer in this volume. See also K. Dunaj, 'Dyktat wersalski i jego kontestacja w Republice Weimarskiej', 18 *Miscelanea Historico-Iuridica* (2019) No.1, 153; A. Peters, 'Treaties, Unequal', in in Anne Peters (ed.), *Max Planck Encyclopedia of Public International Law* (vol IX, Oxford: 2018) para. 60 (online at 6 November 2023).

33 On the peace treaties in general see R. Lesaffer, 'Peace Treaties and the Formation of International Law', in: Bardo Fassbender and Anne Peters (eds), *The Oxford Handbook of the History of International Law*, Oxford 2012, 71.

1969.[34] On the other hand, the practice of the Federal Republic of Germany after WWII pointed to the lack of a peace treaty with Germany (as opposed to the treaties concluded with the Reich's allies) as a reason for questioning the status quo in Europe in the period 1945–1990.

4 Contemporary Approach to Sovereignty

In his discussion on State sovereignty at the background of the *S.S. Wimbledon* judgment Klabbers[35] points out that it is still a basic concept describing the position of the State in international law, even if it is understood differently today than in the 1920s. Even if one can confront the views of outstanding lawyers who attempt to abandon the concept of sovereignty, States consistently and jealously guard their rights, relying on the need to defend sovereignty.

It is difficult to find in contemporary studies an interpretation of State sovereignty other than that developed by the doctrine in the period preceding the *Wimbledon* judgment. Moreover, many authors refer to this judgment in the context of interpreting State sovereignty as the basis for a State to assume international obligations. As in the case of the review of the doctrine of sovereignty from the discussed judgment to the contemporary time, we quote some modern authors on this subject, which resonate with historical arguments. For example Malcolm Shaw[36] claims:

> [T]he capacity to enter into relations with other States is an aspect of the existence of the entity in question as well as an indication of the importance attached to recognition by other states [...] It is essential for a sovereign state to be able to create such legal relations with other units as it sees fit. When it is not present, the entity cannot be an independent state. The outstanding characteristics of the state is its independence, or sovereignty. This was defined [by the ILC in 1949] as the capacity of a state to provide for its own well-being and development free from the

34 We agree with Z. Grochalski, 'The Specific Legal-International Regime of Peace Treaties', 17(4) *The Opole Studies in Administration and Law* (2019) 23, at 29–31. On unequal treaties viewed from the perspective of coercion cf. L. Caflisch, 'Unequal Treaties', 35 *German Yearbook of International Law* (1992) 51. The author does not discuss a category of peace treaties, limiting himself to a general analysis of the validity and voidability of these contracts.

35 Klabbers (n 6) at 347.

36 M. Shaw, *International Law*, 6th ed., Cambridge 2008, at 202, 211.

domination of other states, providing it does not impair or violate their legitimate rights.

According to James Crawford,[37]

> [I]n the Montevideo convention on rights and duties of states, the concept of independence is represented by the requirement of capacity to enter into relations with other States, Independence is the decisive criterion of statehood [...] The state must be independent of other state legal orders, and any interference by such legal orders, or by an international agency, must be based on a title of international law. The competence of states in respect of their territory is usually desribed in terms of sovereignty and jurisdiction [...] the normal complement of state rights, the typical case of legal competence, is described commonly as "sovereignty".

Jan Wouters and the co-authors of modern handbook of international law in European perspective propose as follows:[38]

> '[I]ndependence presupposes that a state is capable of taking part in international relations in its own rights, without being subordinate to another state. Independence does not mean freedom from law – any State is in principle bound by pre-existing customary IL upon its coming into existence – but rather freedom of control from other states'.
>
> According to eminent French writers,[39]
>
> 'Le principe de la souvcrainctć ćtatique est solidement ancré dans le droit positif [...] Non seulement il est impossible de nier la positivité de la notion de souveraineté, mais encore celle-ci apparaît comme l'attribut fondamental de l'Etat. [...] Dans la société contemporaine, largement interétatique, la souveraineté de chaque Etat se heurte à celles, concurrentes et égales, de tous les autres Etats ... La souveraineté apparaît, dans ces conditions, comme la source des compétences que l'Etat tient du droit international ... A travers l'égalité souveraine, c'est l'indépendence de l'Etat qui est affirmée ... La jurisprudence internationale assimile systématiquement souveraineté à l'indépendence. ... La souveraineté

37 J. Crawford, *Brownlie's Principles of Public International Law*, 8th ed., Oxford 2012, at 129 and 204.

38 J. Wouters, C. Ryngaert, T. Ruys, G. de Baere, *International Law. An European Perspective*, Hart, Oxford 2019, at 218.

39 M. Forteau, A. Miron, A. Pellet, *Droit international public*, 9.ed., Paris 2022, at 610.

> n'implique nullement que l'Etat peut s'affranchirn de règles du droit international. Au contraire. L'Etat n'est souverain que s'il est soumis directement, immédiatement au droit international'.

P.M. Dupuy and Y. Kerbrat[40] are of the opinion that '[L]'indépendence est à la fois la conditiion et le critère de la souveraineté: une fois celle-ci reconnue à une collectivité possédant par ailleurs les atributs de l'entité étatique, […] la souveraineté jouera à son tour comme le garant de l'indépendance. Celle-ci constitue une situation de pur fait dont la souveraineté réalise la formalisation juridique'. We also refer to two Polish authors: R.Kwiecień, and J. Kranz, discussing links between State sovereignty and binding force of international law. The former[41] seems to emphasize the transition from the understanding of sovereignty as a certain absolute status of the State, justifying the actions it undertakes in relations with other entities of international law, to the principle of sovereign equality of States, playing a protective function. The latter[42] points to the relationship between sovereignty and independence, distinguishing between the legal and factual understanding of the latter. In our opinion, this view is not entirely correct, because the international legal writers (including the authors quoted above) do not indicate that independence is a legal concept. In our opinion, it is a political concept in the field of international relations, while sovereignty is a legal one.

The *Wimbledon* judgment in the above-mentioned context of the state's capacity to conclude international agreements, which is important as self-limitation of its competences, is referred to, for example, by Dupuy,[43] Pellet,[44] Kau,[45] Crawford,[46] Kranz[47] and Wildhaber.[48]

---

40 P.M. Dupuy, Y. Kerbrat, *Droit international public*, 16th, ed., Paris 2022, at 35.

41 R. Kwiecień, 'Państwo i jego suwerenność a prawo międzynarodowe jako system prawa' (*State and its sovereignty, and international law as a legal system*), in: R. Kwiecień (ed.), *Państwo a prawo międzynarodowe jako system prawa* (*State, and international law as a legal system*), Lublin 2015, at 43.

42 J. Kranz, *Pojęcie suwerenności we współczesnym prawie międzynarodowym* (*The concept of sovereignty in contemporary international law*), Warszawa 2015, at 80–82.

43 Dupuy, Kerbrat (n 40) at 308.

44 Forteau, Miron, Pellet (n 39) at 611.

45 W. Graf Vitzthum, A. Proelß (ed.), *Völkerrecht*, 8th ed., Berlin 2019, at 202.

46 Crawford (n 37) at 9. He claims: 'The apparent paradox of how law could operate between sovereign is resolved by the priority given to consent in the formation of legal obligation and the role of co-operation in interstate affairs – combined with the insight that sovereignty includes the capacity to make commitments not merely temporary in character'.

47 Kranz (n 41) at 87.

48 Cf. L. Wildhaber, 'Sovereignty and International Law', in: R.St.J. MacDonald, D.M. Johnston (eds.), *The Structure and Process of International Law*, Dordrecht 1983, 425, at 442 (noting that '[a]uto-limitations are emanations from, not violations of sovereignty').

The question arises whether the *Wimbledon* statement on sovereignty is still alive. The *Wimbledon* case has survived in legal annals primarily due to the statement that State sovereignty is the basis of State action, enabling the conclusion of international obligations, especially treaty obligations. The legal basis for the binding force of a custom seems to be more complicated, taking into account the fact that not in every situation the State has the opportunity to express its opinion on the binding force of a practice at the stage of custom creation. State sovereignty and its relationship to international law was developed in the Court's judgment in the S.S. *Lotus* case, much more in-depth when it comes to State obligations. More importantly, the *Lotus* judgment was actually the work of two judges, Anzilotti and Huber, who creatively developed their dissenting opinion in the *Wimbledon* case.[49]

5 Conclusion

The concept of State sovereignty elaborated in the first years of the activity of World Court was confirmed by the ICJ, e.g. in the *Nicaragua* judgment, and it was modified in the advisory opinion on *Legality of the threat or use of nuclear weapons*[50] as well as in the *Arrest warrant* judgment.[51] The World Court considered in these decisions whether States did need a clear legal basis for their legitimised actions in international relations. First of all, there is a consensus of opinion that the content of sovereignty varies from one State to another. Calvo[52] stated that each State had its own scope of sovereignty, determined by the State's international obligations. Thus, there was no such thing as an absolute sovereignty. In the modern world, cooperation between States is necessary, which, of course, increasingly requires giving up the exercise of unlimited sovereignty. The interdependence between State sovereignty and the right to self-determination would also require examination, especially in its internal aspect.

49 On relationship between the two judgments and their consequences for the State sovereignty cf. A. Pellet, '*Lotus* que de sottises on profére en ton nom! Remarques sur le concept de souveraineté dans la jurisprudence de la Cour mondiale', in: *Mélanges en l'honneur de J.-P. Puissochet: l'État souverain dans le monde d'aujourd'hui*, Paris 2008, at 215.

50 Advisory opinion of 8 July 1996, ICJ Rep. 1996, 226.

51 Judgment of 14 February 2002, ICJ Rep. 2002, 3.

52 Calvo (n 14) 264.

Sovereignty remains a definitional feature of States. There are other subjects operating in international relations that are not entitled to the attribute of sovereignty. Their legal status would require discussion. It is difficult to ignore the judgment of the ECJ in the *Costa v ENEL* case[53] with the following passus which was a source of heated disputes and discussions among the international legal community:

> By creating a Community of unlimited duration, having its own institutions, its own personality, its own legal capacity and capacity of representation on the international plane and, more particularly, real powers stemming from a limitation of sovereignty or a transfer of powers from the states to the Community, the Member States have limited their sovereign rights, albeit within limited fields, and have thus created a body of law which binds both their nationals and themselves.

Those disputes, as it seems, could not be resolved without the reference to the *S.S. Wimbledon* case.

Bibliography

Anzilotti D., *Cours de droit international*, translated by G. Gidel, Paris 1929.

Bluntschli J., *Droit international codifié*, translated by C. Lardy, Paris 1874.

Bonfils H., *Manuel de droit international public (droit de gens)*, 4th ed., edited by P. Fauchille, Paris 1905.

Caflisch L., 'Unequal Treaties', 35 *German Yearbook of International Law* (1992) 51.

Calvo C., *Le droit international théorique et pratique*, t.1, Patris 1880.

Crawford J., *Brownlie's Principles of Public International Law*, 8th ed., Oxford 2012.

Czaplinski W., Danilenko G., 'Conflict of Norms in International Law', *NethYBIL* 21(1990), 3.

Dahm G., Delbrück J., Wolfrum R., *Völkerrecht*, Band I/1, Berlin-New York 1989.

Dunaj K., 'Dyktat wersalski i jego kontestacja w Republice Weimarskiej', 18/1 *Miscelanea Historico-Iuridica* (2019) 153.

Dupuy P.M., Kerbrat Y., *Droit international public*, 16th, ed., Paris 2022.

Forteau M., Miron A., Pellet A., *Droit international public*, 9.ed., Paris 2022.

53 Case 6/64, 15 July 1964, https://eur-lex.europa.eu/legal-content/EN/TXT/HTML/?uri=CELEX%3A61964CJ0006.

Grochalski Z., 'The Specific Legal-International Regime of Peace Treaties', 17(4) *The Opole Studies in Administration and Law* (2019) 23.

Hall W.E., *International Law. A Treatise*, Oxford 1890.

Klabbers J., 'Clinchinig the Concept of Sovereignty: the Wimbledon Redux', *Austrian Review of International and European Law* 3 (1998) 345.

Kranz J., *Pojęcie suwerenności we współczesnym prawie międzynarodowym* (*The Concept of Sovereignty in Contemporary International Law*), Warszawa 2015.

Kunig Ph., Uerpmann-Witzack R., 'Völkerrecht und staatliches Recht', in W. Graf Vitzthum, A. Proelss (eds), *Völkerrecht*, 8 ed., de Gruyter, Berlin-Boston 2019.

Kwiecień R., 'ańswo i jego suwerenność a prawo międzynarodowe jako system prawa' '(State and its Sovereignty, and International Law as a Legal System)', in R. Kwiecień (ed.), *Państwo a prawo międzynarodowe jako system prawa* (*State, and International Law as a Legal System*), UMCS, Lublin 2015.

Lawrence T.J. and Winfield P.H., *The Principles of International Law*, London 1927.

Lesaffer R., 'Peace Treaties and the Formation of International Law', in Bardo Fassbender and Anne Peters (eds), *The Oxford Handbook of the History of International Law*, Oxford 2012.

Malawer S.S., 'Imposed Treaties and International Law', 7 *California Western International Law Journal* (1977) 62.

Oppenheim L., *International Law. A Treatise*, vol.1 *Peace*, 2nd ed., London 1912.

Pellet A., '*Lotus* que de sottises on profére en ton nom! Remarques sur le concept de souveraineté dans la jurisprudence de la Cour mondiale', in *Mélanges en l'honneur de J.-P. Puissochet: l'État souverain dans le monde d'aujourd'hui*, Préfce Renaud Denoix de Saint-Marc, Pedone, Paris 2008.

Peters A., 'Treaties, Unequal', in in Peters A. (ed.), *Max Planck Encyclopedia of Public International Law* (vol IX, Oxford: 2018).

Shaw M., *International Law*, 6th ed., Cambridge 2008.

Wildhaber L., 'Sovereignty and International Law', in R.St.J. MacDonald, D.M. Johnston (eds), *The Structure and Process of International Law*, Dordrecht 1983.

Wilson G.G. Tucker G.F., *International Law*, New York-Boston-Chicago 1901.

Wouters J., Ryngaert C., Ruys T., de Baere G., *International Law. An European Perspective*, Hart, Oxford 2019.

Treaties

1933 Convention on Rights and Duties of States, 165 *LNTS* 19.

Judgments and Advisory Opinions

PCIJ

Competence of the ILO in regard to International Regulation of the Conditions of the Labour of Persons Employed in Agriculture, Advisory Opinion, PCIJ Publ., [1923] Series B, No. 2.

German Settlers in Poland, Advisory Opinion, [1923] PCIJ Publ. Series B, No.6.

Nationality Decrees in Tunisia and Morocco, Advisory Opinion, PCIJ Publ., [1923] Series B, No. 4.

S.S. Wimbledon (*United Kingdom, France, Italy & Japan v. Germany*) (Poland intervening), [1923] PCIJ Publ. Series A, No.1.

ICJ

Arrest Warrant of 11 April 2000 (*Democratic Republic of the Congo v. Belgium*), Judgment of 14 February 2002, ICJ Rep. 2002.

Legality of the threat or use of nuclear weapons, Advisory opinion of 8 July 1996, ICJ Rep. 1996.

Other Cases

Air service agreement of 27 March 1946 between the USA and France, 9 December 1978, RIAA vol.18.

Costa v ENEL, Case 6/64, 15 July 1964, https://eur-lex.europa.eu/legal-content/EN/TXT/HTML/?uri=CELEX%3A61964CJ0006.

CHAPTER 6

The Sources of International Law and Legal Obligations of States, and the Normative Hierarchy under the Wimbledon Judgment

Or Why 'Relative Normativity' Is Intrinsic to the Development of International Law

Roman Kwiecień

Abstract

This chapter addresses the following problems: 1. the relationship between custom and treaties, and general principles of law; 2. peremptory/categorical norms in the *Wimbledon* decision; 3. interpretation of legal obligations of States, including treaty obligations; 4. 'relative normativity' under the judgment. This author generally seeks to answer the question whether treaties are a real formal source of general international law or merely a source of legal obligations to their parties. According to the PCIJ, Article 380 of the Versailles Treaty contained the 'provision of a general and peremptory character'. The Court also considered the terms of Article 380 as 'categorical'. The Court had to respond to the relationships between Article 380 and other rules of international law, including customary rules, that is a situation when priority had to be given to a specific rule among several that might have been applicable to a legal matter or dispute. Thus, this chapter seeks to address the question whether the Court was in favour of the normative hierarchy in international law or of 'relative normativity' as labelled by Prosper Weil. Another question concerns the problem of formal source of the 'peremptory' or 'categorical' regime. In particular, could just treaty provisions be such a source? It is still a vital problem in international law. The ICJ is known for its long silence about international peremptory norms. It was only its 2006 *Armed activities* judgment that clearly supported the normative significance of such norms. Does this mean that the PCIJ's position was neglected by its successor for such a long time? In the *Wimbledon* judgment legal reconstruction of rights and duties of parties to the proceeding was primarily grounded in the provisions of the Versailles

 | DOI:10.1163/9789004707979_008

Treaty. The Court's interpretation has been criticized for giving too much weight to the wording of Article 380. This was already indicated in the dissenting opinion by judges Anzilotti and Huber. Thus, an issue of interpretation of treaty rights and obligations arises, including the methods of interpretation, which is to be discussed in this chapter. There is another crucial problem addresses in this chapter. It concerns the relationship of treaty obligations to unwritten sources of international law, that is, custom and general principles of law. The judgment was criticized for the absence of a convincing treatment of this issue. In particular, for an unsatisfactory identification of customary rules of international law, their effects and the relation to treaty provisions. Consequently, it is said that the Court gave a poor answer to the question whether and why the treaty provisions could affect the interests of third States, which is discussed in the chapter.

1 Introduction

One of the leading interwar advocates of the development of international judiciary and a judge of the Permanent Court of International Justice (hereafter: PCIJ, or Court) in the last period of its activity – Manley Hudson, claimed that 'the process of finding the applicable international law [...] is not a discretionary process. At every step it calls for the exercise of a judgment disciplined by learning and experience'.[1] This opinion supports the idea that international judges operate within a limited range of discretion. In particular, international courts and their judges should not make laws, but should only find the law as it stands and apply it. Today the International Court of Justice (ICJ) as the successor of the PCIJ evidently underlines that 'it is clear that the Court cannot legislate [...]. It states the existing law and does not legislate'.[2] In this sense the International Court recognizes it as misleading to speak of its decisions as 'law-making' in the true sense of the term, because it is the law that constrains the judges, and not *vice versa*. After the *Wimbledon* decision the PCIJ declared itself to be a body responsible for the knowledge of international law. In the *Brazilian Federal Loans* case it stated '[T]he Court, which is a tribunal of international law, [...] in this capacity, is deemed to know what this law is [...]'.[3] The position of the Court may be understood both as a statement of fact, i.e. the Court's knowledge of law with reference to the specific cases it tried, and as

1 Hudson M.O., *International Tribunals: Past and Future* (Washington D.C.: 1944) 107–108.

2 *Threat or Use of Nuclear Weapons*, Advisory Opinion, ICJ Reports 1996, par. 18.

3 *Case Concerning the Payment in Gold of Brazilian Federal Loans Contracted in France* [1929] PCIJ Ser A No 21, at 124.

the Court's duty to take an authoritative stance on where the law can be found, i.e. on their formal sources. It is the contribution of the PCIJ's reasoning in the *Wimbledon* case to the debate on the sources of international law that is the primary issue discussed in this chapter. Did the Court convincingly indicate the sources of legal norms that were the basis for settling the submitted dispute? The dissenting opinions to the judgment clearly prove the lack of agreement among the judges as to the substantive law in question, and in particular to the relationship between customary and treaty rules.

The current chapter is organized into five parts, including this introduction and the conclusions. Part II addresses the relationship between treaties and custom in the Court's reasoning. In this part the author seeks to indicate the sources of general international law, in particular, to answer the question as to whether law-making provisions of treaties may be seen as its formal source. In the *Wimbledon* case the Court argued they should, in fact, be seen as such. Part III deals with various ways in which the Court interpreted the texts of the treaties when it handed down its final judgement. The aims, methods, and means of treaty interpretation adopted by the Court had a clear impact on the understanding of rights and duties of the parties to the proceedings as well as on third states. Therefore, they are relevant to the Court's doctrine of sources. Part IV discusses the problem of 'relative normativity' under the judgment. The Permanent Court deciding the *Wimbledon* dispute had to address the problem of normative hierarchy, i.e. a situation when priority had to be given to a specific rule among several that might have been applicable to a legal matter or dispute. The Court's pronouncement regarding the provisions of Article 380 of the Treaty of Versailles as a regulation of a 'general and peremptory character'[4] undoubtedly prompts consideration of this problem. The problem is intrinsic to the sources of international law. Discussing this problem, the author seeks to substantiate the proposition that, first, for the sources of international law 'custom is more than treaty, more even than a generally accepted treaty', as James Crawford put it,[5] and, secondly, 'relative normativity' is intrinsic to the practice of international law-making and to the development of international law.

4 *Case of the S.S. "Wimbledon"* [1923] PCIJ Ser A No 1, at 21 (hereafter: *Wimbledon*).

5 Crawford J., *Chance, Order, Change: The Course of International Law* (The Hague: 2014) 139.

2 The Relationship between Treaties and Custom, and General International Law under the Judgment

2.1 *Has the Contribution of the* Wimbledon *Decision to the Debate on Sources Been Less than Expected, and if So, Why?*

The idea of formal sources has been intensely and widely discussed, as well as criticized, by international lawyers. The 'formal sources' approach is championed in international law scholarship for its virtues of distinguishing law from non-law, and consequently as necessary to the ascertainment of international legal norms.[6] That is why the problem of sources of law has traditionally been seen as one of the most important issues for jurists, especially from the perspective of legal certainty. The important function of the formal sources approach is to guarantee the objectivity of law. There is a close link between this approach and the ascertainment of law, since the formal sources show where the law may be found, which makes it possible to know what law is being applied.[7] In every legal order, and perhaps especially in international law which lacks a legislature and a judicial system with compulsory jurisdiction, striving for a precise definition of the formal source of law seems to be a problem of great practical importance, since it makes it possible to identify the formal factors that distinguish binding legal rules from both *de lege ferenda* rules and such rules as may be present in social reality, but are not formally grounded in identifiable legislation. The idea of formal sources matters because its precise understanding makes it possible to determine whether or not certain rules have acquired legal validity in the process leading to their creation. This process gives the rules legal attachment, i.e., it identifies them with the legal order. It is a 'step from the pre-legal into the legal world', as Herbert Hart put it when he spoke of the *secondary rules*.[8] Insofar as the formal sources of international law are concerned, both the processes and forms by which principles and rules

6 See generally d'Aspremont J., *Formalism and the Sources of International Law. A Theory of the Ascertainment of Legal Rules* (Oxford: 2011). See also d'Argent P., "Sources and the Legality and Validity of International Law: What Makes Law 'International'", in Besson S. – d'Aspremont J. (eds.), *The Oxford Handbook of the Sources of International Law* (Oxford: 2017) 541, 543–546; Schachter O., "International Law in Theory and Practice. General Course in Public International Law", *Recueil des Cours* 178 (1982) 9, 60; Thirlway H., "The Sources of International Law", in Evans M.D. (ed.), *International Law* (3 ed., Oxford 2010) 97–98. The ICJ's position should also be taken into account. The ICJ emphasized in the *South West Africa* case that legal rights and obligations must have a 'sufficient expression in legal form'. See *South West Africa* (*Ethiopia v South Africa*) (*Second Phase*) [1966] ICJ Reports 6, 34 [49].

7 d'Aspremont, *Formalism and the Sources* 13.

8 Hart H.L.A., *The Concept of Law* (3rd ed., Oxford: 2012) 94.

are formed, and where they may be found, can be considered as the primary meaning of the term.[9] To put it in other way, the formal sources of law concern both the way in which the legal validity of new rules of conduct is established, and the process by which already existing rules are changed.[10] This definition, naturally, like other definitions, can never be entirely true or false, but only more or less useful. This one seems useful, since it shows well that the formal sources, as 'containers' of valid legal rules and principles, are hardly distinguishable from the very processes that led to their existence. This is why Martii Koskenniemi says that treaties, custom, and general principles of law 'seem, on the one hand, like descriptions of law-creating processes and, on the other, like the objectified results of those processes'.[11]

While deciding a dispute in the *Wimbledon* case, the PCIJ mainly applied treaty law, and, by way of introduction, it is worth considering the opinion of a contemporary researcher in the history of international law related to this issue. Stephen Neff claims that:

> The contribution of the Court's case law to the development of substantive international law was perhaps less than might have been expected. This was because most of the cases brought concerned alleged violations of specific treaty provisions, rather than of general principles of law.[12]

9 See Besson S., "Theorizing the Sources of International Law", in Besson S. – Tasioulas J. (eds.), *The Philosophy of International Law*, (Oxford: 2010)163, 169–170; d'Aspremont, *Formalism and the Sources* 13; Wolfrum R., "Sources of International Law", in Peters A. (ed.), *Max Planck Encyclopedia of Public International Law* (vol IX, Oxford: 2012) para. 6 (online at 6 June 2023).

10 Jennings R. – Watts A., *Oppenheim's International Law* (9th ed., vol 1. London: 1996) 23.

11 Koskenniemi M., *From Apology to Utopia. The Structure of International Legal Argument* (rev. ed., Cambridge: 2005) 306.

12 Neff S.C., *Justice Among Nations. A History of International Law* (Cambridge, Massachusetts: 2014) 356. It needs, however, to be stressed that the influence of the PCIJ's decisions on the development of international law were different in particular periods of its activity. This is well shown in Spiermann O., *International Legal Argument in the Permanent Court of International Justice. The Rise of the International Judiciary* (Cambridge: 2005) 132–133. It is not unfounded that Spiermann most appreciates the PCIJ's decisions at the time of Max Huber's presidency (1924–1931). A similar opinion was expressed, when the PCIJ still existed, by its long-time secretary, and then a judge in the final period of the Court's activity, Ake Hammarskjöld. He wrote: 'During the first years of its existence, the Court displayed a tendency to discuss and to give its views on most of the important questions of principle which arose in the cases submitted to it because it held that to contribute in this way to the restatement of international law was not the least important of its tasks. Subsequently, however, and, curiously enough, more particularly after 1930 [...] the tendency has rather been, following the example of municipal tribunals, to avoid pronouncing upon questions the solution of which does not appear to be indispensable for the decision of the case'. Hammarskjöld A., "The Permanent Court of

This opinion can be applied to the *Wimbledon* case since the Applicants' claim was based on the provisions of Article 380 of the Versailles Treaty. However, it is not, in my view, the large number of disputes based on treaties that is responsible for this less-than-expected contribution of the PCIJ to the development of substantive international law, but an overly superficial presentation by the Court of the relationship between treaties and custom, as evidenced by the *Wimbledon* judgment. Moreover, in this case the Court was rather modestly guided by the interpretative directive known today as the 'systemic integration of international law'. It is clearly visible in the Court's interpretation of the duties of the Respondent under the Versailles Treaty provisions on the Kiel Canal, which will be discussed in part III of this Chapter.

2.2 *Has the* Wimbledon *Decision Contributed to the Theory of General International Law, or Are Treaties the Formal Source of General International Law?*

Ole Spiermann associates the *Wimbledon* case primarily with territorial sovereignty.[13] He discusses the jurisprudence of the Permanent Court in the frameworks of the 'double structure of international legal argument'. The first judgment of the Court, Spiermann contends, was grounded in arguments from 'international law coexistence' which needs no special state consent for its validity, since this validity follows from the very need for this law. That is why, Spiermann argues, the Court assumed that the change of the legal status of the Kiel Canal from a national to an international waterway also changed the status of territorial sovereign. 'International law of coexistence' regulates and protects, *inter alia*, a regime of territories 'permanently dedicated to the use of the whole world', which justifies its essentiality. In this way the majority of the bench avoided considering the issue of the rights of a third state, the Soviet Russia, and the judgment represented a turning away from any 'international law of cooperation' based on a clear state consent, towards an 'international law of coexistence'.[14] According to him, this case provoked a certain tension between two concepts of the state, that is, on the one hand, as an entity subject to international law, and on the other, as an international sovereign. In the judgment, Spiermann argues,

---

International Justice and the Development of International Law", *International Affairs* 14 (1935) 799.

13 Spiermann, *International Legal Argument* 175. See also Barbara Stępień's contribution to this volume, in particular, her remarks on internationalization of canals.

14 Ibid, 185.

> the conception of the State as an international law subject was no longer the main plank of the reasoning. […] And, since the Permanent Court had departed from the conception of the State as an international law subject, its counter argument was grounded on the conception of the State as an international sovereign. Thus, in what may be termed "the *Wimbledon* statement", the Permanent Court held that "the right of entering into international engagements is an attribute of State sovereignty".[15]

The sovereignty issue is not addressed in this chapter.[16] I mention it, however, since the Court's concept of the state clearly influenced the justification of states' compliance with their obligations. It is *nolens volens* linked to the formal sources, the relationships between them, and possible *erga omnes* effects of norms following from them. Thus, the concept of the state had an impact on the Court's doctrine of sources as well as the means of interpreting them. It also affected the Court's understanding of international law as a whole. Indeed, it is a concept of law adopted, although not always clearly articulated, that determines the perception of the structural features of legal order, including the issues of personality, law-making processes, and sources. This is, as it seems, evidenced by the discussed judgment.

It is a truism to recognize that state consent is a crucial matter for the normative validity and legitimacy of international law, and for its formal sources. Consent to be bound by treaties goes without saying. Those, however, who see the rules and principles of international law within the *Lotus* perspective,[17] that is, as 'emanating from the free will' of states, seek to explain the binding force of other sources – custom and general principles of law – in the terms 'tacit agreement' or 'contractual scheme'. Did the Court base its reasoning on this scheme in the *Wimbledon* case, and was the judgment the first step on the way to the 'Lotus statement'? One of the commentators on the PCIJ's contribution to the doctrine of sources argues that generally 'the Court had, in fact, tried to do everything in its power to prevent the incorporation of the contractualist metaphor into the contemporary doctrine of sources debate'.[18] But at the same time, this author poses a question: if this is true, why did the Court enthusiastically endorse the contractualist model in the famous *dictum*

15 Ibid, 181. See also ibid, 177.

16 See Chapter 5 by Władysław Czapliński in this volume.

17 *The Case of the SS "Lotus"* [1927] PCIJ Ser A No 10 at 18.

18 Rasulov A., "The Doctrine of Sources in the Discourse of the Permanent Court of International Justice", in Tams Ch.J. – Fitzmaurice M. (eds), *Legacies of the Permanent Court of International Justice* (Leyden-Boston: 2013) 271, 304.

of the *Lotus* judgment?[19] Regardless of this, he claims that it is too simplistic to force the Court's approach into a contractual and consensual model because there are, in its jurisprudence, decisions within which the Court attempted to go beyond this model.[20] Another issue is whether its overall approach to the sources was coherent as a whole. It is precisely the *Wimbledon* judgment that is not unambiguous as far as the coherence of the Court's approach to sources is concerned. However, one must bear in mind the issue of whether complete coherence of the Court's arguments in its first judgment was at all possible to achieve due to the lack of a predecessor and the different views held by its judges.[21] But this circumstance is not, as it seems, a mitigating factor in assessing the significance of the *Wimbledon* decision for the development of international law, because the consistency and coherence in the jurisprudence is an important value regardless time and place. Thus, the important question is whether some inconsistencies in the Court's arguments presented in the judgment support its constructive contribution to the doctrine of sources. I contend that there are serious doubts in this regard that result from the Court's difficulties in justifying the normative validity and effectiveness of the norms of general international law. To be more precise, the Court, in my view, made an unconvincing attempt to justify an effectiveness of rules applicable *erga omnes* on the basis of treaty obligations. This is the reason for the controversy regarding its presentation of the legal status of the Respondent as a neutral state, and its duties towards third states. As mentioned above, the legal argument in the judgment was based on the international law of coexistence rather than on the international law of cooperation. In respect to the former, what triggers international law is not consent to, but a need for, such law, while, for the latter state consent is crucial. In the judgment, according to the majority of judges, the problems of neutrality and the territorial setting of states came within the international law of coexistence. That is why, Spiermann contends, the majority avoided the problem of Russia not being a party to the Versailles Treaty.[22] Did the Court really avoid this problem? It is the Court's approach to sources that provides an opportunity to consider it.

The Applicants' memorial[23] was based on Article 380 of the Versailles Treaty which stated: 'The Kiel Canal and its approaches shall be maintained free

19 Ibid.

20 Ibid, 282, 299–302, 304.

21 The Author thanks the anonymous Reviewer of the book for pointing this out.

22 Spiermann, *International Legal Argument* 185.

23 *The S.S. "Wimbledon", Documents of the Written Procedure* [1923] PCIJ Ser C No 3 (Additional Volume), 1.

and open to the vessels of commerce and of war of all nations at peace with Germany on terms of entire equality'. Germany as the Respondent claimed in her counter-memorial that it was unable to allow the *s.s. "Wimbledon"*, which had on board a cargo of munitions and artillery stores consigned to the Polish Military Mission at Danzig, to pass through the Kiel Canal, because the German Neutrality Orders of July 25th and 30th, 1920, prohibited the transit of cargoes of this kind destined for Poland or Russia, and that Article 380 of the Treaty of Versailles did not present an obstacle to the application of these Orders to the Kiel Canal.[24] The German Government requested that the Court declare that the German authorities were within their rights in refusing on March 21st, 1921, to allow the "*Wimbledon*" to pass through the Kiel Canal. They claimed that Article 380 of the Versailles Treaty could not prevent Germany from applying the Neutrality Order of July 25th, 1920 to the Canal during the Russo–Polish war of 1920–1921, because the application of this Order was not rendered impossible by the coming into force of the preliminary Treaty of Peace of November 2nd, 1920, but only by the coming into force of the final Treaty of Peace between Poland and Russia of April 30th, 1921.[25] Against this background, the Permanent Court raised a question as to whether the German authorities were entitled to refuse the "*Wimbledon*" access to and passage through the Kiel Canal under the conditions and circumstances in which they did so. The Court answered based on Article 380, which it considered to be a regulation of a 'general and peremptory character', and the terms of this article were 'categorical and give rise to no doubt'.[26] According to the Court,

> the Canal has ceased to be an internal and national navigable waterway [...] and it has become an international waterway intended to provide under treaty guarantee easier access to the Baltic for the benefit of all nations of the world. Under this new régime, the Kiel Canal must be open, on a footing of equality, to all vessels [...], but on one express condition, namely, that these vessels must belong to nations at peace with Germany.[27]

Moreover, the Court recognized that those provisions relating to the Kiel Canal in the Versailles Treaty were 'self-contained', since 'the Kiel Canal is open to the

24 *The s.s. "Wimbledon", Documents of the Written Procedure* [1923] PCIJ Ser C No 3 (Additional Volume), 40.

25 Ibid.

26 *Wimbledon*, 21, 22.

27 Ibid, 22.

war vessels and transit traffic of all nations at peace with Germany, whereas free access to other German navigable waterways [...] is limited to the Allied and Associated Powers alone'.[28] In consequence, the Court claimed that the neutrality orders issued by Germany could not prevail over the provisions of Article 380, and that it was a 'definite duty' of Germany to allow the passage of the "*Wimbledon*" through the Canal.[29] Thus, the Permanent Court rejected Germany's claims and decided that the German authorities were wrong in refusing the "*Wimbledon*" access to the Canal. Moreover, the Court ruled that Article 380 of the Versailles Treaty 'should have prevented Germany from applying to the Kiel Canal the Neutrality Order of July 25th, 1920'.[30]

The Court's judgement that the provisions of Article 380 of the Treaty of Versailles constituted a regulation of a 'general and peremptory character' prompts a discussion as to whether treaty provisions can result in rights and obligations not only *erga omnes partes*, but also those that are applicable to all states, including non-parties to treaties, and their relationship to general international law and its sources. In its report on the fragmentation of international law, the Study Group of the International Law Commission admitted that the very term 'general international law' still has no generally accepted definition.[31] The Study Group has defined what is *general* by reference to its logical counterpart, namely, what is *special*, and has underlined the contextual meaning of this distinction. The Court did not use the term 'general international law' in the judgment. But while defining the provisions of Article 380 as constituting a regulation of a 'general and peremptory character', the Court seemed to support a position that law-making treaties constitute formal sources of general international law, which inclines to address this proposition.

In contemporary studies on the sources of international law, this judgment serves as an example of the explaining and grounding of institutional unilateralism in the decentralized international legal order in willful submission, that is, in the act of a state's granting of its consent, and adhering to *pacta sunt servanda*.[32] After all, the validity of the provisions of the Treaty of Versailles proclaimed by the Court as being 'general and peremptory' is derived from

28 Ibid, 23–24.

29 Ibid, 29, 30.

30 Ibid, 33.

31 International Law Commission, Report of the Study Group of the International Law Commission, *Conclusions of the Work of the Study* Group, *Fragmentation of International Law: Difficulties Arising from the Diversification and Expansion of International Law*, Fifty-eighth session, Geneva, 1 May-9 June and 3 July-11 August 2006, A/CN.4/L.702 18 July 2006, para 2(10) note 11, at 10.

32 d'Argent, "Sources and the Legality" 545.

the consent of its parties. Moreover, it also seems to be true, because probably the best known *dictum* of this decision – the statement on sovereignty – was actually based on the practice of self-limitation by states of their power to exercise their sovereign rights. That is why, as the Court claimed, 'the right of entering into international engagements is an attribute of State sovereignty'.[33] Nonetheless, it is not the problem of basis of obligation in international law that was most relevant to the PCIJ's approach to the sources, but rather the forms in which legal principles and rules existed and were applied. In the *Wimbledon* case the PCIJ seemed to share Manley Hudson's enthusiasm for treaties as the 'most fruitful process by which international law is being developed'.[34] The Court was inclined to believe that modern international relations made treaties more important tools than custom as far as progress in international law was concerned. That is why the Court considered the rights and duties of the parties to the proceedings, in particular the Respondent, primarily in the perspective of treaty law, and derived them only rather modestly and sparingly from other sources.

My contention is that such an approach did not help the Court to comprehensively determinate and convincingly substantiate the legal basis for relations between those states that were parties to the Versailles Treaty and third states that may not have been parties, i.e., the legal relations beyond the treaty regime itself. When the Court focused on the Respondent's international legal status, it derived it primarily from its treaty rights and duties related to the Kiel Canal. The main consequence of this was to marginalize a broader legal perspective, i.e., the perspective of general international law. In particular, the Court gave a very cursory analysis of customary law regarding the duties of the Respondent as a riparian state resulting from its neutrality towards the parties to the international armed conflict, i.e., towards the Soviet Russia and Poland. The Court, on the one hand, in its adjudication of these duties in fact, discredited the significance of general international law arising from custom. On the other hand, the Court's attribution of the 'general and peremptory character' standard to the treaty regulation was made, as it seems, rather exaggeratedly. At that time, speaking of such regulation was undoubtedly a normative novelty and perhaps the beginning of the 'relative normativity' that will be discussed in part IV of this Chapter. But, then as now, it has been doubtful whether law-making provisions of treaties could be the formal source of a regulation of a 'general and peremptory character'. Then and now, treaties have been

33 *Wimbledon*, 25.

34 Hudson M.O., *Progress in International Organization* (Stanford: 1932) 73–74.

indispensable means for the creation of institutions in the international community as well as for the establishment of special territorial regimes. However, their role for the making of principles and rules of substantive general international law seems limited. In the *Wimbledon* decision the Permanent Court rather failed to sufficiently justify any effectiveness *erga omnes* of treaty regulations, even embedded in universal or semi-universal treaties. It also failed to clarify how international custom is determined and what its role is in the international law-making process. The opinion on the normative irrelevance of customary law in this respect has been supported neither by other decisions of the World Court nor by empirical evaluations. In the *Wimbledon* case, the negligence in the Court's approach to the relationship between treaties and custom is noticeable in its reasoning on the obligations arising from the neutrality of states.

2.3 *The Relationship between Treaties and Custom; or Why General International Law Matters*

It is a truism that the relationship between treaties and custom is a complex issue that requires careful consideration to be clarified. It has even been called a 'paradox' in the *Wimbledon* case.[35] Sheila Weinberger argued that in this case the customary law of neutrality in 1921 allowed Germany to do that which the Versailles Treaty prohibited, and the 'paradox' existed because of coequality that treaties and custom share as sources of international law.[36] According to Weinberger, the Permanent Court failed to confront this paradox because it did not treat custom and treaties as coequal sources of law and, instead, it used judicial rhetoric to avoid addressing the issue.[37] In consequence, 'the Court left States in a position of uncertainty', as Weinberger put it.[38] She also accuses the Permanent Court of an 'intellectual dishonesty', claiming that 'rather than acknowledging the conflict which existed in this case, the Court used treaty interpretation and judicial rhetoric to avoid the most important issue. In the process, the Court affected the rights of a third party not before it, Russia'.[39]

There are, however, insufficient reasons to fully share these critical comments. First, it does not seem desirable to evaluate courts' reasoning from

35 Weinberger S., "The *Wimbledon* Paradox and the World Court: Confronting Inevitable Conflicts between Conventional and Customary International Law", *Emory International Law Review* 10 (1996) 397.
36 Ibid, 425.
37 Ibid, 399, 436.
38 Ibid, 399.
39 Ibid, 434–435.

the perspective of 'intellectual honesty' or 'dishonesty'. It should rather be assessed in terms of intellectual correctness and precision. Second, the allegation that the Court declined to treat treaties and custom as 'coequal sources' is unfounded. It is not coequality of treaties and custom that matters in the disputes submitted before the World Court, but normative conflicts between rules and principles following from them. And third, what Weinberger described as a 'paradox' is not a paradox at all, i.e., reasoning that is apparently correct but nonetheless leads to contradictory conclusions. The Court's reasoning in the *Wimbledon* dispute was not paradoxical. What it should be criticized for is its superficiality and inaccuracy in identifying norms of general international law, and in resolving normative conflicts between *lex generalis* and *lex specialis*, which topic will be discussed below.[40]

The method that the PCIJ used in the *Wimbledon* case to determine the applicable customary law has often been the topic of critical commentary. The majority of the bench in the judgment, as in the later *Lotus* judgment, applied an inductive approach to custom, that is, it derived a general rule from few and particular instances. Moreover, it did not actually refer to an *opinio juris* of states.[41] In consequence, the Court found that the general practice of a custom concerning neutrality could be determined from the provisions of no more than two treaties, those being the treaties that governed the Suez and Panama Canals, wherein the number of parties was at best rather limited. The awkward result was that the Court established a customary rule binding upon Germany relying upon treaties that did not involve Germany as a party.[42] Moreover, the

---

40 But cf. Verzijl J.H.H., *The Jurisprudence of the World Court. A Case by Case Commentary. Vol I: The Permanent Court of International Justice (1922–1940)* (Leyden: 1965) 43 (arguing that 'for the appreciation of the *Wimbledon* case it is unnecessary to enter into the difficult but extremely interesting questions as to the relation between general neutrality and special treaty obligations'). As an arbitrator in the *Georges Pinson* case, Verzijl seemed to present a different proposition: 'Every international convention must be deemed tacitly to refer to general principles of international law for all questions which it does not itself resolve in express terms and in a different way', *Georges Pinson (France) v. United Mexican States*, 19 October 1928, *Reports of International Arbitral Awards*, Vol V, 327–466.

41 Simma and Alston speaking of an "identity crisis" of customary law argued persuasively that while the Permanent Court, in the process of identifying rules of customary law had paid attention to practice, its successor emphasized the importance of *opinio juris*, which is particularly noticeable in the *Nicaragua* judgment. Simma B.-Alston P., "The Sources of Human Rights Law: Custom, Jus Cogens, and General Principles", *Australian Year Book of International Law* 12 (1989) 82, 88, 97, 104.

42 *Wimbledon*, 28. For critical comment see D'Amato A., *The Concept of Custom in International Law* (Ithaca N.Y.: 1971) 118–119; Weinberger, "The *Wimbledon* Paradox" 432. Cf. Hudson M.O., *The Permanent Court of International Justice 1920–1943* (New York: 1943) 655, 657; Wolfke K., *Custom in Present International Law* (Wrocław: 1961) 41.

Court did not prove that the stipulations relating to the "neutralization" in the 1901 Treaty between Great Britain and the United States on the Panama Canal were, as it said, 'to a great extent declaratory of the rules which a neutral State is bound to observe'.[43] Indeed, it is the relationship between treaties and custom, and the role of general international law that are probably the weakest parts of the judgment. Its rather poor arguments gave rise to doubts about the duties of the Respondent related to its neutrality towards any third state that is actively participating in an armed conflict. The shortcomings of the Court's justification of the normativity of general international law and its formal sources weaken its statement about the 'general and peremptory character' of Article 380 of the Versailles Treaty.

Spiermann, addressing the origin of the Court's Statute, claims that the discussion in the League of Nations' Advisory Committee of Jurists (ACJ) revealed a need for international law that went beyond positive rules identified with treaty and custom, and an expectation for the Court to fill the scope of general international law.[44] If that was indeed the case, the Permanent Court did not live up to the expectation of most of the ACJ's members. There was another need related to a new international judicial body of general jurisdiction, namely, establishing a broader framework of systemic, coherent and constitutional underpinnings for international law. There were great expectations in this regard after World War I.[45] Andreas Paulus claims from the contemporary perspective that the 'unity of the international legal system was never as great as in the interwar years, when the PCIJ provided some systemic coherence'.[46] Indeed, in the *Wimbledon* judgment the Court did not find a normative incoherence between treaties and custom, and thus it seemed to opt for the substantive unity of international law. However, the fragility of its arguments on application *erga omnes* of the treaty rules of an alleged peremptory character hardly permits one to include this decision in the legacy of the Permanent Court's support for a coherent framing of general international law.

---

43 *Wimbledon*, 26.

44 Spiermann O., "History of Article 38 of the Statute of the International Court of Justice: 'A Purely Platonic Discussion'?", in Besson – Aspremont de (eds.) *The Oxford Handbook of the Sources* 172–173.

45 See Kwiecień R., "The Permanent Court of International Justice and the Constitutional Dimension of International Law: From Expectations to Reality", in Tams – Fitzmaurice (eds.), *Legacies of the Permanent Court of International Justice* 361.

46 Paulus A.L., "The International Legal System as a Constitution", in Dunoff J.L. – Trachtman J.P. (eds.) *Ruling the World? Constitutionalism, International Law, and Global Governance* (Cambridge: 2009) 69, 75.

James Brierly, who also voiced his expectations with the Court's activity, hoped that the Court would produce a body of 'judge-made law'.[47] In his brief 1924 review of the *Wimbledon* judgment, Brierly stated that the Court 'has already, in the only judgment [...] so far reported, given judicial recognition to a new custom of very recent growth relating to international canals'.[48] Brierly touched on one of the most controversial aspects of the *Wimbledon* decision, which is the one concerning how customary rules are established. The question arises as to whether 'judicial recognition of a new custom' have a declaratory effect, or law-making one. Ultimately, it is about which source of obligation – treaties or custom – is more important both in the international law-making process, and for the rights and duties of disputing parties before the Court.

Two authors of comprehensive studies on the jurisprudence of the Permanent Court – Hersch Lauterpacht and Max Sørensen – disagreed in their assessments. In particular, they held disparate views on one point. Sørensen, in his *Les Sources du Droit International*, claimed that in the jurisprudence of the Court, treaty law was of primary importance.[49] Not, however, because the wording of Article 38 of the Court's Statute had had a decisive impact on its decisions, but because the Court proved to be a 'real Court of Justice' (*une veritable Cour de Justice*).[50] Meanwhile, Lauterpacht asserted a different view of the matter. He contended that whenever the Court applied international law, it first referred to international custom unless – expressly or by implication – it was a treaty that provided the basis of the decision.[51] His overall assessment of the impact of the *Wimbledon* decision on the development of international law was as follows:

47 Brierly J.L., "Shortcomings of International Law", in Brierly J.L., *The Basis of Obligations in International Law and Other Papers* (Oxford: 1958) 75.

48 Ibid. See also Deryng A., *Główne tendencje rozwojowe prawa narodów w świetle orzecznictwa Stałego Trybunału Sprawiedliwości Międzynarodowej* [*The Principal Trends in the Development of the Law of Nations under the Jurisprudence of the Permanent Court of International Justice*] (Lwów: 1932) 106–107 (claiming that the interpretation of treaty law on the international canals given in the *Wimbledon* decision had the effect of changing particular treaty rules into generally bindings rules on the legal regime of the international canals).

49 Sørensen M., *Les sources du droit international. Etude sur la Jurisprudence de la Cour Permamente de Justice Internationale* (Copenhague: 1946) 57.

50 Ibid, 252–253.

51 Lauterpacht H., *The Development of International Law by the International Court* (New York: 1958) 392–393.

> The judgment in the *Wimbledon* case, while answering the specific question as to the meaning of Article 380 of the Treaty of Versailles, is now an authority on the status of artificial waterways of an international character, on some aspects of neutrality, on restrictive interpretation of treaties – not to mention such matters as the measure of damages and award of interest.[52]

However, with the exception of the last of the topics mentioned by Lauterpacht, they are all controversial to a greater or lesser extent. Led by the status of neutrality, all have been burdened with some measure of doubt.

The Court defined the regulation of Article 380 of the Versailles Treaty as a 'provision of a general and peremptory character' or 'the general rule', and its terms as 'categorical'.[53] It recognized this regulation as evidence of the rule stating that 'the use of great international waterways, whether by belligerent men-of-war, or by belligerent or merchant ships carrying contraband, is not regarded as incompatible with the neutrality of the riparian sovereign'.[54] According to the Court, this rule had been earlier evidenced by the treaties on the Suez and Panama Canals. These 'precedents', as it claimed,

> are merely illustrations of the general opinion according to which when an artificial waterway connecting two open seas has been permanently dedicated to the use of the whole world, such waterway is assimilated to natural straits in the sense that even the passage of a belligerent man-of-war does not compromise the neutrality of the sovereign State under whose jurisdiction the waters in question lie.[55]

It means that this provision of the Treaty of Versailles was, in the thinking of the Court, of declaratory, and not law-making, character. Thus, it is custom, not the treaty, that was the source of this rule. The mentioned treaties on the international canals were just their supporting justification. This leads to the following conclusion regarding the contribution of the *Wimbledon* reasoning to the doctrine of sources: the difficulties in the Court's identification of customary rules were responsible for an unclear concept of general international law under the judgment.

---

52 Ibid, 29.
53 *Wimbledon*, 21, 22.
54 Ibid, 25.
55 Ibid, 28.

The dissenting judges, along with a number of scholars disapproved of the Court's methodology in the identification of customary rules.[56] Italian Judge Dionisio Anzilotti, who voted to dismiss a case filed by Italy, among others,[57] and Swiss Judge Max Huber in the joint dissenting opinion, pointed to a different custom than that supported by the majority of the bench. Both judges favored the right of each state to take necessary and extraordinary measures that would, in a case of war, temporarily affect the application of conventions concluded for the purpose of giving effect to the principle of freedom of transit. All states were entitled to do so, even if no express reservations were made in the convention. This right, according to Anzilotti and Huber, was based on 'generally accepted usage' and, as such, it had been 'recognised by a clause inserted in the Barcelona conventions concluded for the purpose of giving effect to the principle of freedom of communications which was enunciated in Article 23 of the Covenant of the League of Nations'.[58] Thus, under this opinion, treaty regime, as a *lex specialis*, was not allowed to derogate this right.

German Judge Walther Schücking in his dissenting opinion also drew attention to the relationship between the Versailles Treaty regime and customary law governing the status of neutrality and the resulting obligations. According to Schücking, the Kiel Canal was under the jurisdiction of Germany, and it was not neutralized as the Suez and Panama Canals had been. Its use was rather internationalized, like that of the great inland waterways. Moreover, the right to take special measures, be they in times of war or neutrality, was, Schücking claimed, not expressly renounced; nor could such renunciation be inferred from the fact that the Canal was to be 'maintained free and open'. The fact that the right was granted in perpetuity did not in itself exclude the possibility of regulating or even of temporarily suspending its exercise, since, he argued, the 'essential words' which were used to provide for the neutralization of the Suez

56 See above note 41 and Spiermann, *International Legal Argument* 184 (claiming that 'it can hardly justify a general theory of international canals, as the Permanent Court appeared to have in mind only the conflict between Article 380 of the Versailles Treaty and principles of neutrality'). But cf. Verzijl, *The Jurisprudence of the World Court* 44–45.

57 There were only four cases before the PCIJ where a judge voted against his own State. However, three of them, except the *Wimbledon*, were unanimously decided. See Grewe W.G., *Epochen der Völkerrechtsgeschichte* (2. Auflage, Baden-Baden: 1988) 723 (*The Epochs of International Law*, trans. Byers M. (Berlin: 2000) 615); Hudson M.O., *The Permanent Court of International Justice: A Treatise* (New York: 1934) 337–338.

58 *Wimbledon, Dissenting Opinion by M.M. Anzilotti and Huber*, 36. See Article 8 of the Barcelona Statute on Freedom of Transit, 20 April 1921, vol. 7 *League of Nations Treaty Series* No. 171, 26 ('This Statute does not prescribe the rights and duties of belligerents and neutrals in time of war. The Statute shall, however, continue in force in time of war so far as such rights and duties permit').

Canal and which were reproduced in the treaty relating to the Panama Canal, namely, 'in time of war as in time of peace', did not appear in Article 380 of the Versailles Treaty.[59] Judge Schücking addressed the normative conflict between customary law of neutrality and this treaty regime. He asserted that:

> [N]eutral duties must take precedence over any contractual obligations. The violation of the duties of a neutral no doubt constitutes an offence under international law even when treaty obligations assumed towards third States can be put forward in support of such an act. It cannot have been the intention of the victorious States to bind the Reich by means of the Versailles Treaty, to commit such offences as against third States. It would, moreover, have been impossible to give effect to such an intention, because a legally binding contractual obligation cannot be undertaken to perform acts which would violate the rights of third parties.[60]

Indeed, state neutrality, and its legal status and normative significance is perhaps a crucially substantive topic in the case.[61] That notwithstanding, the issues identified by the German judge *ad hoc*, in particular the intention of the parties to the Versailles Treaty, prompt consideration of the interpretation of treaties in the case.

3 Treaties and Their Interpretation under the Judgment or Does Interpretation Make International Law?

3.1 *Was the Principle of 'Systemic Integration' Relevant to the* Wimbledon *Dispute?*

Hersch Lauterpacht assessed that the majority of the cases, including the *Wimbledon* one, which came before the Permanent Court arose out of a disputed interpretation of a treaty.[62] This view simply declares the inherent interdependence of application and interpretation of legal rules and principles, which leads to a question whether and how interpretation shapes international law.[63] The World Court as a court of general jurisdiction was to 'decide

59 *Wimbledon, Dissenting Opinion by M. Schücking*, 43–44.

60 Ibid, 47.

61 See Chapter 7 by Michał Kowalski in this volume.

62 Lauterpacht, *The Development of International Law* 24.

63 See generally Venzke I., *How Interpretation Makes International Law. On Semantic Change and Normative Twists* (Oxford: 2012).

in accordance with international law' disputes submitted to it. The grammatical or textual interpretation of this stipulation leads to the conclusion that international law as a whole, not only a special treaty regime, should be taken into account by the International Court when deciding disputes. From the substantive point of view, moreover, no treaty regime has is grounded in a legal vacuum but is a part of the normative structure of international law, consisting of general principles of law, custom binding on the parties and their other treaty obligations. Therefore, when international courts and tribunals interpret rights and duties of the parties to treaties, they can be expected to interpret them against the background of 'any relevant rules of international law applicable in the relations between the parties' as indicated in Article 31 of the Vienna Convention on the Law of Treaties.[64] Before the adoption of the Vienna Convention, State delegates at the UN Conference on the Law of Treaties had reaffirmed the normative validity of this customary principle of treaty interpretation known as the principle of systemic integration.[65] The main issue of this part of the chapter is to discuss whether the Court was, when deciding on the treaty rights and duties of the parties to the *Wimbledon* dispute, guided by this systemic directive of interpretation and what were the consequences of its approach to interpretation for the coherence of its reasoning in the dispute.

The Court rejected the argument of the Respondent that the 'general grant of a right of passage to vessels of all nationalities through the Kiel Canal' could deprive Germany of the exercise of her rights as a neutral power in time of war because, the Court claimed, this contention 'conflicts with general considerations of the highest order'.[66] The term 'highest order' may incline to a conclusion that the Court believed in the treaty protection of common interests of the parties as different from bilateral interests strictly based on reciprocity. In this sense, the Court in the *Wimbledon* case, while characterizing the right to enter into international agreements as 'an attribute of State sovereignty', interpreted the notion of legal interest widely to include all the parties to the treaty regime

64 Article 31(3)(c) of the Vienna Convention on the Law of Treaties, 1155 *United Nations Treaty Series* 331.

65 On the origins of this provision of Article 31(3)(c) of the VCLT see Gardiner R., *Treaty Interpretation* (Oxford: 2010) 256–259; McLachlan C., "The Principle of Systemic Integration and Article 31(3)(c) of the Vienna Convention", *International and Comparative Law Quarterly* 54 (2005) 279, 290–293; Zabalza G.O., *The Principle of Systemic Integration. Towards a Coherent International Legal Order* (Zurich: 2012) 211–233.

66 *Wimbledon*, 25.

relating to the Kiel Canal in the execution of its provisions.[67] The Court did not, however, give the systemic approach to the interpretation of rights and duties of Germany as the party to the Versailles Treaty. The dissenting judges Anzilotti and Huber at the very beginning of the join dissenting opinion emphasized an issue of treaty interpretation as 'the essential difference' between their standpoint and that of the majority of the bench.[68] For them, the main legal question which should have been decided was whether the clauses of the Treaty of Versailles relating to the Kiel Canal also applied in the event of Germany's neutrality, or did they only contemplate normal circumstances, that is, a state of peace, without affecting the rights and duties of neutrality.[69] Both judges, as well as judge *ad hoc* Schücking in his dissent, accused in fact the majority of not using a teleological and systemic interpretation of Article 380 of the Versailles Treaty and, in consequence, the status of the Respondent under it. Anzilloti and Huber clearly underlined the limits of grammatical interpretation if such an interpretation would lead to contradictory or impossible consequences or which, in the circumstances, had to be regarded as going beyond the intention of the parties. They claimed: 'The purely grammatical interpretation of every contract, and more especially of international treaties, must stop at this point'.[70] According to them, the legal status of the Respondent was governed not only by Article 380 but also followed from 'generally accepted usage' which gave each State a right to taking extraordinary measures temporarily affecting the application of treaty provisions in order to protect its neutrality or for the purposes of national defense. It is entitled to do so even if no express reservations were made in treaties.[71] They argued:

> The right of a State to adopt the course which it considers best suited to the exigencies of its security and to the maintenance of its integrity, is so essential a right that, in case of doubt, treaty stipulations cannot be interpreted as limiting it, even though these stipulations do not conflict with such an interpretation.[72]

67 Gowlland-Debbas V., "The Role of the International Court of Justice in the Development of the Contemporary Law of Treaties", in Tams Ch.J. – Sloan J. (eds.), *The Development of International Law by the International Court of Justice* (Oxford: 2013) 25, 35.

68 *Wimbledon, Dissenting Opinion by M.M. Anzilotti and Huber*, 35.

69 Ibid.

70 Ibid, 36.

71 Ibid.

72 Ibid, 37.

Moreover, Anzilloti and Huber were against the strictly self-contained regulation of Article 380. They stated that Article 380 'must not be considered alone but in connection with the other provisions of the same section' because 'this Article, the first of the section, lays down the general rule which is supplemented and limited in the following articles'.[73]

Judge *ad hoc* Schücking also based his reasoning on the systemic interpretation of Article 380. He argued that the violation of the duties of a neutral no doubt constituted an offence under international law even when treaty obligations assumed towards third States could be put forward in support of such an act. According to him, however, it could not have been the intention of the parties to bind the Respondent, by means of the Versailles Treaty, to commit such offences as against third States. He finished his dissent as follow: '[A] legally binding contractual obligation cannot be undertaken to perform acts which would violate the rights of third parties'.[74] Meanwhile, the majority of the bench seemed to reject this systemic approach. They primarily believed in the treaties as a main formal source of international law and attributed to Article 380 such a high intrinsic normative significance that they saw no need to interpret it not only against the background of international law as a whole but also in the context of Part XII of the Versailles Treaty. The judgment recognized the regulation of Article 380 as of 'general and peremptory character' and its terms as 'categorical and give rise to no doubt'.[75] The Court agreed that the provisions relating to the Kiel Canal were 'self-contained' and they would lose their *raison d'être* if they had to be supplemented and interpreted by the provisions in the previous Sections of Part XII. Moreover, the Court emphasized that the idea of Article 380 and the following provisions was not to 'be sought by drawing an analogy from these provisions but rather by arguing *a contrario*, a method of argument which excludes them'.[76]

3.2 *The 'Plain Terms', the Intention of the Parties to the Versailles Treaty, and the Interpretation of the Treaty Provisions on the Kiel Canal or Does the Restrictive Interpretation Matter?*

In order to evaluate the presented interpretations of Article 380, it is necessary to refer the maxim *clara non sunt interpretanda* ('what is clear does not require interpretation') in the interpretation process, which concerns the 'plain terms' in treaties or the terms that 'are clear'. The doctrine of 'plain terms' emphasizes

73 Ibid, 38.

74 *Wimbledon, Dissenting Opinion by M. Schücking*, 47.

75 *Wimbledon*, 21, 22.

76 Ibid, 24.

the grammatical interpretation of treaties. Arnold McNair wrote of this doctrine before courts as follows:

> [I]t is submitted that while a term may be 'plain' *absolutely*, what a Court adjudicating upon the meaning of a treaty wants to ascertain is the meaning of the term *relatively*, that is, in relation to the circumstances in which the treaty was made. If that is what is meant by the doctrine of "plain terms", no objection is raised to it. But if it means that the Court must stop short at applying the term in its primary and literal sense and permit no inquiry as to anything further, it is submitted that the doctrine is wrong. The doctrine embodies a presumption but not an irrebuttable one, and it is reasonable to suppose that the Court will lay the burden of proof upon the party seeking to rebut the presumption.[77]

The Permanent Court, when speaking of the terms of Article 380 as 'categorical and give rise no doubt', supported the doctrine of 'plain terms' and gave the grammatical interpretation a crucial role.[78] Besides, the Court's recognition of the provisions relating to the Kiel Canal as 'self-contained' suggests that the Court saw the regime of the Kiel Canal as a strong form of *lex specialis*. It inclines to address the relationship between general international law and self-contained regimes, which was rather failed by the Court and what be discussed in the next part of the Chapter. It is the overall interpretative approach of the Court that needs to be addressed in this place. As said, the Court primarily relied on the grammatical interpretation to determine the rights and duties of the Respondent. Thus, it preferred the objective interpretation to the subjective or intentional one. The latter emphasizes the intention and will of the parties. The Court claimed that the terms of Article 380 'give rise no doubt' and the restrictive interpretation of the limitations of sovereign rights of Germany to the Kiel Canal has to 'stop at the point where the so-called restrictive interpretation would be contrary to the plain terms of the article and would destroy what has been clearly granted'.[79] Nowadays, the 'objective approach'

77 McNair A.D., *The Law of Treaties. British Practice and Opinions* (Oxford: 1938) 175–176 (emphasizes in original). See also ibid his remarks on 'implied terms and conditions' under the *Wimbledon* judgment, at 233 (n 2), 245.

78 *Wimbledon*, 22.

79 *Wimbledon*, 24–5. See Wittich S., "The Permanent Court of International Justice and the Modern International Law of Treaties", in Tams – Fitzmaurice (eds.), *Legacies of the Permanent Court* 89, 107–108 (claiming that the Permanent Court in its jurisprudence gave 'preference to the objective textual approach. This is not to say that the Court ignored the

is the leading approach among commentators of treaty practice based on the Vienna Convention on the Law of Treaties as well as in the practice of the World Court.[80] But it was controversial at the time. The dissenting judges in the case and treaty law experts and commentators of the *Wimbledon* decision of the time paid their attention upon the importance of the intention of the parties to the Treaty of Versailles to the effective interpretation of the treaty.[81] The majority of the bench itself did not completely ignore the intention of the parties to the Versailles Treaty.[82] But the intention of the parties was used by it to confirm the result of grammatical or textual interpretation of Article 380. This means that it served the Court as 'supplementary means' as stipulated in Article 32 of the Vienna Convention on the Law of Treaties.

The Court's approach to the restrictive interpretation of rights and duties of the Respondent against the background of the territorial regime of the Kiel Canal can be useful for addressing an issue of whether and how its interpretative practice shaped substantive law in the case. Essentially, the Court opted for the restrictive interpretation. It argued that the sovereign rights of the Respondent over the Kiel Canal constituted a 'sufficient reason for the restrictive interpretation, in case of doubt, of the clause which produces' their important limitation.[83] However, as already mentioned, the Court decided it was obliged to 'stop at the point where the so-called restrictive interpretation would be contrary to the plain terms of the article and would destroy what has been clearly granted'.[84]

---

common intention of the parties. But first of all, such intention must in any event be reflected in the terms of the treaty').

80 See e.g. *Application of the International Convention on the Elimination of All Forms of Racial Discrimination* (*Qatar v United Arab Emirates*) (Preliminary Objections) ICJ Reports 2021, 71, 98, para. 81 (repeating after its previous decisions: '[i]nterpretation must be based above all upon the text of the treaty').

81 See e.g. Lauterpacht H., *The Development of International Law by the Permanent Court* (Oxford: 1934) 69; Lauterpacht H, "Restrictive Interpretation and the Principle of Effectiveness in the Interpretation of Treaties", *British Yearbook of International Law* 26 (1949) 48; Ehrlich L., "L'interpretation des traités", *Recueil des Cours* 24 (1928) 1, 60, 92, 132–133, 136–137; Hudson, *The Permanent Court* 649–650 (who put on the top of the elements of interpretation under the jurisprudence of the PCIJ the concept of 'authentic interpretation', that is, the interpretation of a treaty on which all parties to it were agreed). Cf. Collette J., *Principes de droit des gens dans la jurisprudence de la Cour Permanente de Justice Internationale* (Paris: 1932) 73; Gardiner, *Treaty Interpretation* 59; Verzijl, *The Jurisprudence of the World Court* 44–45.

82 See *Wimbledon*, 23.

83 Ibid, 24.

84 See on the doctrine of 'plain terms' above note 77.

Wittich claims that in relation to territorial regimes the PCIJ applied a static approach to treaty interpretation that rested upon the political and social background that existed at the time the treaty was entered into force.[85] He also suggests the Court applied the rule of effectiveness interpreting treaties rather than gone for a restrictive approach.[86] Indeed, effectiveness of treaties as a logical consequence of good faith and acknowledgment of the great importance of the object and purpose of treaties played a large role in the case. It is the effectiveness of the treaty regime of the Kiel Canal established in the 'plain terms' that prevailed over the restrictive interpretation of the limitations of the Respondent's rights. Thus, according to the majority of the bench, rights and duties of the parties to the Versailles Treaty should be interpreted in accordance with its object and purpose, and not the other way round. There was an important implication of this interpretative practice concerning state sovereignty. It is known as one of the most famous *dicta* in the international judiciary and sounds that the conclusion of any treaty cannot be seen as an 'abandonment of sovereignty' but 'the right of entering into international engagements is an attribute of State sovereignty'.[87] Therefore, the restrictive interpretation of the limitations of the Respondent's rights was subordinated to the interpretation based on the ordinary meaning of the 'plain terms' of Article 380.[88] In consequence, the Court rejected the argument of Germany that the 'general grant of a right of passage to vessels of all nationalities through the Kiel Canal' could not deprive her of exercise of her rights as a neutral state in time of war. According to the Court, this contention 'conflicts with general considerations of the highest order' and 'is also gainsaid by consistent international practice and is at the same time contrary to the wording of Article 380 which clearly contemplates time of war as well as time of peace'.[89]

85 Wittich, "The Permanent Court" 100.

86 Ibid, 103.

87 *Wimbledon*, 25. See critical comments by Klabbers J., "Clinching the Concept of Sovereignty: *Wimbledon* Redux", *Austrian Review of International and European Law* 3 (1998) 345 and Chapter 5 in this book.

88 See Ehrlich, "L'interpretation des traités" 45, 69; Lauterpacht, *The Development of International Law* 302–303; Sørensen, *Les sources du droit international* 229. But cf. Crawford, *Chance, Order, Change* 91–92 (arguing that in the *Wimbledon* case the Court 'interpreted the provisions in accordance with their ordinary meaning but conceded that in case of doubt the interpretation least restrictive of sovereignty would prevail' and commenting that '[t]oday an international court will not start with such a presumption in interpreting a treaty'). Cf. also Wittich, "The Permanent Court" 105.

89 *Wimbledon*, 25.

The phrase 'consistent international practice' may indicate a systemic interpretation by the Court of the treaty provisions, that is, the interpretation against the background of customary law.[90] However, it does not seem relevant to the case in the face of doubts regarding the identification of customary rules by the Court. Another comment to the Court's position concerns the phrase 'highest order'. According to the Court, this order was made on the basis of the treaty law. Actually, each treaty regime is the highest order for the parties and is protected by the principle *pacta sunt servanda*.[91] But a question arises whether law-making or non-declaratory treaty provisions have a such normative validity to make obligations *erga omnes* in a true sense of the term, that is, obligations which protect not only collective interests of the parties to treaties but interests of the international community as a whole (community interests).[92] Anyway, the interpretative approach of the Permanent Court indicates its willingness to make international law through interpretation.

The analysis of the Court's interpretative practice in its first judgment leads to the conclusion that the Court noticed a new normative quality for the international law-making in treaties. It can be said that the order of enumeration of the grounds for decisions in Article 38 of the Statute was seen by the Court as a hierarchy of the normative validity of the sources. It is in the treaties, as the Court seemed to say, that the cure for the shortcomings of international law should be sought. The entry into force of a multilateral treaty of law-making character (*traite-loi*) was for the Court a clear evidence of the consent of its parties and their common will to ensure the effectiveness of treaty obligations, especially those of 'peremptory and categorical character'. Whether such a position of the treaties in the international normative hierarchy is justified enough to be the source of general international law is discussed in the next part on the 'relative normativity'.

90 Cf. Lauterpacht, *The Development of International Law* 393.

91 See Higgins R., "A Babel of Judicial Voices? Ruminations from the Bench", *International and Comparative Law Quarterly* 55 (2006) 791, 803 (claiming that each treaty regime is a special regime because each of them consists of own substantive primary rules).

92 See Article 48(1)(b) of *The Articles of the ILC: Responsibility of States for Internationally Wrongful Acts*, Annex to General Assembly resolution 56/83 of 12 December 2001, and corrected by document A/56/49 (Vol. I)/Corr.4.

4 'Relative Normativity' and the *Wimbledon* Decision

4.1 *Is the Normative Hierarchy Something Inherent to International Law?*

In the judgment the Court stated that the provisions of Article 380 of the Versailles Treaty could not be modified or affected by the rights and duties of states following from other sources of international legal obligations. However, it did not extensively address, first, whether a treaty itself is effective enough to establish a legal regime that would be applicable *erga omnes*, that is, a regime that would be, in fact, effective beyond the treaty regime itself; and, second, the relationship between treaties and customary rules that were recognized as being effective *erga omnes*. Consequently, the judgment is said to have given a poor answer to the question as to whether and why the treaty provisions could affect the rights of third states. Nonetheless, the Court drew its attention to the normative hierarchy, that is, a situation when priority has to be given to a specific rule among several that might have been applicable to a legal dispute or matter. The normative hierarchy or 'relative normativity', as Prosper Weil famously labeled it,[93] is relevant to the topic of sources of international law as norms in conflicts must come from somewhere, which means they are rooted in the sources understood as 'containers' of valid legal principles and rules.[94]

The Court seemed to perceive the normative differentiation among norms of international law in the case. At the same time, however, it tried to avoid deciding the normative conflict in the submitted dispute. The Court intended to support a 'harmonization attitude' based on a principle that when several norms bear on a single issue they should, to the extent possible, be interpreted so as to give rise to a single set of a compatible

93 Weil P., "Towards Relative Normativity in International Law?", *American Journal of International Law* 77 (1983) 413. See also Fastenrath U., "Relative Normativity in International Law", *European Journal of International Law* 4 (1993) 305; Goldmann M, "Relative Normativity", in d'Aspremont J. – Singh S. (eds.), *Concepts for International Law. Contributions to Disciplinary Thought* (Cheltenham: 2019) 740; Koskenniemi M., "Hierarchy in International Law: A Sketch", *European Journal of International Law* 8 (1997) 566; Shelton D., "International Law and 'Relative Normativity'", in Evans M.D. (ed.), *International Law* (3rd ed., Oxford: 2010) 141; Weiler J.H.H. – Paulus A.L., "The Structure of Change in International Law or Is There a Hierarchy of Norms in International Law?" *European Journal of International Law* 8 (1997) 545.

94 On the relationship between sources and the normative hierarchy in international law, see, e.g. de Wet E., "Sources and the Hierarchy of International Law: The Place of Peremptory Norms and Article 103 of the UN Charter within the Sources of International Law", in Besson – d'Aspremont (eds.), *The Oxford Handbook of the Sources of International Law* 625.

obligations.[95] But this endeavor was not completely coherent, since the Court rather moderately discussed the treaty provisions that were of 'categorical and peremptory character' against the background of general international law. In particular, it substantiated neither whether nor how law-making treaty provisions could be effective beyond the treaty regime, and applicable to third states. Thus, the Court's approach would be susceptible to Weil's criticism towards relative normativity. As known, Weil regarded the normative differentiation of international law as 'pathological'. According to him, international law would no longer be capable of fulfilling its function, i.e., the ordering of international relations in a heterogeneous, pluralist world, where the existence of rights or obligations were to be determined through the importation of material criteria into the law. That would give uncertain weight to such rights and obligations, and would abandon a neutral evaluation to be effected through the application of formal legal criteria. Weil opted for the latter and rejected the material criteria which, by introducing *jus cogens* norms and obligations *erga omnes*, deprive, in his opinion, international law of substantive neutrality, and question the normative significance of the principle of sovereign equality.[96]

These issues are crucial not only to the theory of international law sources, but also to the general theory of international law. Some of Weil's critics argue that what he described as 'relative normativity', that is, a hierarchy of norms, is not an expression of "pathological" development of international law, but a statement of fact inherent in the nature and structure of this law.[97] As Ulrich Fastenrath argues, the gradation of normativity of legal principles and rules is inevitable, which seems to be confirmed in all theories of law, including legal positivism on which Weil based his arguments.[98] Law, as well as other normative orders, always operates in a social context. Therefore, Dinah Shelton claims, the substantive or material criteria of the normative validity of its rules and principles are *nolens volens* elements of *secondary rules*.[99] It is a foundation of international law that the states subject to that law have agreed on the formal sources to identify binding legal obligations for the purpose of resolving their disputes, but, at the same time, they have not clearly determined a

95 See on 'the principle of harmonization', International Law Commission, Report of the Study Group of the International Law Commission, *Conclusions of the Work of the Study Group: Fragmentation of International Law: Difficulties Arising from the Diversification and Expansion of International Law*, para. 1(4), at 8.

96 See Weil, "Towards Relative Normativity" 416, 418, 431–433, 440–441.

97 See esp. Fastenrath, "Relative Normativity" 331–340; Shelton, "International Law and 'Relative Normativity'" 141–144.

98 Fastenrath, "Relative Normativity" 306.

99 Shelton, "International Law and 'Relative Normativity'" 143.

hierarchy of rules and principles – hence, the expectations of the World Court as a court of general jurisdiction regarding the clarification of the international normative hierarchy and the well-justified deciding normative conflicts. The PCIJ, after all, had declared itself to be a body authoritatively responsible for the knowledge of international law.[100]

The normative hierarchy between principles and rules resulting from different sources and conflicts between them are obvious, even natural, in the international legal order. There are many situations when priority must be given to a specific norm among several that may be applicable to a legal matter or dispute. As Shelton put it:

> In practice, conflicts among norms and their interpretation are probably inevitable in the present, largely decentralized international legal system where each State is entitled initially and equally to interpret for itself the scope of its obligations and the means of implementation such obligations require. The interpretations and determinations of applicable rules may vary considerable, making all international law somewhat relative, in the absence of institutions competent to render authoritative interpretations binding on all States.[101]

It is the absence of hierarchy among the formal sources of international law that is responsible for unclear rules governing normative conflicts between international legal regimes. Thus, it is not always unambiguous which conflicting norms prevail and what rules govern the resolution of normative conflicts. In particular, it is relevant when norms of general international law conflict with norms from a special regime. There are, however, a few possibilities to resolve such conflicts, including preventing and solving conflicts of international norms without prioritizing one over the other based on the principle of compliant interpretation or coherence also known as the principle of systemic integration.[102]

---

100 *Payment in Gold of Brazilian Federal Loans Contracted in France* (n 3) at 124.

101 Shelton, "International Law and 'Relative Normativity'" 142. See also Shelton D., "Normative Hierarchy in International Law", *American Journal of International Law* 100 (2006) 291.

102 Besson, "Theorizing the Sources of International Law" 183–184; Fitzmaurice M., "The History of Article 38 of the Statute of the International Court of Justice. The Journey from the Past to the Present", in Besson – Aspremont de (eds.), *The Oxford Handbook of the Sources of International Law* 179, 187–188. See also Part III.A of this chapter on the principle of systemic integration.

4.2 *Did the Court Resolve the Normative Conflict in the Judgment?*

In the *Wimbledon* case, there was a conflict between the regimes on international waterways on the one hand, and those on neutrality on the other. Judging from the terms of the *Wimbledon* decision, the regulation of Article 380 of the Versailles Treaty defined therein as 'peremptory' might have been seen as a specific special regime going beyond the treaty regime.[103] However, this does not go without saying, because the Court's definition of this regulation as 'peremptory' did not in itself confer a peremptory nature onto the regulation. Nor did it necessarily prove that it was *jus cogens*, even to the Court itself.[104] The majority of the bench failed, first, to decide whether the regulation of Article 380 had a law-making character, or declaratory one and, second, to compare customary international law on rights and duties of riparian states in connection with navigation through sea canals, with the treaty regulation on the Kiel Canal. Consequently, the Court did not actually find a normative conflict between the norms of general or customary law and the treaty regime of the Kiel Canal. This interpretation of the relevant law was challenged in the dissenting opinions. At any rate, the Court recognized that the Versailles regulation was a specific and special regime that might modify or qualify rights and duties of states under general international law.[105] However, a crucial issue is whether a treaty regime as a *lex specialis* prevails over norms of general international law that are recognized as being effective and applicable *erga omnes*. This is what the primary problem of the *Wimbledon* case boils down to. It, thus, seems necessary to discuss whether and what rules of general international law should have been applied to the dispute, and whether the Court correctly shaped their relation to Article 380 of the Versailles Treaty.

As mentioned above, the Permanent Court failed to meet the expectations of most members of the Advisory Committee of Jurists, especially Edouard

---

103 The International Law Commission has used the *Wimbledon* case as evidence of the treaty special regime relating to a special subject matter. See Report of the Study Group of the International Law Commission, *Conclusions of the Work of the Study Group, Fragmentation of International Law: Difficulties Arising from the Diversification and Expansion of International Law*, para 12 (note 14) at 12. See also Borgen Ch.J., "Treaty Conflicts and Normative Fragmentation", in Hollis D.B. (ed.), *The Oxford Guide to Treaties* (Oxford: 2014) 448, 467.

104 Orakhelashvili A., *Peremptory Norms in International Law* (Oxford: 2007) 42.

105 Orakhelashvili, *Peremptory Norms* 166 claims that in the *Wimbledon* case general international law was 'irrelevant'. See also Villiger M.E., *Customary International Law and Treaties. A Study of Their Interactions and Interrelations with Special Consideration of the 1969 Vienna Convention on the Law of Treaties* (Dordrecht-Boston-Lancaster: 1985) 35, note 353 (who claimed, referring to the *Wimbledon* case, that 'the PCIJ occasionally preferred a treaty rule to a conflicting customary rule').

Descamps, on the role of general international law as a kind of international law beyond treaties.[106] Spiermann states that there was a great expectation that the Court would fill the scope of general international law which in Article 38 of the Statute was justified as 'international custom', 'general principles of law', 'judicial decisions', and 'teachings of publicists'.[107] If this opinion is correct, the national lawyers sitting on the bench in the *Wimbledon* case squandered an opportunity to clarify the concept and role of general international law, because they marginalized its importance and regarded treaties as the primary source of international law. Hence, difficulties arise in the Court's reasoning in defining the relationship between general international law and treaties. In particular, the majority of the bench addressed the relationship between Article 380 and general international law neither under the rule *lex specialis derogate legi generali* nor under *lex generalis derogate legi speciali*.

The Court's difficulties in identifying customary rules was not the only reason for its non-enthusiastic, so to say, approach to the unwritten sources of general international law. The Court also failed to use the normative potential of general principles of law in the judgment as it has recently been assessed.[108] Instead, the Court based its arguments on the Versailles Treaty, but did not justify the applicability of its rules regarding the Kiel Canal towards third states, including Germany's duties as a neutral state. The problem in the *Wimbledon* case in this context was whether Russia could have legitimate expectations towards Germany as a neutral state under general international law. The Court, in fact, gave a negative answer, since it adopted that free passage through the Kiel Canal was based on only one condition, namely, the belonging of vessels to states that were at peace with Germany.[109] Great Britain and France were at peace with Germany when the "*Wimbledon*" incident occurred, and the Court argued that Germany was free to declare and regulate her neutrality in the Polish–Russian war. But neither Russia nor Poland was at war with Germany at that time either. That is why, the Court claimed, Germany was not only entitled to permit the passage of the "*Wimbledon*", but that it was her 'definite duty' to allow it.[110] The Court, in fact, assumed that the Versailles Treaty regime on the

106 Advisory Committee of Jurists, *Procès-verbaux of the Proceedings of the Advisory Committee of Jurists, June 16-July 24 1920, with Annexes* (The Hague: 1920) 264 (Descamps). For comments see Spiermann, "History of Article 38" 171–173.

107 Spiermann, "History of Article 38" 168.

108 Saunders I., *General Principles as a Source of International Law. Art 38(1)(c) of the Statute of the International Court of Justice* (Oxford: 2021) 57. See also Cheng B., *General Principles of Law as Applied by International Courts and Tribunals* (London: 1958) 29–30.

109 *Wimbledon*, 22.

110 Ibid, 30.

Kiel Canal did not infringe the rights of third states, since, in the view of the Court, free passage through international canals did not undermine the neutrality of the riparian states under customary law. This conclusion was based on the presumption of non-contradiction between the special treaty regime and general international law. But the Court's problems with identification of rules of customary law on neutrality, as the dissenting judges indicated, could lead to the refutation of this presumption.

The crucial problem for the 'relative normativity' issue is whether a special treaty regime, such as the Versailles regime on the Kiel Canal, can legitimately derogate rules of general international law. It seems that while special treaty regimes may make rights effective *erga omnes*, the exercise of these rights when third states are affected is legitimized only if it does not lead to the violation of obligations *erga omnes* under general international law. Therefore, a generally accepted means of interpretation and normative conflict resolution, the maxim *lex specialis derogate legi generali*, is not relevant in every situation concerning normative conflicts. There are certain kinds of general international law from which special treaty regimes simply may not derogate.[111] In the *Wimbledon* case it concerned the duties of the Respondent as a neutral state vis-à-vis the Soviet Russia which might have been affected by the treaty regime on the Kiel Canal. There has been no accepted definition of general international law. The Permanent Court, however, tried to derive general law from the Versailles treaty, since it saw treaties as a remedy for the shortcomings of the international law-making process. This can explain the failings in its arguments regarding custom and the complete marginalization of general principles of law. True, the judges deciding the *Wimbledon* case were, as mentioned, aware of normative conflicts. But the majority of the bench, due to these failings and the adopted interpretation of the rights and duties of the Respondent as the neutral and riparian state, decided that, in fact, there was no normative conflict in the case.

Judge *ad hoc* Schücking in his dissenting opinion offered two important propositions for the 'relative normativity' problem. First, he argued that a treaty regime as a *lex specialis* could not derogate from generally accepted custom, which was also stressed by Anzilotti and Huber. And second, he questioned

111 See International Law Commission, Report of the Study Group of the International Law Commission, *Conclusions of the Work of the Study Group on the Fragmentation of International Law: Difficulties Arising from the Diversification and Expansion of International Law*, para. 2(10), at 10.

whether a treaty, in its limited scope, had the authority to make general international law, that is, to make a law that would be effective *erga omnes*.[112]

The majority of the bench in the *Wimbledon* decision and the dissenting judges disagreed on the normative importance of customary law, the ways of identifying its rules, and their interpretation. These issues, as known, caused considerable problems then as they do now. The majority of the bench argued that

> the precedents [...] afforded by the Suez and Panama Canals [...] are merely illustrations of the general opinion [...] that even the passage of a belligerent man-of-war does not compromise the neutrality of the sovereign State under whose jurisdiction the waters in question lie.[113]

Whose 'general opinion' did the majority of the bench have in mind? Rather not states' but scholars' as most commentators argued.[114] This opinion was therefore not an *opinio juris* of the primary members of the international community, but, 'the teachings of the most highly qualified publicists', that is, 'subsidiary means for the determination of rules of law' as defined in Article 38(1)(d) of the Statute of the World Court. Moreover, the generality of this opinion was not evidenced in the judgment. Therefore, this opinion cannot be considered as a decisive means for the determination of a customary rule that 'passage of a belligerent man-of-war does not compromise the neutrality of the sovereign State under whose jurisdiction the waters in question lie', as the Court claimed. The bench, in its attempt to demonstrate the normative validity of this customary rule, failed to properly identify the relevant state practice. It referred only to the treaties on the Suez and Panama Canals and the mentioned subsidiary means. That is why the Court's position on customary law can hardly be approved.

Germany's refusal to allow the steamship "*Wimbledon*" to pass through the Kiel Canal could qualify in terms of the following possibilities: there was a 'definite duty', as the Court claimed, to allow passage through the Canal, and therefore this refusal violated international law or, alternatively, the Respondent

---

112 *Wimbledon, Dissenting Opinion by M. Schücking*, 43–44. See also *Wimbledon, Dissenting Opinion by M.M. Anzilotti and Huber*, 36.

113 *Wimbledon*, 28.

114 See e.g. Lauterpacht, *The Development of International Law* 24 (writing 'what the Court actually had in mind was opinions of writers'); Sørensen, *Les sources du droit international* 181 (recognizing it as *des opinions doctrinales*); Wolfke, *Custom* 151 (referring to 'opinions of publicists' or 'writers'; but see ibid, 41).

had no such duty. Indeed, a right of free passage through the Kiel Canal was clearly established in the Versailles Treaty. But the Court neglected to provide comprehensive justification for the advantage and superiority of this regulation over rules following from general international law and not clearly defined in this treaty, in particular those concerning the neutrality and security of the riparian state and its duties towards third states.

4.3 *Why General International Law Matters*

Manley Hudson argued that if a problem 'cannot be disposed of by the application of a provision in an agreement in force between the parties, a tribunal must take a wider search, for which numerous guides are available'.[115] This view needs a short comment: even if an international court has jurisdiction to settle a dispute on the basis of a clear treaty regulation, its decision should also be grounded in general international law, since no treaty regulation exists in a legal vacuum. As a consequence, it is necessary to discuss the relationship between *lex specialis* and *lex generalis*. In this context, it is worth remembering ICJ Justice and former President Rosalyn Higgins's dissent in the *Nuclear Weapon* case. She argued: 'It is an essential requirement of the judicial process that a court should show the steps by which it reaches its conclusions'.[116] Did the Permanent Court exercise due diligence in the *Wimbledon* reasoning in this respect? Rather not, since it did not address comprehensively the mutual relationships between treaty obligations on the one hand, and customary sources of rights and obligations of the parties on the other. This problem was referred to much more clearly in the dissents.

The Court in its first judgment took into account, as mentioned, the normative conflict in the submitted dispute. After all, it recognized the Respondent's contention that was submitted in the proceedings as being 'conflicts with general considerations of the highest order', 'gainsaid by consistent international practice', and 'contrary to the wording of Article 380'.[117] This means that the legal obligations of the parties to the proceedings might arise from various sources. But to the Court, among different rules applicable to the parties, those

115 Hudson, *International Tribunals* 107–108.

116 *Legality of the Threat or Use of Nuclear Weapons, Dissenting Opinion of Judge Higgins*, ICJ Reports 1996, par. 7, at 584. Higgins further claimed: 'Nor is the situation changed by any suggestion that the problem is as much one as "antimony" or clashes between various elements in the law as much as alleged "vagueness" in the law. Even were there such an "antimony" (which, as I have indicated above, I doubt), the judge's role is precisely to decide which of two or more competing norms is applicable in the particular circumstances' (ibid, par. 40, at 592).

117 *Wimbledon*, 25.

resulting from the Versailles Treaty comprised the most important legal regime to the parties. Did the priority of this treaty regime follow from a *lex specialis* rule? Unfortunately, the Court did not address this issue, since it found no conflict between the special treaty regime and general customary international law. By this means it avoided any conflict between the treaty duties of the Respondent regarding the Kiel Canal, and its duties as a neutral state in the Polish–Russian armed conflict. However, the Court's superficial determination of the rules of general customary law on neutrality has raised doubts about the legitimacy of this finding, which the dissenting judges subsequently emphasized. Thus, one could hardly contend that the Court evidenced the creation of the 'highest order' of the alleged peremptory character based on the treaty provisions regarding the Kiel Canal. Therefore, their entire effectiveness *erga omnes* can be also questionable. When the successor of the PCIJ spoke about *erga omnes* rules for the first time, it clearly linked them to general international law.[118] While the treaty-established freedom of passage through the Kiel Canal implied the right for all states, and in this sense it was the self-contained regime, the rights and duties of Germany as a territorial sovereign have also been governed by customary law which supplemented this treaty regime.[119] This means that no international self-contained regime has an absolute normative value, but rather only a relative one, because its substantive importance is revealed against the background of general international law. The *Wimbledon* judgment has not been instrumental in elaborating the concept of treaties with a collective interest. The PCIJ tried to give treaties the greatest role in the international law-making process, but its arguments did not show that it is, in fact, treaties that are the primary formal source of general international law. Then as now, the rules of this law that could be effective *erga omnes* could hardly be established in universal or semi-universal treaties. Therefore, no law-making or non-declaratory provisions of a treaty can be applicable *erga omnes* beyond the treaty. Actually, in the practice of international courts and tribunals there has been no international decision confirming the primary role of any law-making provisions of treaties in the international law-making process.

The Court seemed to place too much faith in the normative power of treaties. This, however, can lead to a paradox, characterized by Roger Baxter as 'the more agreement, the less law'.[120] As the Baxter paradox shows, the practice of

118 See *Barcelona Traction, Light and Power Company, Limited*, Judgment, ICJ Reports 1970, 3, 32, paras. 33–34.

119 See Chapter 4 by Malgosia Fitzmaurice and Agnes Rydberg in this volume.

120 Baxter R., "Treaties and Custom", *Recueil des Cours* 129 (1970) 25, 64. See comments on this 'paradox', Crawford, *Chance, Order, Change* 115–118, 134–146.

shaping custom cannot be based exclusively on the activity of the parties to law-making treaties. The states that have not acceded must also participate in this practice. This suggests that the impact and role of treaties in international law-making is not primarily determined by the number of parties to them. Universal or semi-universal treaties seem at first glance to be the only exceptions. However, non-declaratory provisions in universal treaties are not *ipso facto* rules of general international law. There is a gap between the contractual form and the law-making function of treaties which weakens their normative significance.[121] They need *opinio juris* grounded in practice to generate the law. Hence, doubt arises as to whether treaties can be regarded as formal sources of international law,[122] and for the international law-making process, 'custom is more than treaty, more even than a generally accepted treaty', as Crawford put it.[123]

The problems of the relationship between treaties and custom as discussed by Baxter could be more clearly explained by an approach that, on the one hand, takes into account the intrinsic normative conflicts among principles and rules of international law, and on the other hand, seeks to resolve them through systemic interpretation. As it seems, the PCIJ might have avoided the mentioned shortcomings of its reasoning in the *Wimbledon* dispute if it had taken the systemic integration approach, as presented today by the Study

121 Brölmann C., "Law-Making Treaties: Form and Function in International Law", *Nordic Journal of International Law* 74(3–4) (2005) 383, 400.

122 See Fitzmaurice G.G., "Some Problems Regarding the Formal Sources of International Law" in Asbeck F.M. Van et al (eds.), *Symbolae Verzijl. Présentés au Professeur J.H. Verzijl à L'occasion de Son LXX-ième Anniversaire* (Leyden: 1958) 153, 157; Jennings – Watts, *Oppenheim's International Law* 24–25, 31; Besson, "Theorizing the Sources of International Law" 168–169; Brölmann, "Law-Making Treaties" 398; Condorelli L., "Customary International Law: The Yesterday, Today, and Tomorrow of General International Law" in Cassese A. (ed.), *Realizing Utopia. The Future of International Law* (Oxford: 2012) 149–152.

123 Crawford, *Chance, Order, Change* 139. See also Brölmann, "Law-Making Treaties" 383; Charney J., "Universal International Law", *American Journal of International Law* 87 (1993) 529, 551; Dinstein Y., "The Interaction between Customary International Law and Treaties" 322 (2006) *Recueil des Cours* 243, 377–378; Kwiecień R., "The Formal Sources of International Law, the Relationship between Treaties and Custom, and the International Law-Making Process", *Australian Year Book of International Law* 40 (2022) 46, 62–65. But see contra, e.g., *Dissenting Opinion* by Judge Alvarez to the *Reservations to the Convention on Prevention and Punishment of the Crime of Genocide* Advisory Opinion, [1951] ICJ Rep 15, 53 (*'Reservations'*). Judge Alvarez claimed that law-making treaties 'signed by a great majority of States ought to be binding upon the others, even though they have not expressly accepted them'. Likewise D'Amato A., "Treaties as a Source of General Rules of International Law", *Harvard International Law Club Journal* 3(2) (1962) 1, 12–17.

Group of the International Law Commission in its report on fragmentation of international law. It states:

> International law is a legal system. Its rules and principles (i.e. its norms) act in relation to and should be interpreted against the background of other rules and principles. As a legal system, international law is not a random collection of such norms. There are meaningful relationships between them.[124]

Indeed, the interpretative approach matters. But in the *Wimbledon* judgment the Court did not address these 'meaningful relationships' in sufficient depth, and, as a result, general international law receded into the background. In consequence, the Court was unable to clearly identify the relationship between the divergent formal sources of international law in the case.

5 Conclusion

In this chapter, the author generally sought to answer the question as to whether, under the *Wimbledon* judgment, treaties can be seen as a real formal source of general international law, or merely a source of legal obligations to their parties. The problem concerns the relationship of treaty obligations to unwritten sources of international law, that is, custom and general principles of law. The judgment is vulnerable to criticism for the absence of a convincing treatment of this issue. In particular, for its failure to satisfactorily identify any applicable customary rules of international law, their effects, or any relation to treaty obligations. Consequently, the Permanent Court gave a rather modest answer to the question as to whether and why the treaty provisions could affect the interests of non-party states.

Nonetheless, the *Wimbledon* judgment draws attention to crucial issues in the debate on the sources of international law. Firstly, it indicates that normative conflicts are something not only intrinsic to, but also useful for, the development of international law. Addressing these conflicts may contribute to the clarification of international legal norms, and the examination of what is crucial for the normative validity of general international law, that is, the universal *opinio juris* of states. Secondly, contrary to the Court's reasoning, the

124 See Report of the Study Group of the International Law Commission, *Conclusions of the Work of the Study Group on Fragmentation of International Law: Difficulties Arising from the Diversification and Expansion of International Law*, para 1(1), at 7.

Wimbledon case speaks against the identification of the universality of certain treaty obligations resulting from the acceptance of certain treaties by almost all states with the generality of their rules. The binding force of all treaties, governed by consent and *pacta tertiis* rules, is simply limited to the parties. From this point of view treaties would not be able to make a law that binds all subjects in the international legal order. Although law-making treaties are seen to be an important and even necessary means in the international law-making process, treaty regimes cannot bind beyond the treaties themselves. What is more, their normative validity stems from this 'beyond', that is, from general law. This formal and arguably formalist approach supports the idea that treaty obligations have no *raison d'être* outside the treaty regime, unless the treaty confirms the rules of law that arose before its adoption, and third-states choose to conform to these rules. However, the normative validity of such rules does not derive from the treaty itself, but stems from a general practice that is accepted as settled law, that is, from custom. The main doubt about the contribution of the *Wimbledon* decision to the debate on sources arises from the lack of clarification of a scope of customary rules on neutrality binding before the adoption of the Versailles Treaty, and their relationship to the latter. Subsequent jurisprudence of the World Court has explored the relationship between treaties and custom more thoroughly.[125] Indeed, the development of international law is also expressed and visible in the development of its judicial application which can support progress in this law.

Acknowledgments

The publication was funded by the Faculty of Law and Administration of the Jagiellonian University granted within the Priority Research Area Anthropocene under the program "Excellence Initiative – Research University" at the Jagiellonian University in Kraków. The open access publication was funded by the Faculty of Law and Administration of the Jagiellonian University, granted within the Priority Research Area "Heritage" under the program "Excellence Initiative – Research University" at the Jagiellonian University in Krakow.

125 See esp. *Reservations to the Convention on Genocide*, Advisory Opinion, ICJ Reports 1951, 15, 23–24, 53; *North Sea Continental Shelf Cases* (Federal Republic of Germany/Denmark; Federal Republic of Germany/Netherlands) Judgment, ICJ Reports 1969, 3, 43, para. 76; *Continental Shelf* (Libyan Arab Jamahiryia/Malta) Judgment, ICJ Reports 1985, 13, 30, para. 27; *Military and Paramilitary Activities in and against Nicaragua* (Nicaragua v. United States of America), Merits, Judgment, ICJ Reports 1986, 14, 93–96, para. 175–179.

Bibliography

Argent P. de, "Sources and the Legality and Validity of International Law: What Makes Law 'International'", in Besson S. – d'Aspremont J. (eds.), *The Oxford Handbook of the Sources of International Law* (Oxford: 2017) 541.

Aspremont J. de, *Formalism and the Sources of International Law. A Theory of the Ascertainment of Legal Rules* (Oxford: 2011).

Baxter R., "Treaties and Custom", *Recueil des Cours* 129 (1970) 25.

Besson S., "Theorizing the Sources of International Law", in Besson S. – Tasioulas J. (eds.), *The Philosophy of International Law*, (Oxford: 2010).

Borgen Ch.J., "Treaty Conflicts and Normative Fragmentation", in Hollis D.B. (ed.), *The Oxford Guide to Treaties* (Oxford: 2014).

Brierly J.L., "Shortcomings of International Law", in Brierly J.L., *The Basis of Obligations in International Law and Other Papers* (Oxford: 1958).

Brölmann C., "Law-Making Treaties: Form and Function in International Law", *Nordic Journal of International Law* 74(3–4) (2005) 383.

Charney J., "Universal International Law", *American Journal of International Law* 87 (1993) 529.

Cheng B., *General Principles of Law as Applied by International Courts and Tribunals* (London: 1958).

Collette J., *Principes de droit des gens dans la jurisprudence de la Cour Permanente de Justice Internationale* (Paris: 1932).

Condorelli L., "Customary International Law: The Yesterday, Today, and Tomorrow of General International Law" in Cassese A. (ed.), *Realizing Utopia. The Future of International Law* (Oxford: 2012).

Crawford J., *Chance, Order, Change: The Course of International Law* (The Hague: 2014).

D'Amato A., "Treaties as a Source of General Rules of International Law", *Harvard International Law Club Journal* 3(2) (1962) 1.

D'Amato A., *The Concept of Custom in International Law* (Ithaca N.Y.: 1971).

Deryng A., *Główne tendencje rozwojowe prawa narodów w świetle orzecznictwa Stałego Trybunału Sprawiedliwości Międzynarodowej* [*The Principal Trends in the Development of the Law of Nations under the Jurisprudence of the Permanent Court of International Justice*] (Lwów: 1932).

Dinstein Y., "The Interaction between Customary International Law and Treaties" 322 (2006) *Recueil des Cours* 243.

Ehrlich L., "L'interpretation des traités", *Recueil des Cours* 24 (1928) 1.

Fastenrath U., "Relative Normativity in International Law", *European Journal of International Law* 4 (1993) 305.

Fitzmaurice G.G., "Some Problems Regarding the Formal Sources of International Law" in Asbeck F.M. Van et al (eds.), *Symbolae Verzijl. Présentés au Professeur J.H. Verzijl à L'occasion de son LXX-ième Anniversaire* (Leyden: 1958) 153.

Fitzmaurice M., "The History of Article 38 of the Statute of the International Court of Justice. The Journey from the Past to the Present", in Besson S. – d'Aspremont J. (eds.), *The Oxford Handbook of the Sources of International Law* (Oxford: 2017) 179.

Gardiner R., *Treaty Interpretation* (Oxford: 2010).

Goldmann M, "Relative Normativity", in d'Aspremont J. – Singh S. (eds.), *Concepts for International Law. Contributions to Disciplinary Thought* (Cheltenham: 2019) 740.

Gowlland-Debbas V., "The Role of the International Court of Justice in the Development of the Contemporary Law of Treaties", in Tams Ch.J. – Sloan J. (eds.), *The Development of International Law by the International Court of Justice* (Oxford: 2013) 25.

Grewe W.G., *Epochen der Völkerrechtsgeschichte* (2. Auflage, Baden-Baden: 1988).

Hammarskjöld A., "The Permanent Court of International Justice and the Development of International Law", *International Affairs* 14 (1935) 799.

Hart H.L.A., *The Concept of Law* (3 rd ed., Oxford: 2012).

Higgins R., "A Babel of Judicial Voices? Ruminations from the Bench", *International and Comparative Law Quarterly* 55 (2006) 791.

Hudson M.O., *International Tribunals: Past and Future*, (Washington D.C.: 1944).

Hudson M.O., *Progress in International Organization* (Stanford: 1932).

Hudson M.O., *The Permanent Court of International Justice 1920–1943* (New York: 1943).

Hudson M.O., *The Permanent Court of International Justice: A Treatise* (New York: 1934).

Jennings R.,Watts A., *Oppenheim's International Law* (9th ed., vol. 1, London: 1996).

Klabbers J., "Clinching the Concept of Sovereignty: *Wimbledon* Redux", *Austrian Review of International and European Law* 3 (1998) 345.

Koskenniemi M., "Hierarchy in International Law: A Sketch", *European Journal of International Law* 8 (1997) 566.

Koskenniemi M., *From Apology to Utopia. The Structure of International Legal Argument* (rev. ed., Cambridge: 2005).

Kwiecień R., "The Formal Sources of International Law, the Relationship between Treaties and Custom, and the International Law-Making Process", *Australian Year Book of International Law* 40 (2022) 46.

Kwiecień R., "The Permanent Court of International Justice and the Constitutional Dimension of International Law: From Expectations to Reality", in Tams Ch.J. – Fitzmaurice M. (eds.), *Legacies of the Permanent Court of International Justice* (Leyden: 2013).

Lauterpacht H., "Restrictive Interpretation and the Principle of Effectiveness in the Interpretation of Treaties", *British Yearbook of International Law* 26 (1949) 48.

Lauterpacht H., *The Development of International Law by the International Court* (New York: 1958).

Lauterpacht H., *The Development of International Law by the Permanent Court* (Oxford: 1934).

McLachlan C., "The Principle of Systemic Integration and Article 31(3)(c) of the Vienna Convention", *International and Comparative Law Quarterly* 54 (2005) 279.

McNair A.D., *The Law of Treaties. British Practice and Opinions* (Oxford: 1938).

Neff S.C., *Justice Among Nations. A History of International Law* (Cambridge, Massachusetts: 2014).

Orakhelashvili A., *Peremptory Norms in International Law* (Oxford: 2007).

Paulus A.L., "The International Legal System as a Constitution", in Dunoff J.L. – Trachtman J.P. (eds.) *Ruling the World? Constitutionalism, International Law, and Global Governance* (Cambridge: 2009).

Rasulov A., "The Doctrine of Sources in the Discourse of the Permanent Court of International Justice", in Tams Ch.J. – Fitzmaurice M. (eds.), *Legacies of the Permanent Court of International Justice* (Leyden: 2013).

Saunders I., *General Principles as a Source of International Law. Art 38(1)(c) of the Statute of the International Court of Justice* (Oxford: 2021).

Schachter O., "International Law in Theory and Practice. General Course in Public International Law", *Recueil des Cours* 178 (1982) 9.

Shelton D., "International Law and 'Relative Normativity'", in Evans M.D. (ed.), *International Law* (3 rd ed., Oxford: 2010) 141.

Shelton D., "Normative Hierarchy in International Law", *American Journal of International Law* 100 (2006) 291.

Sørensen M., *Les sources du droit international. Etude sur la Jurisprudence de la Cour Permamente de Justice Internationale* (Copenhague: 1946).

Spiermann O., "History of Article 38 of the Statute of the International Court of Justice: 'A Purely Platonic Discussion'?", in Besson S. – Aspremont de J. (eds,) *The Oxford Handbook of the Sources of International Law* (Oxford: 2017).

Spiermann O., *International Legal Argument in the Permanent Court of International Justice. The Rise of the International Judiciary* (Cambridge: 2005).

Verzijl J.H.H., *The Jurisprudence of the World Court. A Case by Case Commentary. vol. I: The Permanent Court of International Justice (1922–1940)* (Leyden: 1965).

Villiger M.E., *Customary International Law and Treaties. A Study of their Interactions and Interrelations with Special Consideration of the 1969 Vienna Convention on the Law of Treaties* (Dordrecht-Boston-Lancaster: 1985).

Weil P., "Towards Relative Normativity in International Law?", *American Journal of International Law* 77 (1983) 413.

Weiler J.H.H., Paulus A.L., "The Structure of Change in International Law or Is There a Hierarchy of Norms in International Law?" *European Journal of International Law* 8 (1997) 545.

Weinberger S., "The *Wimbledon* Paradox and the World Court: Confronting Inevitable Conflicts between Conventional and Customary International Law", *Emory International Law Review* 10 (1996) 397.

Wet E. de, "Sources and the Hierarchy of International Law: The Place of Peremptory Norms and Article 103 of the UN Charter within the Sources of International Law", in Besson S. – d'Aspremont J. (eds.), *The Oxford Handbook of the Sources of International Law* (Oxford: 2017).

Wittich S., "The Permanent Court of International Justice and the Modern International Law of Treaties", in Tams Ch.J. – Fitzmaurice M. (eds.), *Legacies of the Permanent Court of International Justice* (Leyden: 2013).

Wolfke K., *Custom in Present International Law* (Wrocław: 1961).

Wolfrum R., "Sources of International Law", in Peters A. (ed.), *Max Planck Encyclopedia of Public International Law* (vol. IX, Oxford: 2012) (online at 6 November 2022).

Zabalza G.O., *The Principle of Systemic Integration. Towards a Coherent International Legal Order* (Zurich: 2012).

Judgments and Advisory Opinions

PCIJ

Case Concerning the Payment in Gold of Brazilian Federal Loans Contracted in France [1929] PCIJ Ser A No 21.

Case of the s.s. "Wimbledon" [1923] PCIJ Ser A No 1.

The Case of the ss "Lotus" [1927] PCIJ Ser A No 10.

The s.s. "Wimbledon", Documents of the Written Procedure [1923] PCIJ Ser C No 3 (Additional Volume), 1.

The s.s. "Wimbledon", Documents of the Written Procedure [1923] PCIJ Ser C No 3 (Additional Volume), 40.

Wimbledon, Dissenting Opinion by M. Schücking.

Wimbledon, Dissenting Opinion by M.M. Anzilotti and Huber.

ICJ

Application of the International Convention on the Elimination of All Forms of Racial Discrimination (*Qatar v United Arab Emirates*) (Preliminary Objections) ICJ Reports 2021, 71.

Barcelona Traction, Light and Power Company, Limited, Judgment, ICJ Reports 1970, 3.

Legality of the Threat or Use of Nuclear Weapons, Advisory Opinion, ICJ Reports 1996, 226.

Legality of the Threat or Use of Nuclear Weapons, Dissenting Opinion of Judge Higgins, ICJ Reports 1996.

North Sea Continental Shelf Cases (Federal Republic of Germany/Denmark; Federal Republic of Germany/Netherlands) Judgment, ICJ Reports 1969, 3.

Reservations to the Convention on Genocide, Advisory Opinion, ICJ Reports 1951, 15.
Reservations to the Convention on Prevention and Punishment of the Crime of Genocide Advisory Opinion, Dissenting Opinion by Judge Alvarez, ICJ Reports 1951 .
South West Africa (*Ethiopia v South Africa*) (*Second Phase*), ICJ Reports 1966, 6.

Other Sources

Advisory Committee of Jurists, *Procès-verbaux of the Proceedings of the Advisory Committee of Jurists, June 16–July 24 1920, with Annexes* (The Hague: 1920).
Articles of the ICJ on Responsibility of States for Internationally Wrongful Acts, Annex to General Assembly resolution 56/83 of 12 December 2001, and corrected by document A/56/49 (Vol. I)/Corr.4.
International Law Commission, Report of the Study Group of the International Law Commission, *Conclusions of the Work of the Study Group, Fragmentation of International Law: Difficulties Arising from the Diversification and Expansion of International Law,* Fifty-eighth session, Geneva, 1 May–9 June and 3 July–11 August 2006\, A/CN.4/L.702 18 July 2006.

CHAPTER 7

Wimbledon Judgement and the Evolutive Nature of Neutrality: Decline of the Relic

Michał Kowalski

Abstract

The Chapter analyzes the *Wimbledon* judgement's legacy in the context of neutrality. It is argued that this issue strikingly shows the development and transformation of international law throughout the past one hundred years towards the values-based legal system. The Chapter begins with the analysis of the PCIJ's approach towards neutrality in the *Wimbledon* case and the role of the concept in the Court's reasoning. The next section of the Chapter presents the evolutive nature of neutrality as an inevitable consequence of the emergence and evolution of *jus ad bellum*. The subsequent part presents contextual illustrations of neutrality approaches towards two armed conflicts separated by a hundred years: the Polish–Soviet war of 1919-21 and the Russian aggression against Ukraine of 2022. The Chapter concludes with a claim that in the modern international law the concept of neutrality has become a legal relic as it can hardly be reconciled with the prohibition of aggression as a *jus cogens* norm and – more broadly – with States' obligations emanating from the peremptory norms aimed at the protection of community interests.

1 Introduction

There is not any doubt that the neutrality issue was crucial for deciding the *Wimbledon* case by the Permanent Court of International Justice [hereafter: the PCIJ; the Court] in 1923.[1] Yet, the Court barely elaborated on the concept itself. Rather, it addressed the very (non)applicability of neutrality towards the passage through the Kiel Canal in the context of Art. 380 Versailles Treaty regulation. In doing so the PCIJ confronted itself, in the process of identifying the applicable law, with the fundamental problems of international law: with – as

1 *Case of the S.S. Wimbledon* [1923] Publ. PCIJ Ser A. No. 1; For brief summary of the case see: Clemens Feinäugle, *Wimbledon, The*, in Wolfrum R. (ed.), Max Planck Encyclopedia of International Law (Oxford: 2012), online version updated 2013.

 | DOI:10.1163/9789004707979_009

Jan Klabbers put it[2] – the "sovereignty dilemma" as well as with the interrelation of international law sources.[3] The neutrality concept remained in the background of the Court's reasoning also because it seemed to be clear in its scope, were it to be applied.

Nevertheless, it is definitely advantageous to look at the *Wimbledon* judgement and its legacy in the context of neutrality. This issue strikingly shows the development and transformation of international law throughout the past one hundred years towards the values-based legal system. Yet, it also illustrates that, to some extent, the doctrine of international law still remains confined within traditional – or rather old-fashioned – legal concepts and is reluctant to admit their today's inadequacy and decline. In the present chapter it is submitted that such is exactly the case of neutrality. Its function was substantially different in international law before the UN Charter era – i.e. when international law was not based on the prohibition of use of armed force as the leading legal principle aimed at maintaining international peace and security being the founding axiological basis of that legal system. Neutrality has been thus evolving and – in consequence of this transformation – deteriorating. Whether and to what extent it has preserved its significance remains debatable and the Wimbledon case seems to be a good reference point for such a debate.

It is so also because of the practical context and the politics behind the circumstances of the *Wimbledon* case. Whether and to what extent Germany remained neutral towards the Polish–Soviet war of 1919–21 is a historical issue. Yet, it very well exemplifies that the proclaimed legal neutrality (neutrality *de jure*) not necessarily reflects factual and political neutrality (neutrality *de facto*) and – to put it emphatically – neutrality is often not neutral at all. This seems especially topical nowadays when the international community is confronted with Russian aggression against Ukraine and some States again tend to advocate the neutrality concept as a desirable approach towards that armed conflict. Is neutrality towards aggression legally possible in international law as it now stands? Or is it again – as in fact it used to be one hundred years ago – a useful legal excuse to protect individual States' interests preferred over community interests and masked with a pacifist legal narrative?

Addressing the above mentioned questions, the present chapter will start with the analysis of the PCIJ's approach towards neutrality in the Wimbledon case and the role of the concept in the Court's reasoning. The next section of

2 Jan Klabbers, "Clinching the Concept of Sovereignty: Wimbledon Redux", Austrian Journal of International Law 3 (1998) 345–367; see also Chapter 5 in this volume by Władysław Czapliński.

3 See Chapter 6 in this volume by Roman Kwiecień.

the text will present the evolutive nature of neutrality as an inevitable consequence of the emergence and evolution of *jus ad bellum*. That will bring us to the crucial question whether neutrality may be still perceived as a legal concept that can be reconciled with the prohibition of aggression as a *jus cogens* norm and – more broadly – with States' obligations emanating from peremptory norms aimed at the protection of community interests. The next part will present contextual illustrations of neutrality approaches towards two armed conflicts separated by a hundred years but, at least to some extent, surprisingly similar: the Polish–Soviet war of 1919–21 and the Russian aggression against Ukraine of 2022. The text will finish with a brief conclusion addressing the supposed decline of the neutrality concept in modern international law.

2 Neutrality in the *Wimbledon* Judgement

It would seem that the legal problem arising from the case was rather simple and – as it is commonly known – amounted to the question whether Germany was entitled to refuse the passage through the Kiel Canal of the steamship "S.S. Wimbledon". The English ship chartered by the French company was carrying a contraband (munitions and artillery stores) for the Polish armed forces. The incident took place on 21 March 1921, i.e. during the war between Poland and Soviet Russia.[4] The German refusal was based on her neutrality in that war as proclaimed in domestic Neutrality Orders of 25 and 30 July 1920. Yet, the status of the Kiel Canal was specifically regulated in the Versailles Treaty and, according to its Art. 380, the canal and its approaches was to 'be maintained free and open to the vessels of commerce and of war of all nations at peace with Germany on terms of entire equality'. Thus, the question before the Court was

4 Whether the war was still pending on 21 March 1921 may seem to some extent disputable as the Riga Peace Treaty was signed between the Parties on 18 March 1921 and armistice had been formally pending since October 1920 and took effect some months later at the latest. As Norman Davis put it: "At last, on 7 January 1921, the Polish army was put onto a peace footing for the first time in its existence. It was the first moment when one can safely say that a renewal of hostilities between Poland and Soviet Russia was not seriously likely"; Norman Davis, *White Eagle, Red Star. The Polish–Soviet War, 1919–20* (London 1972; 2nd ed. London 2003) 259. Extensively on the Riga Peace Treaty and its repercussions see Jerzy Borzęcki, *The Soviet–Polish Peace of 1921 and the Creation of Interwar Europe* (New Haven 2008). Yet, one has to note that the Riga Peace Treaty formally entered into force upon exchange of ratification documents by the Parties in Moscow on 30 April 1921 and only then the state of war between the parties ended. The PCIJ did consider this issue "useless" as it stated that "[i]n war time as in peace time the Kiel Canal should have been open to the 'Wimbledon' just as to every vessel of every nation at peace with Germany", Wimbledon, 30.

whether Germany, by refusing the passage, violated Art. 380 of the Versailles Treaty or – on the contrary – it was legally entitled to do so as a neutral power.

The dispute regarded foremostly the interpretation of a treaty provision establishing a special territorial regime over the canal and the relation of that treaty regulation with the mainly customary based neutrality concept, i.e. the special status under international law of a State non-party to an armed conflict.[5] Consequently, the PCIJ was not forced to elaborate specifically on the neutrality concept itself. Had Germany enjoyed full territorial sovereignty over the Kiel Canal, she would have been entitled as a neutral power to reject the passage of the S.S. Wimbledon as carrying contraband to the belligerent. The prohibition of transit of a supply movement consisting of transport of weapon seemed to be undisputable under the law of neutrality in that era. Also undisputable was at that time the right of Germany to declare her neutrality towards the Polish–Soviet war. The Court stated explicitly in this context: 'Germany was perfectly free to declare and regulate her neutrality in the Russo–Polish war, but subject to the condition that she respected and maintained intact the contractual obligations which she entered into at Varsailles on June 28th, 1919'.[6] What was decisive, though, was the scope of German contractual obligations under Art. 380 of the Varsailles Treaty regulating the Kiel Canal status and its impact on German neutrality.

However, one should note that there was another question, more general yet preliminary, before the Court. It was accurately and elegantly identified by Jan Klabbers: 'to what extent can Germany actually be considered bound by the Versailles Treaty? Can it actually be said that Germany, a sovereign state, freely and wittingly expressed its consent to be bound by the Versailles Treaty' or was it imposed on Germany?[7] This question remained implicit. Klabbers is right that German pleading, should it have been successful, could not have addressed this issue directly. He noted that

> the German agent must have understood quite well that to present an 'unequal treaty' or 'duress' argument to the Court, and to present it a

5 See generally Michael Bothe, *Neutrality, Concept and General Rules*, Max Planck Encyclopedia of International Law (Oxford: 2012) online version updated 2015. More specifically on the neutrality concept see section 3 below and the literature quoted there.

6 Wimbledon, 30. Note that the PCIJ consistently named the war as "Russo – Polish" whereas more precisely it should be named "Polish–Soviet war." Norman Davis noted in this context that "[i]n English history books, [this war] frequently appears under the erroneous title of the 'Russo – Polish War'", Davis, above note 4.

7 Klabbers, above note 2, 359.

> mere 5 years after the end of the war which had given rise to it, would not enhance his chances of success. Moreover, in an important sense the whole unequal treaty argument is rather awkward, in that it is based on a denial of the sovereignty of one of the parties altogether: in a world of theoretical equals there simply cannot be an unequal treaty without upsetting the theoretical basis of the whole system. That avenue was thus effectively blocked, and consequently another had to be found.[8]

And that another avenue chosen by Germany to relay on was exactly the neutrality argument. And it was deliberately aimed at weakening the limitations of the Varsailles Treaty upon German sovereignty.

German argumentation was, crucially, that the treaty provision of Art. 380 must not have been interpreted in isolation and literally only. On the contrary, it must have been interpreted – as it is plausible to say, although it was not worded this way – in a systemic way in which the spirit of the treaty was reflected in its reconciliation with other basic rights and obligations of States under international law, i.e. – in the context of the case – with Germany's right to be neutral. In other words, Art. 380, regulating the status of the Kiel Canal and imposing certain limitations upon Germany in this respect, must have been compatible with neutrality laws and '[could] not deprive Germany of the exercise of her rights as a neutral power in time of war, and place her under an obligation to allow the passage through the canal of contraband destined for one of the belligerents'.[9] In Germany's argumentation neutrality was identified as 'a personal and imprescriptible right, which forms an essential part of her sovereignty and which she neither could nor intended to renounce by anticipation'.[10] Thus, Germany framed neutrality as intrinsically rooted in a State's sovereignty that must not have been limited contractually.

The Court did not follow the German reasoning and, firstly and famously, stated that treaty obligations of States are compatible with their sovereignty as contractual obligations might place 'a restriction upon the exercise of the sovereign rights of the State' but it was 'the right of entering into international engagements' that was 'an attribute of State sovereignty'. Therefore, the regulation of Art. 380 of the Varsailles Treaty on the Kiel Canal might have introduced upon Germany 'an important limitation of the exercise of [her] sovereign rights'.[11] Yet, the Court did not answer the question whether such

8 Ibid.

9 Wimbledon, 25.

10 Ibid.

11 Ibid., 24.

limitations might have been of such a legal nature that would have deprived Germany of exercising her rights as a neutral power. Rather, it concluded that, because of the terms of Art. 380 being 'categorical' and giving rise 'to no doubt',[12] the 'Germany's neutrality would have remained intact and irreproachable'[13] if "s.s. Wimbledon" had passed the Kiel Canal. The key argument here was that Art. 380, which 'clearly contemplate[d] time of war as well as time of peace',[14] literally included only one exception from transforming the Kiel Canal from German internal navigable waterway to international one open to all vessels with no distinction: they must have belonged to the States at peace with Germany. The Court also added in this respect: '[i]f the conditions of access to the canal were also to be modified in the event of a conflict between two Powers remaining at peace with the German Empire, the Treaty would not have failed to say so'.[15] In consequence of the legal regime introduced to the Kiel Canal by Art. 380, the passage of vessels carrying contraband could not have been attributed ('imputed') to Germany as a violation of her obligations as a neutral power. This was the decisive argument for the Court to decide the *Wimbledon* case and as such – it is worth stressing again – it was derived from Art. 380 of the Varsailles Treaty, i.e. a treaty provision establishing international (or internationalized) regime over the Kiel Canal. The treaty provision over which the domestic Neutral Orders of 1920 must have not prevailed.[16]

The Court based its reasoning also on two additional justifications. It is hard to avoid the impression that they contributed significantly to some ambiguity of the Court's reasoning. The justifications were the following: firstly, that German neutrality argument 'conflict[ed] with general considerations of highest order' and, secondly, that it was 'gainsaid by consistent international practice'. The former claim had not been elaborated at all, whereas the latter was supported by references to two examples only: legal regimes of Suez and Panama Canals. According to the Court, they formed precedents invalidating German arguments that the passage of a vessel carrying contraband

12 Ibid., 22.
13 Ibid., 30.
14 Ibid., 25.
15 Ibid., 23.
16 The Court also referred to the note of the German Delegation to the President of the Conference of Ambassadors of 20 April 1921 in which it was stated that Germany intended to apply neutrality orders to commerce vessels only and war vessels would be beyond the scope of their application. The Court commented that this statement contained appropriate interpretation of Art. 380 in regard of the passage of belligerent war vessels and – *a fortiori* – the same interpretation should have been applied in regard of the passage of neutral vessels carrying contraband of war; ibid. 29.

would have jeopardized her neutrality. The Court also noted in this context that canals connecting two open seas and dedicated to 'the use of the whole world' were 'assimilated to natural straits in the sense that even the passage of a belligerent man-of-war d[id] not compromise the neutrality of the sovereign State under whose jurisdiction the waters in question [lied]'.[17] Indeed, one has to admit that as far as the mentioned additional arguments are concerned, the Court's reasoning reminded somehow underdeveloped and, as such, has been criticized by the dissenting judges[18] and then in the doctrine as inaccurate and less persuasive.[19] The critique was aimed especially at the Court's negligence in its approach or misinterpretation of the relation between treaties and the customary international law.[20] The critical opinions in this regard may be, however, assessed as exaggerated.

It seems doubtful to claim that the Court invoked in its reasoning any new customary norm directly regarding neutrality. Any novelty in customary law the Court to some extent relied on may be only detected as far as the legal status of a canal connecting two open seas is concerned. As James Brierly put it: 'a new custom of very recent growth relating to international canals'.[21] The Court invoked in this regard 'the general opinion according to which when an artificial waterway connecting two open seas has been permanently dedicated to the use of the whole world, such waterway is assimilated to natural straits'[22] and, in consequence, its usage (the passage through) does not affect the neutrality of a riparian State. But first and foremost the Court referred to treaty regulations regarding statuses of the Suez and Panama Canals. Although the mentioned examples were only two (for obvious factual reasons as the number of international canals was and still is limited), they were indeed meaningful. Also, while the regulations of their statuses varied in contexts and in legal details, the rule in question was the same: a passage through the international canal did not impact on neutrality of a riparian State. And, let us repeat this again, regulations were contractually based, as the Kiel Canal status was. The reading of the Court's statements when it spoke – maybe in a slightly unfortunate way – of 'precedents' and, more importantly, on 'the general opinion', may be that it referred to *opinio juris* deriving from States' practice that had

17 Ibid., 28.

18 Wimbledon, Dissenting Opinion by M. Schücking, 46.

19 See, e.g., Klabbers, above note 2, 361.

20 See, e.g., Kwiecień, in this volume, part II and the literature quoted therein.

21 James L. Brierly, *Shortcomings of International Law*, in: James L. Brierly, *The Basis of Obligations in International Law and Other Papers* (Oxford: 1958), p. 75.

22 Wimbledon, p. 28.

been initially based on treaty norms but had started to be independent.[23] The case in which a treaty norm and the States' practice based upon it result in creation of a new customary norm or in modification of a previously existing one is not unique in modern international law. In the late sixties the process was famously declared 'perfectly possible' by the International Court of Justice [hereafter: the ICJ].[24] One should remember, however, that what is absolutely essential in the process is the establishment of distinct *opinio juris*. Without such *opinio juris* the States' practice of treaty obligation application remains nothing more than that and does not result in creation of a parallel customary norm. Thus, one can say that the PCIJ, through its pronouncements in *Wimbledon* judgement, was contributing to the development of customary law – something that was indeed expected from the newly established World Court. Roman Kwiecień comments in his Chapter that 'in the Wimbledon judgement the Court did not find a normative incoherence between treaties and custom'.[25] And this is because – as it is submitted here – such incoherence did not exist.

Nevertheless, as it was mentioned above, the key argument of the Court dismissing Germany's neutrality claim was the strict and literal interpretation of Art. 380 itself. Yet, the Court did not elaborate on the possibility of contractual limitations of neutrality and its relation with State's sovereignty. It is striking in this context that the Court stressed the right to self-defence. It underlined that the only exception to the openness of the Kiel canal to all vessels introduced by Art. 380 referred to vessels of States at war with Germany and in this way '[t]he right of [Germany] to defend herself against her enemies by refusing to allow their vessels to pass through the canal [wa]s therefore proclaimed and recognised'.[26] Also, while analysing the regime governing the Suez Canal under which the canal was to be open also for vessels of States at war with Turkey, her right to self-defence was – according to the Court – 'nevertheless reserved up to a certain point' as other States obliged themselves not to interfere with the use of the canal both at time of peace as well as at time of war.[27] And while referring to the regime of the Panama Canal the Court remarked that the use

23 Cf. Antoni Deryng, *Główne tendencje rozwojowe prawa narodów w świetle orzecznictwa Stałego Trybunału Sprawiedliwości Międzynarodowej [The Principal Trends in the Development of the Law of Nations under the Jurisprudence of the Permanent Court of International Justice]* (Lwów: 1932) 106–107.

24 *North Sea Continental Shelf Cases*, Judgement of 20 February 1969, I.C.J. Reports 1969, para. 71.

25 Kwiecień, in this volume, 183.

26 Wimbledon, 23.

27 Ibid., 26.

of the canal was only restricted to the enemy vessels after the United States had entered into the war (i.e. World War I) in the same vein as Art. 380 forbade the passage of enemy vessel of States at war with Germany. Thus, it seems that for the Court a State's right to defend itself – labelled 22 years later in Art. 51 of the Charter of the United Nations as an inherent right to self-defence – implicitly alluded by the Court as more significant than neutrality, remained not completely beyond possibility of at least some contractual limitations as the Panama Canal case exemplified. This is coherent with the Court's famous stance on sovereignty. Indeed, States are in power to limit the scope of sovereign rights they exercise.

One more argument regarding neutrality in the context of the *Wimbledon* judgement should be referred to. It was invoked by a dissenting judge Walther Schücking. He claimed that because Soviet Russia was not party to the Versailles Treaty, Germany 'remained under an obligation to fulfil her duties as a neutral towards her'.[28] Contrary to the majority's reasoning he claimed that 'neutral duties must take precedence over any contractual obligations' and that 'legally binding contractual obligations cannot be undertaken to perform acts which would violate the rights of third parties'[29] as Germany would have violated her duties of a neutral power towards Soviet Russia. Judge Schücking claimed that the argument to refute Germany's duties as a neutral power used by the majority was based on 'a general consensus of legal opinion to the effect that when an artificial waterway connecting two open seas [had] been permanently dedicated to the use of the whole world, such waterway [was] assimilated to natural straits' and riparian States were no more responsible for passages of vessels in contradiction to neutrality regulations.[30] The dissenting judge stated firmly that such consensus was not sufficiently established by the Court and, consequently, non-existing and that the status of the Kiel Canal might rather resemble the status of international inland waters. Therefore, Germany, in order to comply with her obligations under international law, must have acted as a neutral power towards Soviet Russia and it was obliged to refuse the passage through the Kiel Canal of "S.S. Wimbledon", a vessel carrying a contraband for the Polish State (or rather – as judge Schücking claimed – 'a convoy in the sense of Article 2 [of the fifth Hague Convention]'[31]) at war with Soviet Russia.

Again, it was not disputed that the passage of "S.S. Wimbledon" through a neutral State's territory would have violated duties of a neutral power under

28 Wimbledon, Dissenting Opinion by M. Schücking, 45.
29 Ibid., 47.
30 Ibid., 45–46.
31 Ibid., 46.

then binding neutrality laws.[32] Nevertheless, the majority of the Court stated that internalization of the Kiel Canal did not allow to attribute the potential passage of the "s.s. Wimbledon" to the German State and therefore Germany's neutrality was not affected at all. The Court clearly derived it from the very wording of Art. 380, first presenting the argumentation justifying contractual restrictions upon the exercise of the sovereign rights of the State. As it was mentioned above, 'the general opinion' argument – indeed, framed by the majority, to some extent, in an imprecise way – was only of auxiliary character.

Also, it should be noted in this context that Soviet Russia's rights as a third party to the Versailles treaties were not anyhow violated under Art. 380. The introduced legal status of the Kiel Canal guaranteed the rights of passage to the vessels of all States not at war with Germany. Thus, it was applied on equal footing to both Soviet Russia and Poland as belligerents not at war with Germany. The passage of a vessel carrying contraband (or being a convoy) for Soviet Russia would have been equally permissible under Art. 380. Exercising the German sovereign rights over the Kiel Canal was contractually restricted under the Versailles Treaty to the benefit of all States including the non-parties. The logical consequence was that Germany could exercise its restricted sovereign rights over the Kiel Canal, including those emanating from neutrality laws, neither towards Soviet Russia nor towards any other State not at war with her.

3 Neutrality, Its (Lost) *ratio legis* and Evolution

The concept of neutrality is generally understood as a special status under international law of a State which is not a State party to an armed conflict. This status entails certain rights and obligations in relations of a neutral State (traditionally labelled also as a neutral power) vis-à-vis belligerent States.[33] Thus, neutrality comprises of the body of international legal norms, both of customary and treaty character, regulating this special legal status. This set of norms

32 Interestingly enough, judge Schücking, while referring to the neutrality laws to be applied in the case, mentioned mainly treaty obligations under the fifth Hague Convention, only alluding to their customary character by invoking "the origin" of Articles 2 and 7; ibid., 46–47.

33 Bothe, above note 5, para 1; Generally see, e.g.: James Upcher, *Nautrality in Cntemporary International Law* (Oxford: 2020); Constantine Antonopoulos, *Non-Participation in Armed Conflict: Continuity and Modern Challenges to the Law of Neutrality* (Cambridge: 2022).

may be labelled as neutrality laws or law regulating neutrality[34] and, as such, it is applied in case of a pending international armed conflict.

The above mentioned understanding of neutrality (sometimes labeled as ad hoc neutrality) is distinct from the concept of permanent neutrality declared by some States regardless of the existence of a particular armed conflict.[35] Permanent neutrality results in far reaching legal consequences for a domestic constitutional legal order of a State concerned. In international legal realm permanent neutrality results automatically in neutrality of a permanently neutral State towards every newly emerged armed conflict among third States. Generally, the notion of permanent neutrality is beyond the scope of detailed analysis presented in this chapter. Yet, one has to notice that the contention under consideration according to which a State must not be neutral towards an international armed conflict regardless the legal assessment of the latter, importantly results also in the legal framing of permanent neutrality and its legal consequences, both in domestic and in international contexts.

Neutrality, as a special legal status under international law, is based on two fundamental obligations on the part of a neutral State – non-participation in an armed conflict and impartiality towards the belligerent parties. Thus, a State concerned, while confronted with an armed conflict among third States, may distance itself from that conflict and remain neutral. Complying with obligations of non-participation and impartiality results in certain obligations on the part of the belligerents who are legally obliged to respect the neutral status of a State concerned and not to take any actions that could spread an armed conflict upon a neutral power. It is estimated that such understanding of neutrality had been evolving since the late eighteenth century throughout the nineteenth century and acquired customary status under international law to be finally codified in the two Hague Conventions of 1907: the fifth Convention respecting the Rights and Duties of Neutral Powers and Persons in Case of War on Land;[36] and the thirteenth Convention concerning the Rights and Duties of Neutral Powers in Naval War.[37] Yet, it should be not overlooked that other treaty regulations of that time, including some other Hague conventions of 1907, were also significant in the context of neutrality laws. It is also

34 Note also that the ICJ spoke of "the principle of neutrality." Yet, it has not been clarified in what sense the notion of principle was understood by the ICJ; *Threat or Use of Nuclear Weapons,* Advisory Opinion, ICJ Reports 1996, para 89.

35 Cf. Bothe, above note 5, para 15–18.

36 ICRC, International Humanitarian Law Databases, https://ihl-databases.icrc.org/en/ihl-treaties/hague-conv-v-1907?activeTab=default [as of 1 July 2023].

37 Ibid., https://ihl-databases.icrc.org/en/ihl-treaties/hague-conv-xiii-1907 [as of 1 July 2023].

generally accepted that the then customary law on neutrality was confirmed in the Geneva Conventions of 1949.[38]

It is obvious that the then role of neutrality was especially important in context of the prevention of armed conflicts and their spread as war was made illegal under international law in 1928 only under the Treaty of Paris. Thus, the *ratio legis* of neutrality was originally the limitation of war as a means of international disputes settlement. Neutrality could have been then plausibly perceived as a remedy aimed at maintenance of peace in international relations. This function was predominant but it was accompanied by another one – equally important. Namely, neutrality formed a means of protection of States and their sovereignty, because it limited the scope of armed actions of belligerents towards third states being neutral. Before war became illegal under international law States had not been restricted to recourse to military force under a general prohibiting norm but if they became belligerents they were obliged to respect the neutral status of third States under the laws of neutrality. It was not a coincidence that Art. 1 of the V Hague Convention guaranteed the inviolability of neutral powers' territories. This is also the origin of permanent neutrality declared by States – the permanently neutral States tried to protect their vital interests that could be endangered in case of an armed conflict among third States.

The original dual *ratio legis* of neutrality was strictly pacifist in character. As neutrality preceded the illegalization of war, subsequently transformed into the prohibition of use of force, it may be rightly perceived as a frontrunner of that prohibition and important factor in the process of making the maintenance of international peace and security the leading axiological value of modern international law in the United Nations Charter era. Indeed, neutrality contributed significantly to this process. Yet, it had to change significantly as the result of *jus ad bellum* development. In this context Krzysztof Skubiszewski in 1968 spoke of neutrality's 'gradual invalidation'[39] but he concluded that although neutrality 'underwent a process of change,' 'it nevertheless survive[d] and remain[ed] part and parcel of the life of international community'.[40] This

---

38 Bothe, above note 5, para 8.

39 However, already after the establishment of the League of Nations, and especially after outlawing war in 1928, the opinions perceiving neutrality as a legal anachronism were emerging; Stephen Neff, "A three-fold struggle over neutrality: The American experience in the 1930s", in Lottaz P., Reginbogin H.R. (eds), *Notions of Neutralities* (Lanham: 2018) 3. See also: Przemysław Saganek, *Unilateral Acts of States in Public International Law* (Leiden – Boston: 2016) 323–332 and the literature quoted.

40 Krzysztof Skubiszewski, "Use of Force by States. Collective Security. Law of War and Neutrality", in Sørensen M. ed., *Manual of Public International Law* (London: 1968) 841.

claim prevails also in modern international law scholarship,[41] but it should be critically verified. Is it still so that a third State is – as the PCIJ expressed it in the context of Germany and the Polish–Soviet war – 'perfectly free' to invoke neutrality towards an armed conflict irrespective of its legal assessment under binding *jus ad bellum* norms?

It is modern *jus ad bellum*, based on the prohibition of use of armed force as provided for in the UN Charter and under customary law, that protects the maintenance of international peace and security. The same norms protect States and their sovereignty from forcible interventions of other States. In comparison to the pre-Charter era this is a completely different paradigm of international law in which neutrality traditionally understood lost its original *ratio legis*. Original functions of neutrality were replaced by much more sophisticated and effective *jus ad bellum* norms. It is especially so that modern international law has been consistently developing towards institutionalized values-based legal order in which community interests are increasingly protected. From a purely legal perspective it is foremostly exemplified in the development process of the concept of peremptory norms (*jus cogens*) producing *erga omnes* effects. And the prohibition of aggression remains one of the few uncontested examples of *jus cogens*.[42] It strictly coincides with the development of norms of State responsibility for internationally wrongful acts and particularly with responsibility which is entailed by a serious breach by a State of an obligation arising under a peremptory norm as regulated in Articles 40–41 of the International Law Commission [hereafter: the ILC] Articles of 2001[43] that now reflect the binding customary law in this respect.

Art. 41 that regulates consequences of a breach of a peremptory norm is of special importance in the context concerned. It imposes a triple obligation

41 E.g.: Bothe, above note 5; Upcher, above note 33; Antonopoulos, above note 33; Wolff Heintschel von Heinegg, "'Benevolent' Third States in International Armed Conflicts: The Myth of the Irrelevance of the Law of Neutrality" in Schmitt M.N., Pejic J. (eds.), *International Law and Armed Conflict: Exploring the Faultlines* (The Hague: 2007) 543.

42 Note, however, that doctrinal approaches vary and some authors perceive the very prohibition of use of force as *jus cogens* (generally see: Tom Ruys, *'Armed Attack' and Article 51 of the UN Charter. Evolutions in Customary Law and Practice* (Cambridge: 2010) 24–28 and the literature quoted), whereas some others claim that the whole *jus ad bellum* framework is of the peremptory character (e.g.: Alexander Orakhelashvili, *Peremptory Norms in International Law* (Oxford: 2006) 51). See also: Michał Kowalski, "Original Sin Reaffirmed: The Nicaragua Judgement's Impact on the Notion of Armed Attack as the Most Grave Form of the Use of Force", XXXVI Polish Yearbook of International Law 2016 (2017) 37.

43 ILC Articles on Responsibility of States for Internationally Wrongful Acts, with commentaries, 2001, Yearbook of International Law Commission 2001, vol. II, Part Two.

upon States confronted with a serious breach of a peremptory norm: 1) States are obliged to cooperate to bring such a breach to an end by lawful means; 2) a State must not recognize as lawful a situation created by such a breach; 3) nor must it render aid or assistance in maintaining the situation resulting from such a breach. The same obligations and their customary character have been confirmed in the Conclusion 19 of the Draft conclusions on identification and legal consequences of peremptory norms of general international law (*jus cogens*) adopted by the ILC in 2022.[44] The positive obligation to cooperate may be institutional but also individual in its form. The institutionalized response to the breaches of *jus cogens* under the competent international organizations, including the principal role of the UN, is obviously preferable. Yet, it does not obviate the individual States from the obligation to cooperate, especially when the particular institutional framework fails to be effective. Of course – as the ILC put it in 2001[45] – because of the diversity of circumstances which may be involved it is impossible to determine in detail what forms of cooperation should be taken. Nonetheless, it seems doubtful whether in case of aggression impartiality towards both an aggressor State and a victim State is anyhow reconcilable with the duty to cooperate to bring aggression to an end. It is especially so when a third State invokes neutrality laws in order to release itself from an obligation to cooperate with other States that undertake by lawful means actions aimed at supporting the State which is a victim of aggression and keep fighting to repeal an act of aggression. And in particular circumstances when such a refusal to cooperate results in serious impediment to legal actions supportive to a victim of aggression, such a refusal may amount to illegal aid or assistance to an aggressor State.

Moreover, one should also consider the legal consequences of neutrality for third States supporting a State being the victim of aggression. Out of the two basic obligations on the part of a neutral State, i.e. non-participation and impartiality, it is the former that remains less ambiguous. Any participation in an armed conflict of third states (be it legal under the collective self-defence

44 ILC, Draft conclusions on identification and legal consequences of peremptory norms of general international law (jus cogens), with commentaries, 2022, Yearbook of International Law Commission 2022, vol. II, Part Two. Note that in 2001 the ILC expressed some doubts whether the obligation to cooperate to bring a breach of a peremptory norm to an end by lawful means formed customary international law; yet in 2022 it stated firmly: "the obligation to cooperate to bring to an end serious breaches of obligations arising under peremptory norms of general international law (jus cogens) is now recognized under international law" and extensively supported this statement by references to domestic and international judicial decisions, ibid. 71–72.

45 ILC, above note 43, 114.

framework on the side of a victim State or illegal on the side of an aggressor State) makes the State concerned a party to the armed-conflict with all legal consequences including the termination of neutral status. What may be difficult to establish in this context is the level and character of the involvement that amounts to participation in an armed conflict and that transforms the State concerned into a belligerent. It is especially so in a situation in which vast arms supply and/or other far reaching military support (such as sharing critical intelligence data, training of military personnel etc.) is provided for to a belligerent, yet the third State concerned does not take any armed actions that may be qualified as use of force. Indeed, the border may be very thin. Irrespective of the qualification of such supportive actions as participation or not, they are obviously irreconcilable with the duty to remain impartial towards the belligerents. Thus, a State that is not participating in an armed conflict violates neutrality laws if it is not impartial. And it was exactly the impartiality that was traditionally perceived as of key importance in the early development of neutrality laws. As Krzysztof Skubiszewski put it: 'impartiality towards all belligerents remained the corner-stone of the customary law of the nineteenth century and the Hague Conventions of 1907'.[46] Also according to Rudolf Bindschedler 'as long as war was tolerated as a means of national policy, impartiality was the keystone of neutrality'.[47] But the point is that – as it was already stressed above – war is not tolerated under international law anymore and the peremptory status of the prohibition of aggression invalidates the duty of impartiality towards the aggressor and the victim of aggression.

In the traditional understanding of neutrality there is, in principle, the following alternative only: if an armed conflict occurs a third State remains neutral or becomes a party to the armed conflict (a belligerent). However, due to the emergence of *jus ad bellum* norms an intermediate state was identified that was already addressed above: a third state does not become a state party to the armed conflict (a belligerent) as its actions do not amount to the use of armed force but it is not neutral either as it is not impartial towards belligerents. Thus, it violates neutrality laws and its actions remain illegal under international law. In consequence, the injured belligerent is entitled to take legal (ergo peaceful) countermeasures towards an impartial State. This interpretation leads to the situation in which a State supporting the victim of aggression through non-forcible actions violates its obligations under international law (i.e. neutrality laws) and the aggressor State is entitled to legally target that State through

46 Skubiszewski, above note 40, 841.

47 Rudolf L. Bindschedler, "Neutrality, Concept and General Rules" in Bernhardt R. (ed.) *Encyclopedia of Public International Law*, vol. 4, (Amsterdam – New York – Oxford: 1982), 11.

countermeasures in response. From the perspective of modern international law this interpretation is paradoxical and unsustainable.

There are at least three ways of dealing with this paradox. Firstly, it is possible to address casuistically particular supportive actions towards one of the belligerents and demonstrate that in essence they do not collide with the obligation of impartiality. It is also possible to claim that the States' practice led to the modification of customary scope of impartiality duty making it much broader and encompassing a wide range of peaceful measures. The detail analysis of this claim lies outside the scope of this text. Yet, it seems to remain insufficiently supported by the States' practice and, in fact, it denies the very idea of impartiality. States that support the victim of aggression in principle do not claim that they are impartial but they do claim that they are entitled or even obliged to take action aimed at bringing aggression to an end.

Two other options recognize the effect of *jus ad bellum* norms on neutrality. Secondly then, the actions supporting the victim of aggression, although collide with neutrality laws, remain legal if taken under the framework of collective self-defence. Such an interpretation would be in the sense in which the ILC framed self-defence as a circumstance precluding wrongfulness under Art. 21 of the 2001 Articles. Yet, it seems more appropriate to argue that acting under collective self-defence terminates neutrality as it amounts to participation in the armed conflict concerned. The claim that a State acting under collective self-defence through non-forcible measures does not become a State party to the armed conflict, remains mostly controversial. It is submitted here that invoking collective self-defence makes the State concerned a State party to the armed conflict, whereas beyond the self-defence framework, non-forcible countermeasures by a third State against a State responsible for illegal use of force are permissible under general terms of law of State responsibility and do not result in becoming a State party to the armed conflict.

Thirdly, the concept of "qualified neutrality" (known also as "discriminating neutrality" or "benevolent neutrality") has emerged.[48] It is based on the account of the legal status of the prohibition of aggression in modern international law and modifies neutrality laws in the sense that States are allowed to differentiate their legal approaches towards an aggressor and the victim of aggression and the latter may be supported. As Michael Bothe put it: '[t]he duty of impartiality does not mean that the State is bound to treat the belligerents in exactly the same way'.[49] The exceptional character of this conception

48 Note, however, that, e.g., Rudolf L. Bindschedler stated firmly: 'There is no "strict", "benevolent", "qualified" or "discriminatory" neutrality, and no state of non-belligerency', ibid., 13.

49 Bothe, above note 5, para 3.

is generally supported by the claim that it may be invoked only if the act of aggression is identified by the UN Security Council. In all other cases neutrality encompassing the duties of non-participation and strict impartiality is legally binding.

Whether the above mentioned assertions remain satisfactory is highly questionable. Yet, they prove that approaching neutrality irrespective of the legality assessment of the armed conflict is under modern international law hardly possible. The duty of impartiality towards belligerents responsible for violating the prohibition of aggression is not to be maintained under modern international law. Thus, the traditional understanding of neutrality has evolved so much that the very concept is in decline. What remains crucial is non-participation in an armed conflict. As Krzysztof Skubiszewski argued already in 1968: 'As long as non-belligerent State does not participate in hostilities it retains the status of a neutral State and cannot become the object of any forcible counter-measures on the part of the belligerent against which it lawfully discriminates'.[50] Whether neutrality, being reduced to non-participation in an armed conflict, retains its separate legal value remains highly doubtful. What seems sufficiently adequate today is the legal distinction between the non-belligerent status (non-participation in an armed conflict) and the belligerent status (participation in an armed conflict). The States' practice, as significantly developed following the full-scale Russian aggression against Ukraine on 24 February 2022, is a valuable reference in this context.

4 Neutrality in Context: from the Polish–Soviet War of 1919–21 to the Russian Aggression against Ukraine of 2022

The Polish–Soviet war of 1919–21 was one of the many local armed conflicts which broke out in the Central and Eastern Europe after the end the First World War that resulted in a complete reconfiguration of the political situation in Europe. As Norman Davis put it:

> Yet the Polish–Soviet War was different. Whereas all other disputes in which Poland was involved were simple border disputes, the conflict with Soviet Russia was something more; whereas all the other fronts on which the Red Army was fighting were integral parts of the Russian Civil War, the Polish front had further implications. Unlike all the other post-war

50 Skubiszewski, above note 40, 841.

> squabbles with which it is frequently equated, the Polish–Soviet War raised wider issues – the clash of ideologies, the export of revolution, the future of Europe itself.[51]

No doubt Soviet Russia openly contested the new Polish statehood reestablished in 1918 after 123 years of the partitions of Poland. But also other States, especially those neighbouring with Poland, had their own national goals and interests that often were contradictory to the Polish ones. That includes the post-war Germany. A detailed analysis of the historical and political context is beyond the scope of this chapter,[52] but it should be noted that German neutrality was declared in domestic Neutrality Orders of 25 and 30 July 1920, i.e. exactly when the Red Army was successfully approaching Warsaw and the fall of the Polish capital city seemed inevitable.[53] The Polish–German relations of that time were tense and harsh territorial disputes existed between the two States. Moreover, the German attitude vis-à-vis the Polish–Soviet war was influenced by domestic disturbances and significant internal social, but also political, support for the socialist and communist ideas. The context of domestic disturbances for refusal of the passage through the Kiel Canal of the steamship "s.s. Wimbledon" was explicitly mentioned in the dissenting opinion of judge Schücking.[54] It is to plausible to suggest that German neutrality *de jure* was not necessarily even close to neutrality *de facto* as it is hard to claim that Germany remained impartial and did not discriminate against Poland as one of the belligerents of the Polish–Soviet war. And this was not unique at that time and in that context. Precisely in the context of the Polish–Soviet war one can also point at neutrality declared by the then Czechoslovakia. The Czechoslovak government issued a declaration of non-intervention and strict neutrality on 9 August 1920. Yet, it had its own strategy aimed at weakening Poland (among others, by blocking Poland's main train supply line) due to the territorial disputes[55] and compromising with the Soviets.[56] Again, the

51 Davis, above note 4, 21–22.

52 For the German perspective see, e.g., Gerhard Wagner, *Deutschland und der polnisch-sowjetische Krieg 1920* (Wiesbaden: 1979).

53 Norman Davis noted: "The invasion of Poland from the east inevitably weakened the central government's influence in the continuing territorial disputes in the west and north. The situation was easily exploited by Poland's neighbours", ibid., 162.

54 Wimbledon, Dissenting Opinion by M. Schücking, 45.

55 One of them was addressed by the PCIJ: *Question of Jaworzyna (Polish–Czechoslovakian Frontier), Advisory Opinion* [1923] Publ. PCIJ Ser B No 8.

56 As Norman Davis commented: "There is good evidence to suggest that [Edward] Beneš [the then Minister of Foreign Affairs] was planning to surrender the province of

Czechoslovak neutrality *de jure* had nothing to do with neutrality *de facto* based on impartiality vis-à-vis all belligerents.

The full scale Russian military invasion on Ukraine of 24 February 2022 undoubtedly amounted to a flagrant violation of the prohibition of use of force and to an act of aggression.[57] Although it could not be determined as an act of aggression by the UN Security Council due to the Russian veto and resulting paralysis of the UN Security Council, it was explicitly qualified as such in the UN General Assembly Resolution of 2 March 2022 with 141 States voting for its adoption.[58] As Russian actions formed armed attack under Article 51 of the UN Charter, Ukraine was entitled to act under the framework of self-defence in order to repeal the attack, as she has been doing since then. The widespread condemnation of the Russian aggression was followed by far reaching support for Ukraine, including significant arms transfers from numerous States. As Kevin Jon Heller and Lena Trabucco put it, Russian aggression 'has led many Western states to supply Ukraine with a degree of military support unheard of since the American Lend-Lease Program in 1941'.[59] However, no State supporting Ukraine declared itself explicitly or implicitly as a party to the pending armed conflict. Thus, a few important legal questions arise: how to assess legally the States' practice vis-à-vis the Russian – Ukrainian armed conflict?; do neutrality laws apply to the armed conflict resulting from an act of aggression?; does this practice have far reaching consequences for legal standing of neutrality in modern international law?

The first possible interpretation is that the States supporting Ukraine act under collective self-defence framework. Ukraine as the victim of the armed attack may invoke the right to collective self-defence and other States are entitled to join Ukraine in her defensive endeavours. Acting under the collective self-defence framework does not necessarily amount to military actions and may be limited to non-forcible acts, such as provisions of arms. And the provisions of arms to a belligerent alone does not amount to the use of armed force.[60]

Sub-Carpathian Ruthenia and the city of Užhorod as a sop to the Soviets"; Davis, above note 4, 182.

57 See, e.g.: James A. Green, Christian Henderson, Tom Ruys, "Russia's attack on Ukraine and the jus ad bellum", Journal on the Use of Force and International Law 9 (2022) 4; Patrycja Grzebyk, "Escalation of the Conflict Between Russia and Ukraine in Light of the Law on Use of Force and International Humanitarian Law", XLI Polish Yearbook of International Law 2021 (2022), 145.

58 A/RES/ES-11/1 (141 for, 5 against, 35 abstained, 12 absent).

59 Kevin Jon Heller, Lena Trabucco, "The Legality of Weapon Transfers to Ukraine Under International Law", Journal of Humanitarian Legal Studies (2022), 23.

60 Contrary: Kavin Jon Heller and Lena Trabucco who claim that '[p]roviding weapons to Ukraine constitutes the use of force against Russia', ibid., 4.

Yet, as it is submitted here, acting under collective self-defence would result in States supporting Ukraine becoming parties to the pending armed conflict. In consequence, they would become, subject to necessity and proportionality principles, legitimate targets for the enemy belligerent, i.e. Russia. Invoking collective self-defence would also result in terminating their neutrality.

The proposed interpretation cannot, however, be applied to the case under consideration for the following reasons. States supporting Ukraine, including NATO Member States, do all they can to stress that, although they support Ukraine through provisions of arms and in a various different ways, they are not parties to the pending armed conflict between Ukraine and Russia. What is more, none of the States supporting Ukraine has formally invoked acting under collective self-defence. Nor meet they procedural requirements under Art. 51 of the UN Charter to report immediately to the UN Security Council. This is decisive for the assessment that the States supporting Ukraine, although they would be entitled to, have not been acting under the collective self-defence framework. Thus, it is not necessary to consider more broadly the alternative interpretation of the collective self-defence that was mentioned briefly in the previous section. Namely, that acting under collective self-defence short of forcible measures amounting to use of armed force does not result in becoming a party to an armed conflict. In such a scenario the States supporting Ukraine would be acting in collective self-defence, yet they would not be parties to the pending armed conflict with all legal consequences. As they are openly not impartial, they would not be neutral either, so, presumably, self-defence would be a circumstance precluding wrongfulness of violating neutrality laws. Again, this interpretation seems at least controversial and not supported by States' practice. Nonetheless, it is clearly not the case as far as the armed conflict between Ukraine and Russia is concerned, as the States supporting Ukraine have not invoked collective self-defence as legal basis of their actions.

The second possible interpretation is that, as the States supporting Ukraine have not been acting under collective self-defence, their neutrality has not been terminated and, as they openly and significantly support Ukraine, they are not impartial and, in consequence, they violate neutrality law. Thus, they commit a wrongful act under international law and may be targeted by a belligerent they discriminate against, i.e. Russia, through legal countermeasures under law of State responsibility. This is the interpretation some authors explicitly supported.[61] And this would be exactly the paradox mentioned in the previous section: supporting the victim of aggression and actions aimed

61 Ibid.

at bringing aggression to an end would be qualified as illegal under international law, and, in consequence, an aggressor could legally target the States supporting the victim of aggression through countermeasures. The example of Russian aggression proves like no other how preposterous the consequences of this legal interpretation are.

But also on practical grounds one should note that no support (including transfers of weapons) for Ukraine as the victim of aggression would undoubtedly result in the military victory of the aggressor, i.e. Russia. Thus, the application of the neutrality laws would privilege the aggressor and allow the aggressor to benefit from violation of the very basis of international law. It is barely possible to accept such interpretation with the prohibition of use of force as one of the leading principles of international law constituting the peremptory norm and with corresponding duties binding upon States confronted with a serious breach of a peremptory norm under law of State responsibility. Indeed, as Rosalyn Higgins famously commented: 'International law is not rules. It is normative system. [...] And if international law was just "rules", then international law would indeed be unable to contribute to, and cope with, a changing political world'.[62] Indeed, the interpretation concerned completely misses the systemic approach to international law.

The third possible interpretation that should be seriously considered is the application of the qualified neutrality applied in clear cases of aggression and allowing neutral States to discriminate against an aggressor while remaining neutral. The concept of qualified neutrality has been openly advocated by some States with the prominent example of the United Sates. As the US Law of War Manual states: 'The United States has taken the position that certain duties of neutral States may be inapplicable under the doctrine of qualified neutrality'.[63] Thus, as Russia is clearly responsible for the aggression against Ukraine, third States are entitled to support Ukraine as the victim of aggression and, as long as they do not use armed force against Russia, they remain neutral and comply with their obligations under the laws of neutrality.

What appears to be mostly challenging in the context of qualified neutrality is the problem of qualification of certain armed activities as aggression. Some authors tend to support the concept of qualified neutrality only if such determination is made by the UN Security Council. This is of course not the case in the armed conflict between Ukraine and Russia. Notably, Wolff Heintschel

62 Rosalyn Higgins, *Problems and Process: International Law and How We Use It* (Oxford: 1994) 1 and 3.

63 US Department of Defence, *US Law of War Manual*, June 2015 (last updated December 2016) 952.

von Heinegg proposed 'a more nuanced position' vis-à-vis qualified neutrality and called the Russian aggression of 2022 a game changer.[64] Indeed, firstly the aggressor 'itself prevented the enforcement mechanism under Chapter 7 UN Charter to function'[65] and Russian aggression is manifest as it was qualified as such by a great many of States and subsequently confirmed in the UN General Assembly Resolution of 2 March 2022 (Wolff Heintschel von Heinegg's comment was made available online on 1 March 2022 – just a day before the adoption of the Resolution). Thus, 'the many States supplying Ukraine with military equipment – whether defensive or offensive is irrelevant – are not acting contrary to the law of neutrality, nor are they otherwise committing internationally wrongful acts or aiding and assisting such acts'.[66] So, according to this interpretation, the States supporting Ukraine remain neutral, yet not impartial.

The concept of qualified neutrality definitely forms an attempt to reconcile neutrality with obligations arising in modern international law from *jus ad bellum* and law of state responsibility and to approach it in a more systemic manner. But this assertion does not change the view that it is based on a legal fiction. Neutrality *de jure* has nothing to do with neutrality *de facto* as third Sates are not impartial at all and openly support one of the belligerents. The concept of qualified neutrality deprives neutrality of one of its two founding duties: impartiality. Thus, it reduces neutrality to the very non-participation. And it results in no more than the decline of neutrality as it was originally understood and defined. What is more, in case of the armed conflict between Ukraine and Russia, third States supporting Ukraine do not claim they remain neutral and do not invoke the qualified neutrality concept. They do claim that they are not parties to the pending armed conflict and they refrain from actions that could be qualified as such participation. Neutrality in whatever context is not the legal reference point at all.

One more important aspect regards the status of the States that have not been supporting Ukraine. And one has to admit that this is the majority of the UN Member States. Are those States neutral? It seems that they are not necessarily so as, in general, those third States have not declared their neutrality in the conflict concerned. What is certain is that they do not participate in the armed conflict and their relations with the belligerents are governed

64 Wolff Heintschel von Heinegg, „Neutrality in War against Ukraine", Lieber Institute West Point Articles on War, Mar 1 2022, https://lieber.westpoint.edu/neutrality-in-the-war-against-ukraine/ [as of 1 July 2023].

65 Ibid.

66 Ibid.

by various norms of international law. Thus, as it was clarified above, they are legally obliged not to recognize as lawful a situation created by an act of aggression, nor must they render aid or assistance in maintaining the situation resulting from aggression. Also, they are obliged to cooperate to bring aggression to an end by lawful means. But as the latter obligation is concerned, the third States have a wide range of means at their disposal and enjoy far reaching discretion in this respect. Thus, the practice under consideration could hardly be appealed in support of adequate applicability of neutrality in the armed conflict between Ukraine and Russia.

One more critical argument in defense of neutrality seems possible. Namely, the armed conflict between Ukraine and Russia is unique as it encompasses a clear-cut example of aggression whereas in most cases it is definitely not so. And as Wolff Heintschel von Heinegg put it: '[i]f neutral States were allowed to absolve themselves from their neutrality obligations by a unilateral determination of the aggressor, the law of neutrality could no longer fulfill its function of effectively preventing an escalation of an IAC'.[67] But again, prevention of use of armed force escalation is now governed and secured foremostly by *jus ad bellum* norms and not by neutrality as it has been argued in the previous section. Moreover, Stefan Talmon is perfectly right when he claims that

> [u]nder the Charter, the UN Security Council has been endowed with the 'primary responsibility', but not the exclusive responsibility, for the maintenance of international peace and security. In the horizontal and decentralized legal system of international law, it is the responsibility of each State itself to determine violations of the law and to draw the conclusions therefrom.[68]

Indeed, States are entitled to qualify legally certain actions, react to them adequately under binding international law, and to bear legal responsibility for their own responses. It is far better than maintaining the fiction of neutrality *de jure* that is not neutral *de facto* as Germany or then Czechoslovakia was not vis-à-vis Polish–Soviet war of 1919–21 and as some few States, such as Hungary,[69] are not now vis-à-vis the armed conflict between Ukraine and Russia.

67 Ibid.

68 Stefan Talmon, "The Provision of Arms to the Victim of Armed Aggression: the Case of Ukraine", Bonn Research Papers on International Law, Paper No 20/2022, 6 April 2022 18.

69 Although never formally declared, the Hungarian authorities alluded repeatedly to the neutrality concept in the context of Hungary's participations in the institutionalized responses to the pending armed conflict between Ukraine and Russia under the auspices of NATO and the EU. See, e.g.: Justin Spike, "Hungary's Orban criticized for 'neutrality' in

5 Conclusion

When the PCIJ issued the Wimbledon judgement in 1923, the concept of neutrality played an important role in international legal order as it was then. It prevented armed conflicts and their escalation as war was not outlawed under international law of that time. Moreover, neutrality protected States and their sovereignty, because it limited the scope of armed actions of belligerents towards third states being neutral. In the present chapter this was named dual *ratio legis* of neutrality. Neutrality was rooted in State sovereignty and States were free to declare themselves as neutral. However, this discretion could be limited contractually as it was decided in the *Wimbledon* case. What is more, this limitation was due to the treaty provision regulating the Kiel Canal status and introducing its internationalization in the interests of all States. Thus, the *Wimbledon* judgement formed an early hallmark of the emerging community interests in international society with all the legal consequences international law has accommodated during its development through the last one hundred years.

Thus, one hundred years later, international legal order is significantly different and this transformation has also significantly influenced the concept of neutrality. Nowadays States do not enjoy full discretion in shaping their legal relations towards international armed conflicts irrespective their legal qualification. Neutrality must have and, indeed, it has evolved significantly. Foremostly, neutrality has been deprived of one of its two basic obligations: impartiality. In consequence, it was reduced to the obligation of non-participation in an armed conflict. Has it saved its separate legal standing and the significance in modern international law? It is very doubtful that it has.

One can claim that the significantly pacifist genesis of neutrality still affects how it is framed in modern international law scholarship and forms the main reason why it is still so reluctant to admit the modern decline of the neutrality concept. But there is not much to regret. The *jus ad bellum* framework accompanied by the development of community interests with the concept of peremptory norms resulting in far reaching legal consequences under law of State responsibility provides for powerful legal guarantees. As Paolo Palchetti rightly noted:

Ukraine war", AP News, 22 March 2022 https://apnews.com/article/russia-ukraine-putin-business-budapest-viktor-orban-c289237f0c626ce9447bd1c78ebcd8ae [as of 1 July 2023].

> The main emphasis appears nowadays to be on the effective enforcement of rules aiming to protect the common interests of the international community and on the role which third states may play in that regard. To the extent that this trend will find further confirmation in state practice and will lead to the development of stricter rules imposing duties on third states, the law of neutrality – the scope of applicability of which has already been reduced by the system of collective security by the UN Charter – appears destined to find still less room for application, if not to vanish entirely through obsolescence.[70]

Thus, due to the development of international legal order the initial dual *ratio legis* of neutrality was lost and it was replaced by far more sophisticated legal mechanisms. Naturally, as international law is not static the decline of neutrality is a gradual process but it does not seem necessary to prevent it. It is so also from the purely pragmatic perspective. As evidenced by the examples of the two armed conflicts divided by one hundred years, neutrality *de facto* has never existed, because neutrality *de jure* could and still can be used as a means of securing individual State's interests and/or supporting one of the belligerents under the casing of impartiality. Therefore, nowadays the concept of neutrality became a legal relic and it is justly a relic in decline.

Acknowledgments

The open access publication was funded by the Faculty of Law and Administration of the Jagiellonian University, granted within the Priority Research Area "Heritage" under the program "Excellence Initiative – Research University" at the Jagiellonian University in Krakow.

Bibliography

Antonopoulos C., *Non-Participation in Armed Conflict: Continuity and Modern Challenges to the Law of Neutrality* (Cambridge: 2022).

Bindschedler R.L., "Neutrality, Concept and General Rules" in Bernhardt R. (ed.) *Encyclopedia of Public International Law*, vol.4, (Amsterdam–New York–Oxford: 1982) 9.

70 Paolo Palchetti, "Consequences for Third States as a Result of an Unlawful Use of Force", in Weller M. (ed.) *The Oxford Handbook of the Use of Force in International Law* (Oxford: 2015) 1229–1230.

Borzęcki J., *The Soviet–Polish Peace of 1921 and the Creation of Interwar Europe* (New Haven: 2008).

Bothe M., "Neutrality, Concept and General Rules", in Wolfrum R. (ed.), Max Planck Encyclopedia of International Law (Oxford: 2012), online version updated 2015.

Brierly J.L., "Shortcomings of International Law", in Brierly J.L., *The Basis of Obligations in International Law and Other Papers* (Oxford: 1958).

Davis N., *White Eagle, Red Star. The Polish–Soviet War, 1919–20* (London: 1972; 2nd ed. London: 2003).

Deryng A., *Główne tendencje rozwojowe prawa narodów w świetle orzecznictwa Stałego Trybunału Sprawiedliwości Międzynarodowej* [*The Principal Trends in the Development of the Law of Nations under the Jurisprudence of the Permanent Court of International Justice*] (Lwów: 1932).

Feinäugle C., *Wimbledon, The*, in Wolfrum R. (ed.), Max Planck Encyclopedia of International Law (Oxford: 2012), online version updated 2013.

Green J.A., Henderson Ch., Ruys T., "Russia's attack on Ukraine and the jus ad bellum", Journal on the Use of Force and International Law 9 (2022) 4.

Grzebyk P., "Escalation of the Conflict Between Russia and Ukraine in Light of the Law on Use of Force and International Humanitarian Law", XLI Polish Yearbook of International Law 2021 (2022) 145.

Heintschel von Heinegg W., "'Benevolent' Third States in International Armed Conflicts: The Myth of the Irrelevance of the Law of Neutrality" in Schmitt M.N., Pejic J. (eds.), *International Law and Armed Conflict: Exploring the Faultlines* (The Hague: 2007) 543.

Heintschel von Heinegg W., "Neutrality in War against Ukraine", Lieber Institute West Point Articles on War, Mar 1 2022, https://lieber.westpoint.edu/neutrality-in-the-war-against-ukraine/ [as of 1 July 2023].

Heller K.J., Trabucco L., "The Legality of Weapon Transfers to Ukraine Under International Law", Journal of Humanitarian Legal Studies (2022) 1.

Higgins R., *Problems and Process: International Law and How We Use It* (Oxford: 1994).

Klabbers J., "Clinching the Concept of Sovereignty: *Wimbledon* Redux", *Austrian Review of International and European Law* 3 (1998) 345.

Kowalski M., "Original Sin Reaffirmed: The Nicaragua Judgement's Impact on the Notion of Armed Attack as the Most Grave Form of the Use of Force", XXXVI Polish Yearbook of International Law 2016 (2017) 37.

Neff S., "A three-fold struggle over neutrality: The American experience in the 1930s", in Lottaz P., Reginbogin H.R. (eds), *Notions of Neutralities* (Lanham: 2018) 3.

Orakhelashvili A., *Peremptory Norms in International Law* (Oxford: 2006).

Palchetti P., "Consequences for Third States as a Result of an Unlawful Use of Force", in Weller M. (ed.) *The Oxford Handbook of the Use of Force in International Law* (Oxford: 2015) 1224.

Ruys T., *'Armed Attack' and Article 51 of the UN Charter. Evolutions in Customary Law and Practice* (Cambridge: 2010).

Saganek P., *Unilateral Acts of States in Public International Law* (Leiden – Boston: 2016).

Skubiszewski K., "Use of Force by States. Collective Security. Law of War and Neutrality", in Sørensen M. (ed.), *Manual of Public International Law* (London: 1968) 739.

Talmon S., "The Provision of Arms to the Victim of Armed Aggression: the Case of Ukraine", Bonn Research Papers on International Law, Paper No 20/2022, 6 April 2022.

Upcher J., *Neutrality in Contemporary International Law* (Oxford: 2020).

Wagner G., *Deutschland und der polnisch-sowjetische Krieg 1920* (Wiesbaden: 1979).

Weinberger S., "The *Wimbledon* Paradox and the World Court: Confronting Inevitable Conflicts between Conventional and Customary International Law", *Emory International Law Review* 10 (1996) 397.

Judgments and Advisory Opinions

PCIJ

Case of the S.S. "Wimbledon" [1923] Publ. PCIJ Ser A No 1.

Question of Jaworzyna (Polish – Czechoslovakian Frontier), Advisory Opinion [1923] Publ. PCIJ Ser B No 8.

The S.S. "Wimbledon", Documents of the Written Procedure [1923] PCIJ Ser C No 3 (Additional Volume), 1.

The S.S. "Wimbledon", Documents of the Written Procedure [1923] PCIJ Ser C No 3 (Additional Volume), 40.

Wimbledon, Dissenting Opinion by M. Schücking.

Wimbledon, Dissenting Opinion by M.M. Anzilotti and Huber.

ICJ

North Sea Continental Shelf Cases (Federal Republic of Germany/Denmark; Federal Republic of Germany/Netherlands) Judgment, I.C.J. Reports 1969.

Threat or Use of Nuclear Weapons, Advisory Opinion, ICJ Reports 1996.

Other Sources

ILC *Articles on Responsibility of States for Internationally Wrongful Acts, with commentaries, 2001*, Yearbook of International Law Commission 2001, vol. II, Part Two.

ILC, *Draft conclusions on identification and legal consequences of peremptory norms of general international law (jus cogens), with commentaries, 2022,* Yearbook of International Law Commission 2022, vol. II, Part Two.

US Department of Defence, *US Law of War Manual,* June 2015 (last updated December 2016).

CHAPTER 8

Legal Status of International and Internal Waterways

Barbara Stępień

Abstract

The emblematic *Wimbledon* case decided by the Permanent Court of International Justice (PCIJ) in 1923 still provokes debate on multiple legal matters. This Chapter examines the contemporary international regime of waterways, tracing its inception to the *Wimbledon* judgment and exploring whether including a broader array of waterways in an international regime with analogous regulation can be justified. To address judicial and scholarly attempts to theorize the existence of a unified legal regime on international waterways, the author explains the notion of international waterways, the concept of canal internationalization, and the problem of objective legal regimes. Multiple examples bolster the legal analysis, especially regarding the three main interoceanic canals of Kiel, Suez, and Panama. In conclusion, the author states that even though the analyzed scenarios do not support the existence of a unified international regime of waterways, the *Wimbledon* judgment marked a starting point in the development of the common framework for them and acts as a cornerstone for the concept of the objective legal regime.

1 Introduction: Earth's Cardiovascular System

The ubiquitous network of international and internal waterways, like the circulatory system of a living organism, surges as the lifeblood of global maritime connectivity. This metaphorical comparison with the vascular system likens the oceans to the main vital organs, providing the well-being of the entire maritime body. In drawing this parallel, straits and canals assume a pivotal role in facilitating the smooth movement of marine traffic, ensuring the exchange

 | DOI:10.1163/9789004707979_010

of goods for the prosperity of nations. As in the case of veins and arteries, a notable resemblance exists between straits and canals. Nonetheless, careful examination reveals important differences between them, most obviously in their creation. While canals are crafted by human hand, straits represent natural formations. This crucial distinction is reflected in the legal and operational frameworks applicable to them. But is it so simple?

The wide variety of waterway types, categories, and characteristics poses significant challenges for legal scholarship in establishing a legal regime of international waterways. Therefore, during the last hundred years, scholars and international courts have focused on searching for common denominators, allowing them to provide for some generally applicable rules. The Permanent Court of International Justice (PCIJ) used this approach for the first time in the 1923 *Wimbledon* case, where the World Court searched for similarities between the Kiel, Suez, and Panama canals to compare applicable precedents and existing State practices.[1] Thus, the *Wimbledon* judgment –until today provoking debate on various legal matters analyzed in detail in this book – serves as a starting point for analyzing the development of the international regime of waterways during the last century.

This Chapter examines the contemporary international regime of waterways, tracing its inception to the *Wimbledon* judgment and exploring whether including a broader array of waterways in an international regime with analogous regulation can be justified. The remainder of this Chapter is organized as follows. Section 2) introduces the notion of international waterways, a narrower term than international watercourses entailing navigational characteristics and the possibility of substantial exploitation. Section 3) addresses judicial and scholarly attempts to theorize the existence of a unified legal regime on international waterways. It explains that the PCIJ first attempted to construct a systematic, unified legal regime, although on the disputable basis of a limited number of examples with significant legal differences. Section 4) addresses the internationalization of the Kiel Canal through the Versailles Peace Treaty, which set the stage for the *Wimbledon* case. Since the Versailles Peace Treaty had a limited number of State Parties but simultaneously conceded rights to other States, Section 5) addresses the concept of objective legal regimes. It examines the notion of objective legal regimes, the controversial concept of common interests, and the disputable competency that such regimes grant states to act on behalf of the international community. Section 6) takes

1 *S.S. Wimbledon* (*United Kingdom, France, Italy & Japan v. Germany*) (Poland intervening), 1923 PCIJ Ser A, No. 1 (hereafter: *Wimbledon*).

a peek beyond the three main Canals, describing a dynamic of nationalization, namely, the assertion of the respective states to exercise jurisdiction over them, which partially reverses a tendency to understand that such waterways have an inherently international nature. Finally, Section 7) concludes that the available examples do not support the existence of an objective legal regime internationalizing waterways nor advance a notion that a homogeneous regulation may be derived from international law or state practice.

2 The Notion of an International Waterway

The metaphor of Earth's cardiovascular system sets the scene for a detailed analysis of the legal norms governing international waterways. Before analyzing whether a general international regime for waterways exists, the concept and criteria of an international waterway must be unpacked. An international waterway forms part of the broader concept of international watercourses.[2] The distinctive features of an international waterway are its navigational character[3] and 'substantial' exploitation by merchant and naval shipping.[4] However, this broad concept of an international waterway has not led to any binding legal definition, given its complications.[5]

The notion of an international waterway covers rivers, straits, and canals.[6] Subsequently, they can be divided into artificial and natural waterways, which poses further legal complexities. Even though an inland canal could be compared to a river and an international canal to a natural strait, there are considerable differences in how they should be approached legally.

Furthermore, the differences between the interoceanic and *other* types of canals are also notable, especially in the context of this analysis. Whereas many canals and straits of international consequence exist, the maritime or

2 One definition of watercourse may be found in the 1997 Convention on the Law of the Non-Navigational Uses of International Watercourses. According to article 2 a) 'a watercourse is a system of surface waters and groundwaters constituting by virtue of their physical relationship a unitary whole and normally flowing into a common terminus'; article 2 b) states that an 'international watercourse' may be defined as 'a watercourse, parts of which are situated in different States'.

3 McCaffrey S.C., "International Watercourses", in Peters A. – Wolfrum R. (eds.), *Max Planck Encyclopedia of Public International Law* (Oxford: 2023) para. 1.

4 Baxter R., *The Law of International Waterways: With Particular Regard to Interoceanic Canals* (Cambridge: 1964) 3.

5 Ibidem, 3.

6 Ibidem, 3.

interoceanic canals linking two oceans are few;[7] thus, they must be distinguished from the canals forming part of the international river systems.[8] In the latter case, suffice it to say that their regime is often 'assimilated to that of the rivers upon which they are dependent or which they link'[9] as they aim to 'duplicate or improve' the existing river system.[10] Purely in terms of rivers, their navigational character, the possible usage of their waters (e.g., for power generation, land irrigation, consumption, etc.) and their exact geographical location (e.g., in bordering regions of one or more countries) all contribute to the question of their national or international character.[11]

In terms of international canals, central for the analysis in this Chapter, their transit capacity –translated into their significance for the world economy and well-being – is one of the decisive factors in their genuinely international nature. Even though there are numerous international canals from the geographical perspective, the world tonnage that passes through them reflects the international interest they represent, not only in littoral but also in non-littoral states. Consequently, while discussing the regime of international canals, scholarship usually focuses, similar to the PCIJ in the *Wimbledon* judgment on the Kiel, Suez, and Panama Canals, on what scholarship calls the interoceanic canals.[12]

Over the years, these artificial arteries of the world have raised many legal questions, ranging from sovereignty and neutrality issues to effects of reservations and interpretative declarations to third-party effects.[13] The scholarly interest in their legal regime is strongly related to their economic and strategic importance for the international community. A complete comparative analysis of the history of legal developments of the Panama and Suez Canals

7 A maritime or interoceanic canal means a canal which links two different parts of the high seas or exclusive economic zones. Arcari M. – de Andrade M.C., "Canals", in Peters A. – Wolfrum R. (eds.), *Max Planck Encyclopedia of Public International Law* (Oxford: 2023) para. 12.

8 Baxter, *The Law of International Waterways* 10.

9 Ibidem, 10.

10 For example, the provisions of the Versailles Peace Treaty on Elbe, the Oder, the Niemen and the Danube. Also provisions on Rhine and Moselle river systems, articles 361–362.

11 Baxter, *The Law of International Waterways* 16.

12 Ibidem, 12.

13 While this Chapter focuses on the legal status of international waterways, other chapters in this book address at length the concepts of sovereignty and neutrality through the relationship of international and national law to responsibility, among other things, also present in the *Wimbledon* case.

is beyond this Chapter's scope.[14] Nonetheless, suffice it to say that their legal evolution may be considered more complicated than the Kiel Canal's.

3 In Search of a Common Denominator for International Waterways

The definitions and characteristics of international waterways established in the previous section allow us to delve into the complex analysis of the advances towards a common regime of international waterways. The plethora of different types and categories of waterways, sharing certain similarities but differing from one another, has thwarted efforts over the last hundred years in the international legal system to find one set of rules to regulate them. Nevertheless, scholars and international courts have attempted to systematize their legal regime, seeking common points for constructing broadly applicable rules.

The PCIJ was the first to employ such a method in the *Wimbledon* judgment, where it searched for parallels between the interoceanic canals as the basis for precedents and State practices. The World Court stated that:

> The precedents therefore afforded by the Suez and Panama Canals invalidate in advance the argument that Germany's neutrality would have necessarily been imperiled if her authorities had allowed the passage of the 'Wimbledon' through the Kiel Canal, because that vessel was carrying contraband of war consigned to a State then engaged in an armed conflict. Moreover, they are merely illustrations of the general opinion according to which when an artificial waterway connecting two open seas has been permanently dedicated to the use of the whole world, such waterway is assimilated to natural straits in the sense that even the passage of a belligerent man-of-war does not compromise the neutrality of the sovereign State under whose jurisdiction the waters in question lie.[15]

---

14 A Reader interested in a detailed analysis of the Suez and Panama Canals may consult respectively: Lawrence T. J., *The Suez Canal in International Law*, 2nd ed., (Cambridge: 1885); Huang T. F., "Some International and Legal Aspects of the Suez Canal Question", *American Journal of International Law* 51, no. 2 (1957) 277–307; Manyin Lee J. – Yin-cheung Wong E., "Suez Canal Blockage: An Analysis of Legal Impact, Risks and Liabilities to the Global Supply Chain", in Khvedelidze P. – Gechbaia B. – Goletiani K. (eds.), *MATEC Web of Conferences* 339 (2021) 01019; Smit H., "The Panama Canal: A National or International Waterway?", *Columbia Law Review* 76, no. 6 (1976) 965; Bakenhaus R.E. – Knapp H.S. – Johnson E. R., *The Panama Canal: Comprising Its History and Construction, and Its Relation to the Navy, International Law, and Commerce* (New York: 1915); Aguirre R.W., *The Panama Canal* (Leiden: 2010).

15 *Wimbledon*, 28.

Over the years, scholarship has been critical of the PCIJ's reasoning in *Wimbledon*, which relied on State practice in merely two questionably similar cases, the Panama and Suez Canals, including a limited number of State parties.[16] In his dissenting opinion, Judge Schücking criticized such a comparison, noting different characteristics of the canals, the circumstances of their construction, and the applicable legal regimes.[17] On the other hand, Judges Anzilotti and Huber also argued in their dissenting opinion, that the treaties regulating the other two canals included provisions in time of war, which was not the case of Kiel Canal.[18] Judge Schücking supported this view, also highlighting that the Kiel Canal was never neutralized like the other two canals.[19]

Even though the Court's line of reasoning could probably be better supported, its search for common points of comparison seemed unavoidable. In 1885, Lawrence reflected upon the precedents regarding international canals, stating that:

> Now, since there are no precedents to guide us, and since the analogies applicable to the case are many and diverse, we are forced to the purely negative conclusion that, agreement apart, International Law does not afford any rules for the conduct of states in reference to the Suez Canal… If we ask for precedents, none are forth coming; if we reason from analogy, we are lost in confusion; if we search for an agreement, we cannot find one.[20]

Although resolved many years ago, the *Wimbledon* judgment was the first attempt to systematize the international law of waterways and remains the starting point of any attempt at a legal reconstruction of the international law of waterways.

4 Internationalization of Canals

The explored conceptual framework and complex legal nature of international waterways pose a challenge to creating a uniform legal regime for international

16 *Wimbledon*, 25–29. Feinäugle C., "Wimbledon, The", in Peters A. – Wolfrum R. (eds.), *Max Planck Encyclopedia of Public International Law* (Oxford: 2023) para. 16.

17 *Wimbledon, Dissenting Opinion by M. Schücking*, 46–47.

18 *Wimbledon, Dissenting Opinion by M.M. Anzilotti and Huber*, 39–40.

19 *Wimbledon, Dissenting Opinion by M. Schücking*, 46–47.

20 Lawrence, *The Suez Canal* 56–57.

waterways. Furthermore, the internationalization of the mentioned interoceanic canals at different historical periods constitutes a critical moment in analyzing their legal statutes. This concept, examined in detail in this section, marks a crucial departure from traditional sovereignty principles enjoyed by the riparian States towards a more open, international legal framework. The transition of the legal status of the Kiel Canal based on the Versailles Peace Treaty discussed below is one example of this.

The construction of the Kaiser-Wilhelm-Kanal took eight years, starting on 3 June 1887.[21] It operated solely under German sovereignty during the first 25 years (1895–1919), which was also confirmed by the PCIJ in the *Wimbledon* judgment.[22] Its status changed after World War I, when the Treaty of Peace between the Allied and Associated Powers and Germany (Versailles Peace Treaty) was signed on 28 June 1919, entering into force on 10 January 1920. Since then, the Kiel Canal emerged in the place of the Kaiser-Wilhelm-Kanal.

Part XII Section VI (Articles 380–386) of the Versailles Peace Treaty regulated the Kiel Canal. Article 195 of the Versailles Peace Treaty also obligated Germany to demilitarize its approaches to an indicated area to provide all nations free passage into the Baltic Sea. Article 380 of the Versailles Peace Treaty stated, 'The Kiel Canal and its approaches shall be maintained free and open to the vessels of commerce and of war of all nations at peace with Germany on terms of entire equality'.

---

21 On 16 March 1886 Reichstag passed the Imperial Law Concerning the Creation of the North Sea – Baltic Canal (Reichsgesetz betreffend die Herstellung des Nord-Ostseekanals). An extensive debate on the necessity of the Canal's construction followed the legislation. Two opposite views were competing. Chancellor Bismark, supporting the Canal's construction, aimed to obtain a delicate equilibrium between the powers in the region. As the British navy had a prevalent position therein, Bismark saw a possibility of strengthening the Reich's position on both seas – North and Baltic – by providing its navy a shortcut between them. Opponents of the Canal based their skepticism on unproportionally high, in their opinion, construction costs in comparison to possible benefits. Field Marshal von Moltke was one of the main opponents of the Canal. On 23 July 1873 during his intervention in Reichstag he stated that it would be possible to build a second fleet for the cost of the Canal. Another reason against it was the lesser strategic military importance of the Canal since Helgoland belonged to the Brits. Bismark resolved the latter issue, however, by the onset of negotiations with the British Government on the exchange of Helgoland for Zanzibar. Based on Article XII (1) of the Agreement between Germany and Great Britain respecting Zanzibar (known as Heligoland-Zanzibar Treaty) Helgoland was handed over to the German Empire in 1890. Bohmer A., "One Hundred Years: The Kiel Canal in International Law", *German Yearbook of International Law* 38 (1995) 327; Hattenhauer Ch., "Heligoland", in Peters A. – Wolfrum R. (eds.), *Max Planck Encyclopedia of Public International Law* (Oxford: 2023) para. 5.

22 *Wimbledon*, 23.

Article 380 constituted what doctrine calls an *internationalization* of a canal.[23] This term has two understandings: a territorial and a functional one.[24] While the first refers to a scenario when some territory of a State comes under the control, safeguard, or administration of another State or a group of States, the second – the functional one – has a more limited nature.

The scholarship distinguishes three categories of functional internationalization: 1) when a special international organization gains authority to exercise jurisdiction within the State's territory, leading to a corresponding restriction of the State's sovereignty, 2) when States acting as 'custodian' of the international community exercise specific functions beyond their national jurisdiction for the benefit of the global community, and 3) when a special international regime, with more limited approach, is established to regulate parts of a territory, which remain under the sovereignty of the respective State.[25] In such a situation, the State is sovereign, although bound to comply with certain obligations aiming to benefit the interests of other States or the international community. International supervision may be exercised over fulfilling the State's obligations, sometimes delegated to a concrete international organization (a mechanism known as indirect international administration).[26]

The concept of functional internationalization in maritime navigation was further expanded by the right to transit passage through straits used for international navigation,[27] which was embodied in Part III of the 1982 United Nations Convention on the Law of the Sea (UNCLOS).[28] However, the mentioned provisions regulate the natural straits and do not apply to artificial waterways such as canals.[29] State practice shows that even though the right of transit passage through straits used for international navigation became a part of general international law, there is still no consensus on its exact content and

23 For examples of the terminological usage, *see* Bohmer, "One Hundred Years" 328; Arcari – de Andrade, "Canals" para. 12; Arcari M. – de Andrade M.C., "Suez Canal", in Peters A. – Wolfrum R. (eds.), *Max Planck Encyclopedia of Public International Law* (Oxford: 2023) paras. 5 and 22; Baxter, *The Law of International Waterways* 43.

24 Wolfrum R. – Pichon J., "Internationalization", in Peters A. – Wolfrum R. (eds.), *Max Planck Encyclopedia of Public International Law* (Oxford: 2023) para. 2.

25 Ibidem, para. 16.

26 Ibidem, para. 16.

27 A Reader interested in straits used for international navigation may consult: Stelakatos-Loverdos M.C., "The Contribution of Channels to the Definition of Straits Used for International Navigation", *The International Journal of Marine and Coastal Law* 13, no. 1 (1998) 71.

28 Wolfrum – Pichon, "Internationalization" para. 23.

29 Mahmoudi S. – Ratcovich Leopardi M., "Transit Passage", in Peters A. – Wolfrum R. (eds.), *Max Planck Encyclopedia of Public International Law* (Oxford: 2023) para. 13.

the scope of its application.[30] In 1949, the International Court of Justice (ICJ) pronounced this right for the first time in the *Corfu Channel Case,*[31] where it stated that:

> It is...generally recognized and in accordance with international custom that States in time of peace have a right to send their warships through straits used for international navigation between two parts of the high seas without the previous authorization of a coastal State, provided that the passage is innocent. Unless otherwise prescribed in an international convention, there is no right for a coastal State to prohibit such passage through straits in time of peace.[32]

The Kiel Canal case and Article 380 of the Versailles Peace Treaty fall under the second type of functional internationalization. Through them, a special international regime was created, and the Canal transformed from an internal to an international waterway. The PCIJ confirmed this in its *Wimbledon* judgment, stating that:

> [The] canal has ceased to be an internal and national navigable waterway, the use of which by the vessels of States other than the riparian State is left entirely to the discretion of that State, and that it has become an international waterway intended to provide under treaty guarantee easier access to the Baltic for the benefit of all nations of the world.[33]

The cases of Panama and Suez Canals were similar in this regard. The 1901 Hay-Pauncefote Treaty stated that the Panama Canal was 'free and open to the vessels of commerce and of war of all nations observing these Rules'.[34] Also, the 1888 Convention Respecting the Free Navigation of the Suez Maritime Canal (Constantinople Convention) provided that '[T]he Suez Maritime Canal shall always be free and open, in time of war as in time of peace, to every vessel of commerce or of war, without distinction of flag'.[35]

---

30 Ibidem, para. 38.

31 Lowe V. – Tzanakopoulos A., "The Development of the Law of the Sea by the International Court of Justice", in Tams Ch. J. and Sloan J. (eds.), *The Development of International Law by the International Court of Justice* (Oxford: 2013) 191.

32 *Corfu Channel* (*United Kingdom of Great Britain and Northern Ireland v. Albania*), ICJ Reports 1949, 28.

33 *Wimbledon*, 21.

34 The 1901 Hay-Pauncefote Treaty, article 3.

35 The 1888 Convention Respecting the Free Navigation of the Suez Maritime Canal, article 1.

The applicable treaties regulating the legal status of the Kiel, Panama, and Suez Canals were concluded between several States. Nonetheless, all established an international legal status of waterways, granting rights to third States not parties to the conventions. Thus, the legal nature of such a mechanism must be examined. Scholarship has termed them *objective legal regimes*.

5 Objective Nature of 'Objective Legal Regimes'

The internationalization of canals, akin to the internationalization of territories, is frequently cited as an example of an objective legal regime.[36] What are objective legal regimes? And why has scholarship occasionally posited that they constitute the basis for an arguable international common regulation of waterways?[37]

5.1 *The Notion of an Objective Legal Regime*

Objective regimes are controversial.[38] They refer to a situation when a treaty generates *erga omnes* effects, binding third States that are not State Parties to a particular treaty.[39] As the creation of rights or obligations *vis-à-vis* third States is not subject to their acceptance, it questions the sacred principle of international law *pacta tertiis nec nocent nec prosunt* (hereinafter, *pacta tertiis*) stating that a treaty does not create obligations or rights for a third State without its consent.[40] Thus, they are considered to be an exception to the established rule.[41]

The doctrine of objective regimes dates back primarily to the XIX century when the major European powers were establishing territorial and peace settlements as a consequence of wars.[42] Nevertheless, it was not until the XX century

36 Barnes R.A., "Objective Regimes Revisited", *Asian Yearbook of International Law* 9 (2000) 133.

37 As the creation of an objective regime for the Kiel Canal is central to the analysis presented in this book, these and other related questions are also explored in other chapters from various perspectives. For in-depth analysis of this topic, *see* Chapter Four in this volume: 'The S.S. Wimbledon Judgment: General International Law, Objective Regimes, Self-Contained Regimes, and the Fragmentation of International Law: Then and Now' by Fitzmaurice M. and Rydberg A.

38 Ryngaert C., "Objective Regime", in Peters A. – Wolfrum R. (eds.), *Max Planck Encyclopedia of Public International Law* (Oxford: 2023) para. 3.

39 Ibidem, para. 1; Salerno F., "Treaties Establishing Objective Regimes", in Cannizzaro E. (ed.), *The Law of Treaties Beyond the Vienna Convention* (Oxford: 2011) 225.

40 Ryngaert, "Objective Regime", para. 3.

41 Barnes, "Objective Regimes Revisited" 139.

42 Ryngaert, "Objective Regime", para. 10.

when the International Law Commission (ILC), drafting the 1969 Vienna Convention on the Law of Treaties, debated the codification of the objective regime and its inclusion in the text of the convention. Two Special Rapporteurs, Fitzmaurice and his successor Waldock, advocated, although from two different perspectives, for objective regimes therein.[43] In 1960, Fitzmaurice proposed draft articles 14 and 18 of his Fifth Report, which aimed to 'describe the types of cases that have been regarded as having *erga omnes* effect under the old public law theory'.[44] However, the ILC did not analyze Fitzmaurice's proposal. Subsequently, in 1964, Waldock suggested a more extensive and different approach to the content of article 63, where he also included the third states' rights to object to the creation of an objective regime.[45] His proposal was, however, not accepted by the International Law Commission.[46]

Article 63 (1) stated that:

> [a] treaty establishes an objective regime when it appears from its terms and from the circumstances of its conclusion that the intention of the parties is to create in the general interest general obligations and rights relating to a particular region, State, territory, locality, river, waterway, or to a particular area of the sea, sea-bed, or airspace; provided that the parties include among their number any State having territorial competence with reference to the subject matter of the treaty, or that any such State has consented to the provision in question.[47]

Whereas the concept of objective regimes did not explicitly appear in the 1969 Vienna Convention, it is possible to trace it to the 1978 Vienna Convention on Succession of States in respect of Treaties, where Articles 11 and 12 supported the view that the succession of states would not affect the boundary arrangements and reaffirmed their legitimacy even in the case of succession.[48] Although the notion of an objective regime does not appear explicitly in the

---

43 Fitzmaurice M., "Third Parties and the Law of Treaties", *Max Planck Yearbook of United Nations Law Online* 6, no. 1 (2002) 72.

44 Fitzmaurice, "Third Parties" 73; United Nations, *Yearbook of the International Law Commission 1960* II (New York: 1961) 80.

45 Draft article 63, para 2 of the 1969 Vienna Convention on the Law of Treaties. United Nations, *Yearbook of the International Law Commission 1964* II (New York: 1965) 26–27.

46 Salerno, "Treaties" 225; Fitzmaurice, "Third Parties" 74.

47 United Nations, *Yearbook of the International Law Commission 1964* 26.

48 For a more extensive analysis of the objective regime in the 1978 Vienna Convention on Succession of States in Respect of Treaties, see Chapter Four by Fitzmaurice M. and Rydberg A in this volume.

1978 Vienna Convention, it was categorized as such by the International Law Commission during the preparatory works on the convention.[49] Consequently, as they do not explicitly appear in any of the international conventions, objective regimes are mainly doctrinal constructions.[50]

5.2 *Is a Common Interest So Common?*

The fundamental principle of international law and relationships – *pacta tertiis* – arises from the State's sovereignty.[51] Whereas it aims to safeguard the State's interests, it also creates practical problems in reaching an agreement related to common interests[52] between the States. Given that a treaty-making process, from negotiations to entry into force, is rather lengthy, there arises a danger that once it is concluded, the common interest may no longer exist.[53]

Advocates of objective regimes have highlighted the weakness of the international law-making process and the lack of an objective form of drafting international law to address the international collective interest.[54] As a supranational institution or body competent to prepare binding international regulations and impose them *de facto* on States does not exist, creating objective regimes could constitute a remedy when the agreement cannot be achieved through negotiations. Therefore, some scholars claim that a collective interest, as the central feature of an objective regime, can 'legitimize' the departure from the *pacta tertiis* principle and the establishment of an objective regime.[55]

Klein underscored that the 'decisive criterion for establishing whether an objective regime valid *erga omnes* exists is whether or not a general interest is served'.[56] Similarly, Lauterpacht agreed that *ius cogens* and *ordre public* recognized the category of general interest,[57] and he stated that: '[A]s international

49 United Nations, "Draft Articles on Succession of States in Respect of Treaties with Commentaries", *Yearbook of the International Law Commission* II (1974) 204.

50 Ryngaert, "Objective Regime", para. 3.

51 Chinkin Ch., *Third Parties in International Law* (Oxford: 1993) 25.

52 The concept of a common interest is also referred to in the doctrine as collective, public or general interest. Thus, the mentioned terms are employed interchangeably in this Chapter to describe the same idea of an interest shared by all or a group of States. Feichtner I., "Community Interest", in Peters A. – Wolfrum R. (eds.), *Max Planck Encyclopedia of Public International Law* (Oxford: 2023) paras. 1–2.

53 Fitzmaurice M. and Rydberg A. also offer an interesting analysis of common interest in Chapter Four in this volume.

54 McNair A., *The Law of Treaties* (Oxford: 1961) 259; Barnes, "Objective Regimes Revisited" 99.

55 Barnes, "Objective Regimes Revisited" 140.

56 Klein E., *Statusverträge Im Völkerrecht: Rechtsfragen Territorialer Sonderregime, Beiträge Zum Ausländischen Öffentlichen Recht Und Völkerrecht* (Berlin-Heidelberg- New York: 1980) 352.

57 Ibidem, 353.

society is transformed into an integrated community, a departure from the accepted principle (*pacta tertiis*) becomes unavoidable, in particular in the sphere of international peace and security'.[58] Moreover, Lauterpacht emphasized that Article XXVII of the League of Nations' Convent and Article 2(6) of the United Nations Charter imposed a limit on the principle that the treaty should not impose obligations upon third States, which was the general interest of the entire international community.[59]

Nonetheless, not all scholars have accepted the notion. Opposition to objective regimes firmly claims that the notion of common interest is rather vague and, thus, can be subject to possible strategic usage by strong States in pursuing their policy aims. Such usage would allow them to attribute their own aims and goals to shared interests.[60]

Given that common interest remains a largely undetermined concept, the debate on objective regimes seems to rely partially on ascribing normative content to it. Scholarship has been divided on how to define common interest and what aims may be considered as covered by it. While some scholars considered that world peace and security, and consequently demilitarization and neutralization, were primary candidates,[61] others identified international settlements of a territorial dimension,[62] especially the boundary agreements,[63] as suitable examples. The peace settlements and territorial arrangements concluded in the XIX and XX centuries,[64] such as the Versailles Peace Treaty,[65] are also often cited as examples. Moreover, the International Court of Justice recognized the

58 Lauterpacht H., *Oppenheim's International Law* 8th ed., I (Oxford: 1955) 528.

59 Ibidem, 529.

60 Chinkin, *Third Parties* 142.

61 For example, the neutralization of the Congo Basin based on the 1885 General Act of the Conference of Berlin respecting the Congo. Ryngaert, "Objective Regime", para. 11.

62 For example, the 1713 Treaty of Utrecht, the 1990 Treaty on German Re-unification. Barnes, "Objective Regimes Revisited" 105. According to Crawford, "[M]ultilateral territorial settlements may well possess certain special features as a matter of general international law" Crawford J.R., *The Creation of States in International Law*, 2nd ed. (Oxford: 2007) 318.

63 The 1978 Vienna Convention on Succession of States in respect of Treaties, articles 11 and 12 support this view by reaffirming the legitimacy of boundary agreements *vis-à-vis* a succession of States. See also *Free Zones of Upper Savoy and the District of Gex (France v Switzerland)* (Judgment of 7 June 1932) PCIJ Series A/B No. 24 and No. 46. Also *Case Concerning the Temple of Preah Vihear (Cambodia v. Thailand)* (Judgment of 15 June 162) ICJ Reports 1962, 6.

64 Chinkin, *Third Parties* 142.

65 Barnes, "Objective Regimes Revisited" 105.

internationalization of territories on multiple occasions as one of the exceptions to the *pacta tertiis* principle.[66]

More recently, the ICJ, while analyzing the emergence of new peremptory norms of general international law under Article 64 of the 1969 Vienna Convention, also pointed out that a concept of general interest exists:

> newly developed norms of environmental law are relevant for the implementation of the Treaty and that the parties could, by agreement, incorporate them through the application of Articles 15, 19 and 20 of the Treaty. These articles do not contain specific obligations of performance but require the parties, in carrying out their obligations to ensure that the quality of water in the Danube is not impaired and that nature is protected, to take new environmental norms into consideration when agreeing upon the means to be specified in the Joint Contractual Plan.[67]

In *Wimbledon*, the PCIJ ruled that the new international regime of the Kiel Canal would be 'for the benefit of all nations of the world'.[68] The World Court based its decision on grammatical, structural, and teleological methods of treaty interpretation.[69] It also extensively focused on grammatical interpretation, particularly of Article 380 of the Versailles Peace Treaty, although this was subsequently criticized.[70]

Moreover, the World Court, while analyzing the intention of the treaty's authors, stated that it was to 'facilitate access to the Baltic by establishing an international régime, and consequently to keep the canal open at all times to foreign vessels of every kind'.[71] The World Court's considerations on

66 *International Status of Southwest Africa,* Advisory Opinion, ICJ Reports 1950, 132 including the *Separate opinion by Sir Arnold McNair,* 153–155. Also, *Certain Phosphate Lands in Nauru* (*Nauru v Australia*) (Preliminary Objection), ICJ Reports 1992, 240, 251- 253. *Free City of Danzig and the ILO Advisory Opinion,* 1930 PCIJ Ser. B, No. 18.

67 *Gabcikovo-Nagymaros Case* (*Hungary v Slovakia*) ICJ Reports 1997, 67.

68 *Wimbledon,* 21.

69 Feinäugle, "Wimbledon, The", para. 15. A Reader interested more in the PCIJ's methods of interpretation employed in Wimbledon, especially the restrictive interpretation of the limitations of rights of a sovereign State, may consult Kwiecień R., "The Permanent Court of International Justice and the Constitutional Dimension of International Law: From Expectations to Reality", in Tams Ch. J. and Fitzmaurice M. (eds.), *Legacies of the Permanent Court of International Justice* (Leiden: 2013) 373–74; Wittich S. "The PCIJ and the Modern International Law of Treaties", in Tams Ch. J. and Fitzmaurice M. (eds.), *Legacies of the Permanent Court of International Justice* (Leiden: 2013) 89–123.

70 Feinäugle, "Wimbledon, The", para. 15.

71 *Wimbledon,* 23.

the authors' intentions were crucial in this context as it was one of the decisive factors in establishing an objective regime. The PCIJ later confirmed this approach in the *Free Zone Case*, while referring to a method in which an objective regime emerged, stating that:

> it cannot be lightly presumed that stipulations favourable to a third State have been adopted with the object of creating an actual right in its favour [...] it must be ascertained whether the States which have stipulated in favour of a third State meant to create for that State an actual right which the latter has accepted as such.[72]

Later, the ICJ underscored in the *North Sea Continental Shelf* cases that the third States interested in the establishment of rights or obligations for them should search for a prescribed basis for it:

> In principle, when a number of States, including the one whose conduct is invoked, and those invoking it, have drawn up a convention specifically providing for a particular method by which the intention to become bound by the régime of the convention is to be manifested-namely by the carrying out of certain prescribed formalities (ratification, accession), it is not lightly to be presumed that a State which has not carried out these formalities, though at all times fully able and entitled to do so, has nevertheless somehow become bound in another way. Indeed if it were a question not of obligation but of rights,-if, that is to say, a State which, though entitled to do so, had not ratified or acceded, attempted to claim rights under the convention, on the basis of a declared willingness to be bound by it, or of conduct evincing acceptance of the conventional régime, it would simply be told that, not having become a party to the convention it could not claim any rights under it until the professed willingness and acceptance had been manifested in the prescribed form.[73]

5.3 *The States' Competence to Act on Behalf of the Community*

An objective regime gains legitimacy by the State parties' competence to act on behalf of the community to protect the common interest.[74] Over the years, three views on this matter arose in the doctrine: territorial competence, the

---

72 *Free Zones of Upper Savoy and the District of Gex*, 1932 PCIJ Ser. A/B, No 4, 147–148.

73 *North Sea Continental Shelf Cases* (Federal Republic of Germany/Denmark; Federal Republic of Germany/Netherlands), ICJ Reports 1969, 25–26.

74 Barnes, "Objective Regimes Revisited" 135.

Great Powers theory, and the 'liberal approach' to competence.[75] Territorial competence refers to a situation with a territorially competent State among the contracting parties. The Great Powers theory suggests that a group composed of the most dominant States is capable of imposing its will on the others.[76] Lastly, the 'liberal approach' simply means that the 'manifestation of actual State interest' is predominant over the strict adherence to territorial requirement.

The Versailles Peace Treaty is an example of the Great Powers' competence, as a group of the victorious powers drafted its provisions in the aftermath of World War I.[77] Nevertheless, the Great Power theory also has its deficiencies as it refers only to a concrete, usually post-war period when international stability is a priority. It also fails to recognize the need to participate in a decision-making process by the 'lesser States' and does not provide for their inclusion in the extra-territorial regimes (e.g., Zones of Peace or Antarctica).[78] Moreover, it challenges the fundamental rule of equality between the States. The Great Power theory was also subject to judicial opinions and decisions. For example, in the Aaland Islands case, the Committee of Jurists indicated that: 'An examination of the political conditions in which this agreement was entered into shows that the convention, in reality, has a much more extended bearing… the provisions settled upon in Paris between the Powers and Russia went beyond the limit of purely Swedish interests'.[79]

On the other hand, in the *Southwest Africa Advisory Opinion*, it was stated that:

> From time to time it happens that a group of great Powers, or a large number of States both great and small, assume a power to create by a multi-partite treaty some new international regime or status, which soon acquires a degree of acceptance and durability extending beyond the limits of the actual contracting parties, and giving it an objective existence. This power is used when some public interest is involved, and its

75 Ibidem, 135.

76 For interesting remarks on the 'Great Powers' theory on competence, refer also to Chapter Four by Fitzmaurice M. and Rydberg A in this volume.

77 Schorkopf F., "Versailles Peace Treaty (1919)", in Peters A. – Wolfrum R. (eds.) *Max Planck Encyclopedia of Public International Law* (Oxford: 2023) para. 3.

78 Barnes, "Objective Regimes Revisited" 137.

79 *Aaland Islands Case*, League of Nation Official Journal, Special Supplement No. 3, (1920), 17.

> exercise often occurs in the course of the peace settlement at the end of a great war.[80]

Exploring the concept of objective legal regimes allows a better understanding of the implications for the international community and the international law they generate, particularly for the legal status of international waterways. Objective regimes underpin the delicate interplay between the established legal principles related to the State's sovereignty, especially *pacta tertiis*, and the global community's evolving needs. Thus, the internationalization of the Kiel Canal under Article 380 of the Versailles Peace Treaty may be considered a creation of an objective regime of an international waterway as all the indicated requirements necessary to create and 'legitimize' an objective regime, as analyzed above, were met.[81]

6 From Internationalization to Nationalization of the International Canals

In the end, XX century history and the political, economic, and military situation in the international arena did not allow for any further development of the idea of objective regimes of international canals or any general international regime of international waterways. Important shifts in political power, economic interests, and legal interpretations have influenced the balance between international cooperation and national sovereignty.

Even though the three interoceanic canals – Kiel, Suez, and Panama – were either internationalized or their management was private since their inaugurations, they all became nationalized and 'returned' to the riparian States over the years. One could say that this reversal was critical for the ongoing quest for a cohesive international legal framework for international waterways that often had to reconcile opposite interests at play.

---

80 *Separate opinion by Sir Arnold McNair* to *International Status of Southwest Africa, Advisory Opinion, ICJ Reports 1950*, 29.

81 Fitzmaurice and Rydberg arrived at a similar conclusion, further expanding on the concept of an objective legal regime for the Kiel Canal. They underscored that, even though the Versailles Peace Treaty provisions established its basis, the subsequent recognition of the Kiel Canal's objective regime depended on a more general international consensus. Thus, a complex relationship between treaty provisions and norms of international law must always be considered. *See* Chapter Four by Fitzmaurice M. and Rydberg A in this volume.

On 14 November 1936, the German Government issued the Memorandum on German waterways (German Memorandum) stating that it no longer considered the provisions of the Versailles Peace Treaty as binding on the Kiel Canal, which awoke different reactions of the State Parties, ranging from protests to silence.[82]

Instead, Germany drafted a new regulation stating that:

> The navigation of waterways within German territory is open to all countries at peace with the German Reich. No differentiation takes place in the treatment of German and foreign ships. This also applies to shipping fees. The German Government assumes that this will be reciprocated on the waterways of the other participating countries.[83]

In this way, the German Memorandum *de facto* terminated the international status of the Kiel Canal, although its lawfulness has been questioned over the years, and the scholarship has analyzed the impact of Germany's unilateral act on the Versailles Peace Treaty.[84] According to Bohmer the outbreak of World War II could also be a possible reason for the termination of the international status of the Kiel Canal, although opinions among scholars vary on this matter.[85]

Regarding the Suez Canal, suffice it to say that at the beginning, it was managed by a private company – Universal Suez Maritime Canal Company – based on the 1854 Concession granted by the Viceroy of Egypt to the Canal's constructor.[86] The Canal was inaugurated in 1869, and the Constantinople Convention has governed it since 1888.[87] The following years were, as in the case of the other canals, full of political tensions between the interested states. Finally, on 26 July 1956, the operator of the Suez Canal – the Company and its assets – was nationalized by a presidential decree.[88] Egypt's decision was supported by the

82 Two States – Czechoslovakia and France – issued a protest memorandum on 2 of December 1936. The same day, three countries, Great Britan, Yugoslavia and Poland, expressed their regret over the German decision. Rumania expressed a similar position on 3 of December 1936. The rest of the State Parties did not react. Bohmer, "One Hundred Years" 333.

83 Ibidem.

84 Ibidem, 333–38.

85 Ibidem, 339.

86 Arcari – de Andrade, "Suez Canal", para. 2.

87 Lee – Wong, "Suez Canal Blockage" 3.

88 Decree of Gamal Abdel Nasser on the nationalisation of the Suez Canal Company (Cairo, 26 July 1956, Law No. 285 of 1956).

examples of the Turkish Straits, Gibraltar, and Panama, which individual States unilaterally controlled.[89] What is interesting is the fact that the examples of both natural straits and artificial canals were invoked to bolster the same claim.

In the case of Panama, the last package of international treaties governing the Panama Canal included the 1977 Panama Canal Treaty and the Treaty concerning the Permanent Neutrality and Operation of the Panama Canal.[90] Panama regained complete control over the Canal when the first treaty terminated on 31 December 1999. The Constitution of Panama, title XIV, addressed the new regime of the Panama Canal, stating that it was an '*inalienable patrimony of the Panamanian Nation*'.[91]

Further analogies, often marking differences, between the legal norms regulating international straits and canals may be found in the events of the XX century. For example, the provisions of the 1920 Treaty of Sevres regarding the Turkish Straits, which was never ratified, mirrored the 1888 Constantinople Convention on Suez Canal provisions. Similarly, the 1901 Hay-Pauncefote Treaty on the Panama Canal, especially Article 3, also borrowed text from the 1888 Constantinople Convention. Some authors even suggested that the similarities between the two treaties established the foundation for '*un droit commun des canaux internationaux*'.[92]

In 1936, the Montreux Convention Regarding the Regime of the Straits (Montreoux Convention) was adopted, establishing the freedom of transit and navigation through the natural straits of Bosporus and Dardanelles for the vessels of all States.[93] It granted Turkey the authority to regulate access to the Black Sea, striking a compromise between international navigational rights and Turkey's concerns about security and sovereignty. Furthermore, based on the Montreux Convention, Turkey holds strong discretional power over the transit of warships through the Straits depending on the circumstances, such as during peacetime, times of war, and when perceiving imminent threats.[94] A further

89 Baxter, *The Law of International Waterways* 43.

90 The mentioned treaties are also known as the Panama Canal Treaties and the Torrijos-Carter Treaties. Arcari M. – de Andrade M.C., "Panama Canal", in Peters A. – Wolfrum R. (eds.), *Max Planck Encyclopedia of Public International Law* (Oxford: 2023) para. 22.

91 The constitutional amendment was introduced by Public Law (Legislative act) No. 1 of 27 December 1993 (Gaceta Oficial de Panamá No 22674).

92 Guillien R., "Un Cas de Dédoublement Fonctionnel et de Législation de Fait Internationale: Le Statut Du Canal Du Suez", *La Technique et Les Principes Du Droit Public; Études En l'honneur de Georges Scelle* 2 (Paris: 1950) 743.

93 Plant G., "Dardanelles and Bosporus", in Peters A. – Wolfrum R. (eds.), *Max Planck Encyclopedia of Public International Law* (Oxford: 2023) para. 3.

94 The 1936 Montreoux Convention, Section 2.

example of the related legal complexities is the ongoing Russo-Ukrainian armed conflict and the 'closure' of the Black Sea by Turkey, which raised questions on its legal grounds, given the absence of explicit clarification from Turkey regarding its reliance on Articles 19 or 21 of the Montreux Convention.[95]

Additionally, the new Istanbul Canal project sparked a discussion on the legal framework of waterways and the possible applicability of the Montreux Convention to it. Conversely, the Corinth Canal, established in 1893 and consistently under Greek jurisdiction, underpins an individualistic approach to waterway governance. Another example supporting this view was the creation of the Panama Canal Authority (Autoridad del Canal de Panamá – ACP), overseeing the administration, functioning, conservation, maintenance, and modernization of the Canal and related activities.[96] As the ACP may restrict access to the Canal for vessels not complying with the existing regulations on navigation, transit, pollution prevention, hazardous cargo regulations, and others, the Canal is governed by a 'specific treaty system'.[97] Probably, for similar reasons, Judge Krylov, in his dissenting opinion on the ICJ *Corfu Channel* case, underscored that 'there is no such thing as a *common* regulation of the legal regime of straits. Every strait is regulated individually (…). The legal regime of all those straits is defined by the respective international conventions'.[98] And this opinion seems to still be valid today.

7 Conclusions

More than a hundred years later after the *Wimbledon* judgment, legal scholarship still cannot clearly answer the question of whether the international regime of waterways exists and if the applicable regulations are more customary or treaty-based in nature. In 1885, Lawrence wrote that there were no guidelines on how to approach the regulation of the interoceanic canals. Then, in 1923, the PCIJ stated that the legal status of artificial canals should be assimilated to the natural straits.[99] Years later, the initially internationalized or privately managed canals, such as Kiel, Panama, and Suez, returned to the riparian States. Currently, all the major international canals are regulated by

95 Pedrozo R., "Closing the Turkish Straits in Times of War", *International Law Studies* 99 (2022) 519–520.

96 The organization and competencies of the ACP were established by the Public Law no 19 of 11 June 1997 (Ley No 19 de 11 de Junio de 1997, Gaceta Oficial de Panamá No 23309).

97 Arcari – de Andrade, "Panama Canal" para. 45.

98 *Corfu Channel Case, Dissenting Opinion by Judge Krylov*, 74.

99 *Wimbledon*, 28.

particular international treaties and generally remain under the coastal states' national control.

Other examples present during the last century regarding similar, although distinctive, scenarios affecting different types and categories of waterways – rivers, canals, and straits – whether natural or artificial in nature, do not really permit the determination of any particular customary law development of this area of international law. Baxter suggested that the fact that each of these waterways is usually regulated by a concrete international treaty 'handicapped rather than aided' the development of the customary regulations.[100] On the other hand, he underscored that 'certain principles of international law having common application to a particular category of international waterways or to two such types of watercourse' could be drawn from the *Wimbledon* and *Corfu Chanel* cases.[101] Kwiecień augmented this view, stating that 'the practice of shaping custom cannot be based only on the activity of the parties to law-making treaties. The states that have not accessed must also participate in this practice'.[102]

Nevertheless, the *Wimbledon* judgment marked the starting point in developing the common framework for international waterways and set a cornerstone for the objective legal regime. Currently, even if in the light of the 1969 Vienna Convention on the law of treaties and customary law, the *raison d'être* of an objective legal regime may seem questionable, the evolving nature of international law must be considered. Moreover, since the *Wimbledon* decision, scholars and international courts have searched for common denominators, state practices, and widely applicable rules to govern the world's veins and arteries. Even though the existence of the common regime of international waterways is, at present, rather questionable, *Wimbledon* greatly impacted the development of international law in many areas, analyzed in detail in other parts of this book.

To summarize, political shifts and legal challenges mark the continuous evolution of the applicable legal framework for international waterways. This Chapter underscores the legal struggle between national sovereignty and the international community's collective interests, a struggle crucial for establishing the rules for global maritime routes. As past precedents and emerging global challenges strongly shape international law, the international waterways framework will develop further. As the maritime arteries of global trade and connectivity continue to evolve, so too must the legal order prevailing at sea.

---

100 Baxter, *The Law of International Waterways* 48.

101 Ibidem, 48.

102 Kwiecień R., "The Formal Sources of International Law, the Relationship between Treaties and Custom, and the International Law-Making Process", *Australian Year Book of International Law* 40 (2022) 65.

Acknowledgments

This chapter presents results of a research project entitled 'Autonomous and Unmanned Vessels in International Law: Yara Birkeland as a Challenge to the Law of the Sea' that has received funding from the European Union's Horizon 2020 Research and Innovation Programme under the Marie Sklodowska-Curie grant agreement No 101038097. The open access publication was funded by the Faculty of Law and Administration of the Jagiellonian University, granted within the Priority Research Area "Heritage" under the program "Excellence Initiative – Research University" at the Jagiellonian University in Krakow.

Bibliography

Aguirre R.W., *The Panama Canal* (Leiden: 2010).

Arcari M. ,de Andrade M.C., "Canals", in Peters A. – Wolfrum R. (eds.), *Max Planck Encyclopedia of Public International Law* (Oxford: 2023).

Arcari M., de Andrade M.C., "Panama Canal", in Peters A. – Wolfrum R. (eds.), *Max Planck Encyclopedia of Public International La w* (Oxford: 2023).

Arcari M., de Andrade M.C., "Suez Canal", in Peters A. – Wolfrum R. (eds.), *Max Planck Encyclopedia of Public International Law* (Oxford: 2023).

Bakenhaus R.E., Knapp H.S., Johnson E. R., *The Panama Canal: Comprising Its History and Construction, and Its Relation to the Navy, International Law, and Commerce* (New York: 1915).

Barnes R.A., "Objective Regimes Revisited", *Asian Yearbook of International Law* 9 (2000).

Baxter R., The Law of International Waterways: With Particular Regard to Interoceanic Canals (Cambridge: 1964).

Bohmer A., "One Hundred Years: The Kiel Canal in International Law", *German Yearbook of International Law* 38 (1995).

Chinkin Ch., *Third Parties in International Law* (Oxford: 1993).

Crawford J.R., *The Creation of States in International Law*, 2nd ed. (Oxford: 2007).

Feichtner I., "Community Interest", in Peters A. – Wolfrum R. (eds.), *Max Planck Encyclopedia of Public International Law* (Oxford: 2023).

Feinäugle C., "Wimbledon, The", in Peters A. – Wolfrum R. (eds.), *Max Planck Encyclopedia of Public International Law* (Oxford: 2023).

Fitzmaurice M., "Third Parties and the Law of Treaties", *Max Planck Yearbook of United Nations Law Online* 6, no. 1 (2002).

Guillien R., "Un Cas de Dédoublement Fonctionnel et de Législation de Fait Internationale: Le Statut Du Canal Du Suez", *La Technique et Les Principes Du Droit Public; Études En l'honneur de Georges Scelle* 2 (Paris: 1950).

Hattenhauer Ch., "Heligoland", in Peters A. – Wolfrum R. (eds.), *Max Planck Encyclopedia of Public International Law* (Oxford: 2023).

Huang T. F., "Some International and Legal Aspects of the Suez Canal Question", *American Journal of International Law* 51, no. 2 (1957).

Klein E., *Statusverträge Im Völkerrecht: Rechtsfragen Territorialer Sonderregime, Beiträge Zum Ausländischen Öffentlichen Recht Und Völkerrecht* (Berlin-Heidelberg-New York: 1980).

Kwiecień R., "The Formal Sources of International Law, the Relationship between Treaties and Custom, and the International Law-Making Process", *Australian Year Book of International Law* 40 (2022).

Kwiecień R., "The Permanent Court of International Justice and the Constitutional Dimension of International Law: From Expectations to Reality", in Tams Ch. J. – Fitzmaurice M. (eds.), *Legacies of the Permanent Court of International Justice* (Leiden: 2013).

Lauterpacht H., *Oppenheim's International Law*, 8th ed., vol. I (Oxford: 1955).

Lawrence T. J., *The Suez Canal in International Law*, 2nd ed., (Cambridge: 1885).

Lowe V., Tzanakopoulos A., "The Development of the Law of the Sea by the International Court of Justice", in Tams Ch. J. and Sloan J. (eds.), *The Development of International Law by the International Court of Justice* (Oxford: 2013).

Mahmoudi S., Ratcovich Leopardi M., "Transit Passage", in Peters A. – Wolfrum R. (eds.), *Max Planck Encyclopedia of Public International Law* (Oxford: 2023).

Manyin Lee J., Yin-cheung Wong E., "Suez Canal Blockage: An Analysis of Legal Impact, Risks and Liabilities to the Global Supply Chain", in Khvedelidze P. – Gechbaia B. – Goletiani K. (eds.), *MATEC Web of Conferences* 339 (2021).

McCaffrey S.C., "International Watercourses", in Peters A. – Wolfrum R. (eds.), *Max Planck Encyclopedia of Public International Law* (Oxford: 2023).

McNair A., *The Law of Treaties* (Oxford: 1961).

Pedrozo R., "Closing the Turkish Straits in Times of War", *International Law Studies* 99 (2022).

Plant G., "Dardanelles and Bosporus", in Peters A. – Wolfrum R. (eds.), *Max Planck Encyclopedia of Public International Law* (Oxford: 2023).

Ryngaert C., "Objective Regime", in Peters A. – Wolfrum R. (eds.), *Max Planck Encyclopedia of Public International Law* (Oxford: 2023).

Salerno F., "Treaties Establishing Objective Regimes", in Cannizzaro E. (ed.), *The Law of Treaties Beyond the Vienna Convention* (Oxford: 2011).

Schorkopf F., "Versailles Peace Treaty (1919)", in Peters A. – Wolfrum R. (eds.) *Max Planck Encyclopedia of Public International Law* (Oxford: 2023).

Smit H., "The Panama Canal: A National or International Waterway?", *Columbia Law Review* 76, no. 6 (1976).

Stelakatos-Loverdos M.C., "The Contribution of Channels to the Definition of Straits Used for International Navigation", *The International Journal of Marine and Coastal Law* 13, no. 1 (1998).

Wittich S. "The PCIJ and the Modern International Law of Treaties", in Tams Ch. J. – Fitzmaurice M. (eds.), *Legacies of the Permanent Court of International Justice* (Leiden: 2013).

Wolfrum R., Pichon J., "Internationalization", in Peters A. – Wolfrum R. (eds.), *Max Planck Encyclopedia of Public International Law* (Oxford: 2023).

Judgments and Advisory Opinions

PCIJ

Free City of Danzig and the ILO Advisory Opinion, 1930 PCIJ Ser. B, No. 18.

Free Zones of Upper Savoy and the District of Gex (*France v Switzerland*) (Judgment of 7 June 1932) PCIJ Series A/B No. 24 and No. 46.

S.S. Wimbledon (*United Kingdom, France, Italy & Japan v. Germany*) (Poland intervening), 1923 PCIJ Ser A, No. 1.

Wimbledon, Dissenting Opinion by M. Schücking, 1923 PCIJ Ser A, No. 1.

Wimbledon, Dissenting Opinion by M.M. Anzilotti and Huber, 1923 PCIJ Ser A, No. 1.

ICJ

Case Concerning the Temple of Preah Vihear (*Cambodia v. Thailand*) (Judgment of 15 June 162) ICJ Rep 1962.

Certain Phosphate Lands in Nauru (*Nauru v Australia*) (Preliminary Objection), ICJ Rep1992.

Corfu Channel (*United Kingdom of Great Britain and Northern Ireland v. Albania*), ICJ Rep 1949.

Corfu Channel Case, Dissenting Opinion by Judge Krylov, ICJ Rep 1949.

Gabcikovo-Nagymaros Case (*Hungary v Slovakia*), ICJ Rep 1997.

International Status of Southwest Africa, Advisory Opinion, ICJ Rep 1950.

North Sea Continental Shelf Cases (*Federal Republic of Germany/Denmark; Federal Republic of Germany/Netherlands*), ICJ Rep 1969.

Separate opinion by Sir Arnold McNair to International Status of Southwest Africa, Advisory Opinion, ICJ Rep 1950.

Other Sources

Aaland Islands Case, League of Nation Official Journal, Special Supplement No. 3, (1920).

United Nations, *Yearbook of the International Law Commission* 1960 II (New York: 1961).

United Nations, *Yearbook of the International Law Commission* 1964 II (New York: 1965).

United Nations, "Draft Articles on Succession of States in Respect of Treaties with Commentaries", *Yearbook of the International Law Commission II* (1974).

Conclusion: Persistent Problems of International Law in the Changing World

Roman Kwiecień

The legal issues decided by the PCIJ in the *Wimbledon* case are still relevant to the international community as a legal community, which has been affected by many major geopolitical, social, ideological and cultural changes over the past 100 years. In this sense, these issues are persistent legal problems related to the properties of the normative architecture of the international community. At the same time, the *Wimbledon* case, its legal background and its consequences show the close relationships of international law and politics, as Raphael Schäfer points out in his chapter. He draws attention on the twofold effects of the *Wimbledon* case for Germany. On the one hand, the Treaty of Versailles and the judgment were strongly criticized both in academia and by politicians in Germany. Some scholars of that time believed that Germany unconsciously presented itself as the defeated of the war even though this fact was without any relevance for the legal question before the Court. Others claimed, Schäfer argues, that the German Reich wanted to see it confirmed that the spirit of the Treaty of Versailles was not the mutual recognition as *'entités politiques indépendantes'* but the embodiment of the control over Germany. On the other hand, however, this assessment does not capture the *Wimbledon* judgment in its entirety because this decision created a new awareness in Germany of the importance of international law. The judgment simply sparked the development of expertise in international law in Germany, as Schäfer put it. This is evidenced by the renewal in 1926 of the activity of the Institute for International Law of the University of Kiel founded in 1914 and initially headed by the German judge *ad hoc* in the *Wimbledon* case, Walther Schücking.

The new circumstances in the changing world allow us to draw attention to new dimensions of well-known legal problems. This new background of the old problems also points to the need to reevaluate the suitability and significance of their ruling in the *Wimbledon* decision. Changes in the normative core of international law go without saying. These changes concern especially the law on the use of force, which has gone from *jus ad bellum* to *jus contra bellum.* The legal status of neutrality and obligations of non-parties to armed conflicts were most affected by these changes, as Michał Kowalski argued in his chapter. In connection with these questions he presents contextual illustrations of neutrality approaches towards two armed conflicts separated by a

 | DOI:10.1163/9789004707979_011

hundred years but, at least to some extent, similar: the Polish–Soviet war of 1919–21 and the Russian aggression against Ukraine of 2022. Kowalski emphasizes the changing nature and role of neutrality in the international legal order. He argues thar when the PCIJ issued the *Wimbledon* judgement in 1923, the concept of neutrality played an important role in international legal order as it was then, since it prevented armed conflicts and their escalation as war was not outlawed under international law of that time. Then states were free to declare themselves as neutral but this discretion could be limited contractually as it was decided in the *Wimbledon* case. However now, Kowalski claims, the international legal order is significantly different and this transformation has also significantly influenced the concept of neutrality. According to him, it is definitely advantageous to look at the *Wimbledon* judgement and its legacy in the context of neutrality as this issue strikingly shows the development and transformation of international law throughout the past one hundred years. But at the same time, neutrality is also political question as evidenced the *Wimbledon* case. For Germany – the guardian of the Kiel Canal, the incident came at a period of extreme uncertainty and fragile domestic stability. In 1921, Raphael Schäfer claims in his chapter, the German Reich was psychologically still under the immediate impact of the conclusion of the Treaty of Versailles and the overall political future seemed uncertain. Due to the unstable domestic political situation, the government was dependent on maintaining strict neutrality towards the Russian–Polish war if it wanted to preserve the fragile constitutional body of the Weimar Republic. Nonetheless, the political situation cannot be an excuse for a state to free itself from its legal obligations related to neutrality, as Kowalski broadly argues. According to him, the case of neutrality illustrates how strongly the scholarship of international law still remains confined within traditional – or rather old-fashioned – legal concepts and is reluctant to admit their today's inadequacy and decline. He states that the function of neutrality was substantially different in international law before the UN Charter era – i.e. when international law was not based on the general prohibition of the use force. Neutrality has been thus evolving and – in consequence of this transformation – deteriorating. Whether and to what extent it has preserved its significance remains debatable and the *Wimbledon* case seems to be a good reference point for such a debate, Kowalski claims. The issue of neutrality seems especially topical nowadays when the international community is confronted with the Russian aggression against Ukraine and some states again tend to advocate the neutrality concept as a desirable approach towards that armed conflict. Kowalski poses important questions in the light of this conflict: Is neutrality towards aggression legally possible in international law as it now stands? Or is it again – as in fact it used to be one hundred years ago – a useful legal excuse to protect individual states' interests preferred over community interests and masked with a pacifist legal narrative? Nowadays, Kowalski claims, states do not enjoy full discretion in shaping their legal relations towards international armed conflicts irrespective their legal qualification. Thus, as he put it, neutrality must have and, indeed, it has evolved significantly. Foremostly, neutrality has been deprived of one of its two basic obligations: impartiality. In consequence, it was reduced to the obligation of non-participation in an armed conflict. He doubts whether neutrality has saved its separate legal standing and the significance in modern international law and concludes that due to the development of international legal order the initial dual *ratio legis* of neutrality was lost and it was replaced by far more sophisticated legal mechanisms. According to him, the examples of the two armed conflicts divided by one hundred years – the Polish–Soviet Russia war of 1919–1921 and the Russian aggression against Ukraine of 2022 – evidence that neutrality *de facto* has never existed, because neutrality *de jure* could and still can be used as a means of securing individual state's interests and/or supporting one of the belligerents under the casing of impartiality. Therefore, nowadays the concept of neutrality became a "legal relic" and it is justly a "relic in decline", as Kowalski put it.

We have also seen different approaches to other issues of international law over the last hundred years. They are related not only to substantive and procedural international law but also to the World Court's reasoning and interpretative practice. Law, including international law, is not only a set of norms, but also a system of reasonings about norms. That is why, the argumentative practice of both courts and parties to disputes before them matters. This practice is particularly relevant to systemic or constitutional issues of the legal order, i.e. sources of law, law-making, hierarchy of norms and normative conflicts. It is indicated in Chapter 6 on the sources of international law that there is a significant improvement to the sources issue in the subsequent case law of the ICJ as compared to the *Wimbledon* decision. The ICJ has given, as especially evidenced in its 1969 judgment in *North Continental Shelf* cases, a more comprehensive clarification, than the PCIJ did, of the process of identification of customary rules, the relationship between treaties and custom, and, as a result, the sources of general international law. The development and changes in judicial application of international law enhance the belief that international law is not only a mere set of rules and principles, but also a dynamic system within which the sources of legal obligations are a "living instrument" as the European Court of Human Rights named the European Convention of Human Rights and Fundamental Freedoms.

The Permanent Court's approaches to the treaty interpretation and the fragmentation of international have been rather rejected in the subsequent judicial practice and the ILC's works. At present, under the rules of treaty interpretation, the guidance for states in relation to fragmentation is found in the systemic interpretation of treaty rules. The main tool for coherence and harmonisation in international law is based on the principle of systematic integration as contained in Article 31(3)(c) VCLT. This is clearly emphasized by the authors of Chapter 4 on self-contained regimes, objective regimes and fragmentation of international law. Fitzmaurice and Rydberg claim that the approach and definition of self-contained regimes as adopted by the PCIJ was significantly different from its contemporary legal characteristics. They argue that in respect to the question of fragmentation, recourse to the principle of systemic integration would have enabled the PCIJ to take material sources external to the Treaty of Versailles and the broader normative environment into consideration when interpreting its provisions so that Article 380 of the Treaty of Versailles could have remained integrated within the legal system as a whole. And lastly, Fitzmaurice and Rydberg state that the approach and definition of self-contained regimes as adopted by the PCIJ was significantly different from its contemporary legal characteristics. First of all, the PCIJ treated self-contained regimes as rules of primary international law; whilst self-contained regimes as understood by the law on state responsibility and the work of the ILC on the subject, are secondary norms of international law. Nonetheless, they note that the development of this notion through the work of the ILC has not been without complexities and lack of clarity. They also underline that the ILC working group on fragmentation further defined the notion of self-contained regimes, most importantly the relationship to general international law. Fitzmaurice and Rydberg, however, argue that the *Wimbledon* judgment put the foundation of present international law in the above-discussed areas, even taking into consideration differences in approaches and structural considerations between legal circumstances then and now.

Taking into account the number of references in the scholarship to the Court's statement on state sovereignty in the *Wimbledon* decision, this famous *dictum* is probably the most durable part of the heritage of the judgment. State sovereignty is still a crucial problem in theory and practice as it has a multidimensional character. In particular, it is clearly connected to the relationships between international law and national law, as well as the state consent as a basis of obligations in international law. The PCIJ clearly referred to both problems in the *Wimbledon* case. The judgment is alluded as an example, even the pattern, of how to escape the difficulty or dilemma that results from the confrontation between the binding character of treaty obligations and the sovereign rights of states based on their consent. The Court, on one hand, famously stated that "the right of entering into international engagements is an attribute of State sovereignty" and "sovereignty is not above law", and, on the other hand, it rejected the opinion that national legal acts could prevail over the treaty provisions. Władysław Czapliński in his chapter addressed this understanding of state sovereignty and its influence on the relation of national law to international law. Thus, this chapter seeks to offer answers to the questions, first, whether the *Wimbledon* judgment established an interpretative canon for understanding of state sovereignty in international law, second, whether this canon is worth defending under the law, and, third, how the sovereignty issue affects the problem of mutual relations between international law and national law, which is especially visible in the time of populism. According to Czapliński, the *Wimbledon* case has survived in legal annals primarily due to the statement that state sovereignty is the basis of state action, enabling the conclusion of international obligations, especially treaty obligations. He claims that the *Wimbledon* decision is still a good guide to address legal controversies regarding the relationship between the limitations of powers of states and the needs of international cooperation.

The Court's findings regarding the legal status of the international waterways turn out to be less controversial from the contemporary perspective. In present international law, all the canals are treated as examples of objective regimes. The regime established in Article 380 of the Versailles Treaty sought to protect a general community interest of preserving international peace and security and constituted an exception to the *pacta tertiis* rule. From present-time point of view, the PCIJ set the fundamental framework for objective regimes concerning international waterways, taken into consideration the peculiarities of the Kiel Canal as reflected in Article 380. Barbara Stępień in her chapter argues that the *Wimbledon* judgment marked the starting point in developing the common framework for international waterways and set a cornerstone for the objective legal regime. Since the *Wimbledon* decision, scholars and international courts have searched for common denominators, state practices, and widely applicable rules to govern the world's veins and arteries. Stępień claims that even though the existence of the common regime of international waterways is, at present, rather questionable, the *Wimbledon* case greatly impacted the development of the law on international waterways. Political shifts and legal challenges mark the continuous evolution of the applicable legal framework for international waterways. Stępień underscores the legal struggle between national sovereignty and the international community's collective interests, a struggle crucial for establishing the rules for global maritime routes. According to her, as past precedents and emerging global challenges strongly shape international law, the international waterways framework will develop further.

The part of the book devoted to the protection of the legal interests of both states and the 'international community as a whole' in judicial proceedings offers interesting reflections about *locus standi* before the World Court. Christian Tams in his chapter pointed to the importance of the *Wimbledon* judgment for *locus standi* of states not directly affected by a violation of the law. Tams recognizes the *Wimbledon* judgment as a starting point leading through the *Barcelona Traction* case to the 2022 judgment in the *Rohingya* dispute between the Gambia and Myanmar based on the *Genocide Convention*. He focuses on what he calls a *prequel* to the ICJ's debates. This prequel was, according to him, set in the *Wimbledon* judgment and it offers insights into an early approach to what might be called 'public interest litigation'. For Tams, this approach is characterised by a degree of healthy pragmatism that would get lost afterwards, and that it is now perhaps possible to reclaim. The decision in the *Wimbledon* case, Tams argues, proves that 'public interest litigation' can be handled pragmatically, and that it need not be seen as exceptional. According to him, this is the central lesson of the *Wimbledon* judgment.

In turn, Michał Balcerzak addressed the problems of third-party intervention before the World Court, including the concept of legal interest. He argues that it would be hard to claim that the Polish intervention in the *Wimbledon* case set any firm precedent or contributed to a better understanding of what "an interest of a legal nature" referred to in Article 62 of the Statute entails. As Balcerzak claims, we have not learned from the *Wimbledon* judgment whether Poland's legal interest in the case could have been regarded as surpassing the ordinary interest of a state party to the Treaty of Versailles. According to him, in the early 1920s, it was premature to adopt a more progressive approach towards interests of a legal nature, let alone to facilitate states in invoking the legal interests of the international community as a whole. But Balcerzak seems to join the proposition pointed out by Christian Tams in this volume, namely, that the approach of the PCIJ to the notion of interest was – perhaps even surprisingly – broad. As Balcerzak emphasizes, the Polish symbolic intervention in the *Wimbledon* case remains the sole example of this kind in the PCIJ's practice. The first three decades of the ICJ saw only two states invoking Article 63 of the Statute. The situation started to change in the first half of the 1980s. Balcerzak argues that it is not excluded that the relatively broad and open-minded interpretations of (legal) interests offered by the PCIJ in the *Wimbledon* case have impacted modern trends in public or common interest litigation at the ICJ. By it as it may, one must admit that the concept of third-party intervention has come a long way from the humble and somewhat symbolic presence of Poland in the *Wimbledon* case to the robust engagement of thirty-three states as expressed in their declarations to intervene in the pending Ukraine v. Russia proceedings. Hence, as he concludes, what might have seemed unthinkable in 1923 when the PCIJ adjudicated its first contentious case with the intervention of a third state, i.e., litigation in the interest of the international community, has become a reality in 2023.

The legal problems addressed by the PCIJ in the *Wimbledon* case are still meaningful problems in the modern international community. The Permanent Court had no predecessors and therefore no argumentative pattern to safely follow. Rather, it is the *Wimbledon* decision that, for better or for worse, shaped such a pattern. Some changes in approaches to the problems decided in the *Wimbledon* case result not only from changes in substantive international law, but also from the strengthening belief of the systemic nature of international law among judges, scholars and experts. As a legal system, international law is not a random collection of rules and principles. There are meaningful relationships between them and should be interpreted against the background of other rules and principles, as the ILC put it in its report on the fragmentation of international law. But at that time such a belief was not shared by the majority of judges. On the contrary, they held different perceptions of what international law was. In this respect, the *Wimbledon* judgment was not a groundbreaking decision. However, it passed the test of time in other respects. The development of the international legal system also generates new measures to protect the rights and legitimized interests of its various actors, not only states. Without the willingness of theses actors, however, it is not possible to communitarise their mutual legal relations. The first judgment of the World Court indicates that expectations placed on international law are justified to the extent that the remedies to protect them are available. Indeed, rights without remedies are not rights at all. Sometimes this leads to the normative conflicts, as the *Wimbledon* case shows. The PCIJ had to resolve a conflict between the public or community interest and the individual interests of the respondent and the third state. To this day, these are fundamental problems of international law. The *Wimbledon* case is worth recalling for indicating that the first international court of general jurisdiction was to face these problems already in its first judgment. This is not the only reason. The development of international law from the *Wimbledon* case, through the *Continental Shelf*, or the *Barcelona Traction* cases, to the recent decisions of the ICJ may allow us to focus on what is the lasting legal legacy, and, on the other hand, what in international law has not stood the test of time. But new circumstances in the changing world do not removed the old legal problems. Better reasoned approaches to these problems, including the interpretation of legal principles and rules by impartial bodies, may, however, provide them with new and effective solutions that meet the legitimate expectations of international actors. Before courts and tribunals as impartial bodies "justice must not only be done, but must be seen to be done". That is why it is crucial for courts and tribunals to indicate in their reasonings whose rights and interests should be protected in the law, why they should be protected, on what basis their protection is to be granted, and, last but not least, by what remedies.

Index

Printed in the United States
by Baker & Taylor Publisher Services